Child soldiers in international law

Melland Schill Studies in International Law
Series editor Professor Dominic McGoldrick

The Melland Schill name has a long-established reputation for high standards of scholarship. Each volume in the series addresses major public international law issues and current developments. Many of the Melland Schill volumes have become standard works of reference. Interdisciplinary and accessible, the contributions are vital reading for students, scholars and practitioners of public international law, international organisations, international relations, international politics, international economics and international development.

Child soldiers in international law

Matthew Happold

Juris Publishing

MANCHESTER 1824

Manchester University Press

Published by Manchester University Press
Altrincham Street, Manchester M1 7JA, UK
www.manchesteruniversitypress.co.uk

British Library Cataloguing-in-Publication Data
A catalogue record for this book is available from the British Library

First published in the USA and Canada by Juris Publishing, Inc.
71 New Street, Huntingdon, New York 11743
www.jurispub.com

Library of Congress Cataloging-in-Publication Data applied for

ISBN 978 0 7190 6586 6 *hardback*

First published 2005

This edition first published 2015

Printed by Lightning Source

Contents

Acknowledgements

In writing this book I have received much help and encouragement, and I am grateful to a great number of people for their support. Christopher Greenwood supervised my first efforts at writing on the subject when I chose to write my LLM dissertation on the treatment of child soldiers in international law. Guy Goodwin-Gill encouraged me to think that despite his book on child soldiers there might be room for another work on the subject. Dominic McGoldrick, series editor of the Melland Schill Studies in International Law, was willing to believe that I could produce such a book. Tony Mason, commissioning editor at Manchester University Press, kept me to my deadlines. Paul Eden was consistently encouraging.

A number of my colleagues at the University of Nottingham provided aid and comfort. Thanks are due, in particular, to Peter Bartlett, Peter Cartwright, Robert Cryer and Robert McCorquodale. The book was finished during a sabbatical spent at the Human Rights Program at Harvard Law School. Tawhida Ahmed compiled the index.

Rob Cryer and Dominic McGoldrick also both read and commented on the draft manuscript. My mother proofread a number of chapters and my brother Tom read Chapter 2 for content. I am grateful to my hosts, Henry Steiner and James Cavarallo, for the opportunity to spend time in such a congenial environment. Needless to say, any remaining errors are my own.

Most of all, I am grateful for the support given to me by my wife Nuriye. Cliché it may be, but I couldn't have done it without her.

Child soldiers in international law: introduction

In recent years, the participation of children in armed conflict has become an issue of international concern. There are a large number of child soldiers in the world today and it is believed that their number is growing. Pictures of children toting AK-47s in various conflicts around the globe have appeared on television and in our newspapers. Child soldiers have been stereotyped as either feral children, amoral and dangerous, or the innocent and helpless victims of adult wiles. Non-governmental organisations (NGOs) have taken up the issue. Governments and international organisations have come under increasing pressure to do something.

This growth in international concern has resulted in significant legal developments, including the conclusion of new treaties on the subject. Unsurprisingly, the emphasis has been on seeking to regulate the recruitment and use of child soldiers. Much effort in recent years has gone into raising the minimum legal age of recruitment. In addition, however, there has been a shift in focus with regard to whose actions the law seeks to regulate. Originally, prohibitions with regard to the recruitment and use of child soldiers were directed against states and, to a lesser extent, non-state actors such as armed opposition groups; against collectivities rather than individuals. More recently, however, the individual recruiters themselves have been targeted. Child recruitment is now a crime in international law. A number of prosecutions are in progress and more are anticipated.

However, this concentration on restricting the participation of children in armed conflict has meant that less attention has been paid to what rules govern the treatment and activities of child soldiers themselves. The unfortunate reality is that large numbers of children are participating in a number of armed conflicts ongoing around the world today. A number of legal issues arise from that fact. How should child soldiers be treated when combatants? What is the situation when they fall into the hands of an adverse party to the conflict? States are under an obligation to demobilise and reintegrate child soldiers back into their communities, but what does that obligation mean in practice? What are child soldiers' rights and duties as combatants; in particular, in what circumstances can they be held liable for violations of international humanitarian law?

This book seeks to answer these questions and to provide a critical exposition of the international law concerning child soldiers. It starts by looking at the situation of child soldiers in the world today, examining, in particular, why children are recruited into armed forces and groups; why they volunteer for military service; and, once recruited, what treatment they receive (Chapter 1). There follows a brief discussion of how perceptions of childhood and children's rights have changed, and how this has affected the ways in which child soldiers have been treated (Chapter 2). Chapter 3 describes the activities of the United Nations (UN) with regard to the child soldier phenomenon. Over the past decade or so, the issues of war-affected children in general, and child soldiers in particular, have shot up the UN's agenda. Consideration of children's rights and welfare has been 'mainstreamed' into the UN's peacemaking and peacekeeping activities, while the Security Council has increasingly acted to put pressure on both states and non-state groups to cease the illegal recruitment and use of child soldiers.

Chapters 4, 5 and 6 examine the legal regulation of the recruitment and use of children in hostilities. The relevant international humanitarian and human rights treaties are discussed (Chapters 4 and 5), as are the role of customary international law and the extent to which the law regulates the activities of non-state armed groups (Chapter 6). This is the issue which has received most attention, with the adoption of two new treaties in the past five years.[1] Indeed, efforts continue to encourage a 'straight 18' consensus prohibiting all recruitment and use of children in armed conflict. However, it will be shown that although international law comprehensively regulates the recruitment and use of child soldiers, owing to the plethora of treaties on the subject, states' obligations continue to differ and children can still lawfully be recruited and used to participate in armed conflict.

Chapter 7 discusses how, once recruited into armed forces and groups, international law treats child soldiers. The chapter considers the status of child soldiers as combatants and as persons in the power of an adverse party in both international and internal armed conflicts, and states' obligations with regard the disarmament, demobilisation and reintegration of child soldiers.

An unusual feature of how child soldiers are viewed is that they are often seen as both victims of human rights abuses and as human rights violators. Chapter 8 examines the extent to which the recruitment and use of child soldiers is an international crime. This is an area which has seen considerable recent developments and the first prosecutions for child recruitment are presently proceeding before the Special Court for Sierra Leone.[2] It will be argued that child recruitment is not only a war crime but in some cases can also constitute a crime against humanity.

[1] The Optional Protocol to the Convention on the Rights of the Child on the Involvement of Children in Armed Conflict (2000) and ILO Convention 182 on the Worst Forms of Child Labour (1999).

[2] See *Prosecutor v. Samuel Hinga Norman*, Case No. SCSL-2004-14-AR729E, Special Court for Sierra Leone (Appeals Chamber), Decision on preliminary motion based on lack of jurisdiction (child recruitment), 31 May 2004.

Chapter 9 then considers the issue of the criminal responsibility of child soldiers themselves for international crimes. Child soldiers are immature, are fed drink and drugs by their commanders, and are coercively recruited and forced to participate in atrocities. Accordingly, special attention is placed on the extent to which child soldiers might be able to avoid liability for their actions by pleading infancy, intoxication or duress.

Chapter 10 covers child soldiers as asylum seekers and refugees. It discusses whether service as a child soldier, or the threat of being recruited as such, can found a claim for refugee status. Also considered, in light of the discussion in Chapter 9, is the extent to which child soldiers' activities might serve to exclude them from refugee status even if they were otherwise eligible.

Finally, there is a brief conclusion (Chapter 11), which is intended to reprise and analyse the various themes appearing throughout the previous chapters.

Two caveats should be announced before entering into the substance of the book. First, throughout the book the concentration is on the *lex lata*.[3] There exist numerous 'soft law' instruments in this area – resolutions of conferences, principles of good practice, and so on – but unless they are useful as means of interpreting legally binding rules, they are not considered. Indeed, one of the themes of the book is how far what states have been willing to accept has lagged behind what campaigners have advocated. Second, only UN activities with regard to child soldiers are examined. A number of states and international organisations[4] have announced the reduction of child soldiering to be a policy priority. Dealing with all such initiatives, however, would have ensured this book were considerably longer without adding to its conclusions as to the law. The intention has been to state what the law is, not what it is thought it should be. This should not be seen as representing a belief that the present situation is satisfactory, but unless we know where we are now, and why, we are unlikely to be able to get to where we want to be.

[3] I have endeavoured to state the law as it existed as of 30 June 2004.

[4] Such as Canada and the European Union (EU).

1

Child soldiers in the world today

'J'ai été officier à l'âge de seize ans, quinze jours'[1]

Introduction

Children have always participated in armed conflicts. For most of history, Napoleon's admission would have been seen as giving rise to no moral conundrum. Over the past few decades, however, the recruitment and use of child soldiers has become a matter of increasing international concern. There appears to be two reasons for this: first, an increase in the use of child soldiers and, second, a change in our perceptions of what childhood is and when it ends.

In the past, to a large extent adulthood and the ability to bear arms went together. The age at which a man was able to bear arms was the age of majority. For a number of Germanic tribes this was 15 years of age.[2] Later, in the Middle Ages, as the strength and training needed to be able to handle a lance and warhorse while wearing heavy armour took longer to develop, the age of majority for nobles was fixed at 21.[3] Those below the age of majority might participate in hostilities but only as auxiliaries, although as such they might be exposed to the dangers of battle in much the same ways as combatants. This remained the case into the nineteenth century, as with drummer boys and powder monkeys, boys enlisted in the British armed forces in their early teens.[4] Today, the link between adulthood and the ability to bear arms no longer exists. Developments in modern weaponry

[1] Napoleon Bonaparte, *Mémoires*, quoted in Alain Louyot, *Gosses de Guerre*, Paris: ed. Robert Laffont, 1989, p. 13.

[2] See T.E. James, 'The Age of Majority' (1960) 4 *American Journal of Legal History* 22, p. 24.

[3] *Ibid.*, pp. 26–7.

[4] See Michael Smith, 'End of an Era for Little Drummer Boys and the Powder Monkeys', *Daily Telegraph*, 29 March 2002.

have permitted children to participate in hostilities at a younger age. The worldwide availability of cheap, lightweight automatic weapons has meant that children can participate in combat on a far more equal footing with adult combatants than in any previous period. Even a generation ago, battlefield weapons were heavy and cumbersome, restricting children's ability to carry and aim them. Bolt action and semi-automatic weapons required far more training for their effective use than modern automatic weapons. Now, as Ilene Cohn and Guy Goodwin-Gill have stated: 'More children can be more useful with less training than ever before'.[5] Children continue to be used where their size and agility is particularly useful, for espionage, carrying communications and (more recently) de-mining, but they now serve in many other ways and, increasingly, participate in hostilities as combatants.

However, we no longer consider the ability to bear arms to be a relevant criterion in assessing adulthood, although physical maturity does remain a factor. Instead, psychological maturity is stressed, the ability to make decisions for oneself and to participate in public affairs. Today, the generally accepted legal definition of childhood is contained in Article 1 of the Convention on the Rights of the Child (the CRC), which provides that: 'a child means every human being below the age of eighteen years unless, under the law applicable to the child, majority is attained earlier'. This book will use that definition, and all references to children or childhood should be assumed to include all persons under the age of 18 unless otherwise specified. However, although the CRC is the most ratified human rights treaty, its view of when childhood ends and adulthood begins is still not universally accepted.

Our increasing concern about children's participation in hostilities is the result of both our changed views about childhood, and about warfare and soldiering. Children are excluded from participating in hostilities not because they are too young to engage effectively in combat, in which case they could serve in auxiliary roles, but because the experience is seen as damaging to them. Previously, children participating in hostilities could be seen as heroic. One of the heroes of the First World War, for example, was Boy First Class John Travers Cornwall, who was mortally wounded at the Battle of Jutland aged 16 and awarded the Victoria Cross posthumously.[6] Today, war is no longer seen as glorious or as a rite of passage into adulthood. War is hell and child soldiers are victims.

There has been a tendency to focus on child combatants to the exclusion of other children associated with armed force and groups. However, children can participate in conflict in a variety of ways. In the Cape Town Principles and Best Practices,[7] adopted at a symposium on the prevention of recruitment of children

[5] Ilene Cohn and Guy S. Goodwin-Gill, *Child Soldiers: The Role of Children in Armed Conflicts*, Oxford: Oxford University Press, 1994, p. 3.

[6] Smith, *op. cit.* note 4.

[7] Cape Town Principles and Best Practices, adopted at the symposium on the prevention of recruitment of children into the armed forces and on demobilisation and social reintegration of child soldiers in Africa, Cape Town, South Africa, 27–30 April 1997.

into the armed forces and on the demobilisation and social reintegration of child soldiers in Africa organised by the NGO working group on the Convention on the Rights of the Child and the United Nations Fund for Children (UNICEF) in 1997, child soldiers are defined as: 'Any person under 18 years of age who is part of any kind of regular or irregular armed force or group in any capacity, including but not limited to cooks, porters, messengers and anyone accompanying such groups, other than family members. The definition includes girls recruited for sexual purposes. It does not, therefore, only refer to a child who is carrying or has carried arms'. It will be seen that international law does not always comport with this definition. However, it provides a useful heuristic tool for examining the child-soldier phenomenon.

Statistics

The nature of warfare across much of the world is not the traditional clash of armies. Conflicts involve guerrilla warfare, with civilians and civilian objects often the combatants' main targets. In the First World War, admittedly an exception, civilians accounted for only 5 per cent of casualties. In the Second World War, the figure rose to 48 per cent. Today, however, up to 90 per cent of combat casualties around the world are civilians.[8] Children disproportionately suffer from the effects of war, not only because they are themselves targeted, but also because the family and community structures and educational and health systems on which they rely are disrupted or destroyed. UNICEF has estimated that between 1986 and 1996, armed conflicts killed two million children, injured six million, traumatised over ten million and left more than one million orphaned. Almost half the world's twenty-one million refugees are children, while another thirteen million children have been displaced within the borders of their own countries.[9] Moreover, children, particularly conflict-affected children, have been and are continuing to be recruited into a variety of armed forces and groups.

Precise statistics are impossible to come by, but more than 300,000 children are believed to be serving as soldiers in conflicts across the world today.[10] According to the Coalition to Stop the Use of Child Soldiers, in the period between 1999 and 2001 children were fighting in some thirty-six armed conflicts, and in more than eighty-five countries children had been recruited into 'governmental armed forces, paramilitaries, civil militia and a wide variety of non-state armed groups'.[11] Child

[8] See Report of the Special Representative of the Secretary-General for Children and Armed Conflict: Protection of Children Affected by Armed Conflict, 12 October 1998 (A/53/482), para. 9.

[9] See Report of the Secretary-General: Children and Armed Conflict, 19 July 2000 (A/55/163-S/2000/712), para. 2.

[10] See Coalition to Stop the Use of Child Soldiers, *Child Soldiers Global Report 2001*.

[11] *Ibid.*

soldiers have served in recent and ongoing conflicts in Africa, Asia and South and Central America. Most of such children were aged between 15 and 18 but the youngest age reported was 7. For example, it was estimated that in 2000 between 10,000 and 20,000 children under the age of 15 years were serving as combatants within the various forces fighting the conflict in the Democratic Republic of Congo (DRC).[12] And, if the statistics are accurate, the recruitment of children is growing.

Inevitably, these statistics conceal considerable differences in the experiences of child soldiers, differences that are often concealed by the stereotyped view of the child soldier as a pre-adolescent African boy toting an AK-47. Child soldiers vary in age, in how they are recruited and by whom, and in the treatment they face during their military service. Not all child soldiers are boys. Girls also serve, not only in auxiliary roles – cooking, cleaning and serving as 'wives' to adult combatants[13] – but also as combatants themselves, and their gender conditions the treatment they receive.

Although most child soldiers are to be found in governmental armed forces, younger child soldiers are more likely to be found in armed opposition groups. In the admittedly partial lists of parties to conflicts recruiting or using child soldiers in breach of their international obligations produced by the UN Secretary-General in 2003,[14] only seven out of the fifty-two parties listed were governments. However, there are exceptions. In Burma, there are believed to be some 70,000 children serving in the Tatmadav Kyi (the government army) and reports state that children as young as eleven have been forcibly recruited into its ranks. In addition, the Secretary-General's list only covered situations of armed conflict where parties were in breach of their obligations under international law. As we will see, international law does not prohibit all recruitment or use of children to participate in armed conflict, although this is the objective to which many NGOs are working. A number of developed states, including the USA and the UK, recruit children into their national armed forces. The US armed forces recruit from high school graduation, which can be at 17 years of age. The British army recruits from age 16, the age at which compulsory schooling ends in the UK.[15] Opposition from these developed states has prevented the adoption of a 'straight-18' standard prohibiting all recruitment or use in hostilities of children under 18. Indeed, Rachel

[12] See *op. cit.* note 10, at Box 2.

[13] A number of the accused before the Special Court for Sierra Leone have been arraigned on charges of 'inhumane acts' – a crime against humanity – relating to forced marriage. See the Office of the Prosecutor, Special Court for Sierra Leone, press release, 'Prosecutor Welcomes Arraignment of RUF and AFRC Indictees on Charges Relating to Forced Marriages', 17 May 2004.

[14] Report of the Secretary-General: Children and Armed Conflict, 10 November 2003 (A/58/546-S/2003/1053*), Annexes 1 and 2. The national armed forces listed were those of Burundi, Côte d'Ivoire, the Democratic Republic of Congo, Liberia, Somalia, Burma and Uganda. In addition, several governmental-allied militias were listed.

[15] For further details on US and UK recruitment practices, see pp. 19–20.

Brett and Margaret McCallin have suggested that, taking all recruitment of under-18s into account, including that undertaken in peacetime and in conformity with applicable national legislation, the real number of child soldiers in the world today may be more than double the usual estimate.[16]

How and why are children are recruited?

Children are recruited into armed forces and groups in a number of ways. They are compulsorily and forcibly recruited. They also frequently volunteer to serve in armed forces and groups.

Compulsory recruitment: Compulsory recruitment, or conscription, occurs when persons falling within a particular category are under a legal obligation to perform a specified period of military service. Most states today only conscript from age 18 or above.[17]

Forced recruitment: Children are also forcibly recruited, that is, simply taken out of school or seized at road checkpoints, etc., and enrolled into a national armed force or armed opposition group. For example, on 8 November 2002 in Mudzi Pela in Ituri in the Democratic Republic of Congo, the UPC, an armed opposition group, reportedly entered the *ecole primaire* and rounded up the entire fifth grade, some forty children, for military service.[18] Such treatment shades into abduction.

Volunteering: However, children also enlist voluntarily in armed forces and groups, although the extent to which a child can meaningfully consent to join an armed force or group is a matter of controversy. Indeed, this is the main way in which children become soldiers. Given this, we might want to ask both not only why are children recruited into armed forces and groups but also why they volunteer to do so.

Few states now admit to conscripting children into their armed forces, even when they are not parties to the Optional Protocol to the Convention on the Rights of the Child on the Involvement of Children in Armed Conflict (the OP), which prohibits the practice. However, the existence of a legal minimum age at which a person is liable to conscription does not always protect children from being compulsorily recruited. Individuals' lack of documents verifying their age may be used against them when the government recruiters come, or conscription may be conducted on a 'quota' basis, where it is the number, not the identities of the conscripts which is predetermined, and local authorities determine who is chosen.[19] Nor does the existence of a system of conscription prevent some governments

[16] R. Brett and M. McCallin, *Children: The Invisible Soldiers*, Stockholm: Rädda Barnen, rev. edn 1998, p. 12.

[17] See the statistics in Chapter 6, p. 80.

[18] Human Rights Watch, *Ituri: 'Covered in Blood': Ethnically Targeted Violence in Northeastern DR Congo*, New York: HRW, 2003, p. 47.

[19] See R. Brett and M. McCallin, *op. cit.* note 16, pp. 80–3.

from forcibly recruiting children into their armed forces. For example, in Sudan in 1995, following widespread draft evasion, boys as young as 12 were forcibly recruited into the army after having been picked up at checkpoints or taken from buses and other vehicles, football stadia and other recreation centres.[20] In addition, a number of insurgent armed groups have systematically engaged in the forced recruitment of children, including undertaking raids on villages and towns to kidnap children for enrolment into their forces.

According to Cohn and Goodwin-Gill, government armed forces are primarily motivated by manpower shortages. Forced recruitment may be a response to an immediate shortage of manpower. Children are forcibly recruited alongside young men. The age of those taken is a matter of indifference. Another reason why forced recruitment is resorted to, however, is class discrimination. Forcible recruitment targets the most vulnerable and disenfranchised groups in society, such as street children, whose families cannot effectively complain about their treatment. This might explain why forced recruitment has taken place even when governments have imposed conscription. A fairly applied system of conscription can be unpopular among a government's most influential supporters, whose children may be vulnerable to recruitment. Even if their children are recruited, rich parents are able to buy them out from military service. Indeed, forcible recruitment is frequently utilised as a method of repression aimed at minority or dissident groups, taking away from the group those members most likely to resist government measures and holding them as hostages for the good behaviour of those remaining. In addition, as many developing states have weak administrative systems and are unable to record or track the identities, ages and addresses of their population, even when they do not compulsorily or forcibly recruit children, their desire for new blood can lead them to accept recruits without enquiring about their age.

The motives of armed opposition groups who forcibly recruit children seem to be slightly different. Unable to conscript, as conscription is a governmental prerogative, insurgent groups frequently resort to forced recruitment to alleviate manpower shortages. The Sri Lankan Tamil Tigers, for example, only started recruiting children following the intervention of the Indian Peacekeeping Force in 1987, which, by excluding them from their traditional areas of recruitment, led to a manpower shortage.[21] In such cases, the youth of those recruited is a matter of indifference. However, elsewhere it appears that armed opposition groups have made a positive choice to recruit children. In Mozambique in the 1980s, RENAMO systematically targeted children for forced recruitment. As a RENAMO deserter forcibly recruited at the age of 10 explained: 'RENAMO does not use many adults to fight because they are not good fighters ... kids have more stamina, are better at surviving in the bush, do not complain, and follow orders'.[22] Indeed, RENAMO

[20] Human Rights Watch, *Children of Sudan: Slaves, Street Children and Child Soldiers* (HRW: New York, 1995), pp. 55–6.

[21] *Op. cit.* note 5, p. 29.

[22] Quoted *op. cit.* note 5, p. 26.

made substantial efforts to indoctrinate their child recruits, sever the links between them and their families and communities, and develop a dependency relationship between the child recruits and their captors. Brutal initiation rituals, such as forcing recruits, on pain of death themselves, to kill a comrade or a village elder in front of their neighbours, rendered child recruits both unable to return home and accustomed to killing.

> The strategy of the MNR [RENAMO] was to intimidate young boys until their socialization pattern was broken down and they actually accepted a gun willingly. Then they were forced to kill someone. The typical process entailed taking a boy back to his own village and forcing him to kill someone known to him. The killing took place in such a way that the community knew that he had killed, thus effectively closing the door to the child ever returning to his village.[23]

Child soldiers are recruited because they are more docile and more easily manipulated. They are also more fearless, being less able to assess the risks of combat and lacking the strong streak of self-preservation adults have. A relief worker in Liberia commented: 'I think they [the warring factions] use kids because the kids don't understand the risk and children are easier to control and manipulate. If the commanding officer tells a child to do something, he does it'.[24]

Indeed, in some cases, it appears that children are targeted for recruitment specifically because they can be more easily persuaded to commit atrocities. As Rachel Brett and Margaret McCallin state: 'the greater suggestibility of children and the degree to which they can be normalized into violence means that child soldiers are more likely to commit atrocities than adults'. In Sierra Leone, children were singled out for recruitment both by the armed opposition and by groups fighting in support of the government.[25] More than 5,000 children are estimated to have fought as combatants, with another 5,000 associated with rebel forces as porters, servants and sexual slaves. Most of the children in the rebel forces were forcibly recruited from their homes. They were extremely brutally treated and ordered to commit atrocities. One former Revolutionary United Front (RUF) child soldier reported that in 1998: 'We were ordered to kill any civilian we might come across. Any fighter or children suspected of being reluctant to do the killings were severely beaten. We are asked to advance and to do everything possible to terrorize the civilians. It was during this period that people's hands and limbs were cut off'.[26] Child soldiers were beaten and killed if they refused to obey such orders. Similarly, in the Lord's Resistance Army (LRA) in Uganda, child abductees

[23] Cole P. Dodge, 'Child Soldiers of Uganda and Mozambique', in Cole P. Dodge and Magne Raundalen (eds), *Reaching Children in War: Sudan, Uganda and Mozambique*, Bergen: Sigma Forlag, 1991, p. 57.

[24] Quoted in Human Rights Watch, *Easy Prey: Child Soldiers in Liberia*, New York: HRW, 1994, p. 23.

[25] See Amnesty International, *Sierra Leone: Childhood – a Casualty of Conflict*, 2000, AI Index AFR/51/69/00.

[26] *Ibid.*, p. 4.

were forced to abduct other children, to participate in the killings of children who attempted to escape or were captured, to beat and sometimes kill civilians in looting operations, and steal from and burn down houses.[27]

Children associated with armed forces and groups undertake a variety of tasks. They often start in support roles. Destitute or unaccompanied children attach themselves to individual soldiers, working as servants in exchange for food and shelter. Children are used for guard duty, patrolling and staffing checkpoints, or as porters, often being required to carry very heavy loads. A former child soldier for UNITA in Angola, recalling his experiences as a porter, stated that: 'For our work, we had to carry heavy things. Mortar shells for example ... Our main job was to carry ammunition from the bases in the *altura* (heights) to the front lines. It was difficult work because the loads were heavy. We were often hungry and without proper clothes and sometimes it would happen that people would "disappear" [die]'.[28]

Children, it appears, are often preferred for some jobs, such as messengers, spies, scouts and mine layers, for which their age, size and agility are deemed to render them particularly suitable. As a consequence, even if not defined as combatants, children are often given hazardous assignments. Another UNITA child soldier stated: 'I ... had to carry messages back and forth to the front lines. It was dangerous because you were on the front, in combat. If you didn't have luck you could be captured or killed'.[29] Children, however, are frequently also employed as combatants, either routinely or when shortages in the numbers of combatants are considered to require it, especially as they grow older.

Why do children volunteer?

After examining the ways in which children were recruited, the 1996 Machel report concluded that: 'While young people may appear to choose military service, the choice is not exercised freely. They may be driven by any of several forces, including cultural, social, economic or political pressures'.[30] Children might enlist to ensure that they and their families are fed, or for their own protection. It was remarked that 'The lure of ideology was particularly strong in early adolescence', with often 'disastrous consequences', instancing the child *genocidaires* in Rwanda and the child suicide bombers in the Lebanon and Sri Lanka.[31] However, the

[27] Human Rights Watch, *Stolen Children: Abduction and Recruitment in Northern Uganda*, New York: HRW, 2003, p. 9.

[28] Human Rights Watch, *Forgotten Fighters: Child Soldiers in Angola*, New York: HRW, 2003, p. 9.

[29] *Ibid.*

[30] *Impact of Armed Conflict on Children*: Report of the Expert of the Secretary-General, Ms Graça Machel, submitted pursuant to GA Res. 48.157, 26 August 1996 (A/51/306) para. 38.

[31] *Ibid.*, para. 43.

report also stated that: 'Children may also identify with and fight for social causes, religious expression or national liberation, as happened in South Africa or in occupied territories, they may join the struggle in pursuit of political freedom'.[32] This appraisal of children's motives for volunteering neatly illustrates the ambiguities of many responses to the phenomenon. On the one hand, children are not seen as having sufficient psychological maturity to consent meaningfully to joining an armed force or group. On the other hand, however, there is a tendency to categorise children's motives for volunteering as permissible or impermissible depending on whether the observer agrees with them or not. It is undoubtedly correct that volunteering, compulsory and forced recruitment form parts of a continuum rather than being sharply defined and distinct categories. However, no decision, whether made by a child or an adult, is made in a vacuum. The argument is not so much that children are exposed to pressures which adults are not, but that children are more easily manipulated into making decisions which are not in their own best interests.

A study of child soldiers by Rachel Brett and Margaret McCallin described child soldiers as coming from three groups: from the poor or otherwise disadvantaged in society; from the population of the actual conflict zones themselves; and, over and above the overlap with the other two categories, from those with disrupted or non-existent family backgrounds.[33] More recently, a survey by Rachel Brett and Irma Specht[34] concluded that five major factors underpinned adolescents' volunteering for armed forces and groups: war, poverty, education, employment and family. Other motivating factors referred to in the literature include societal attitudes to violence as a means of effecting change and military life, and national, ideological or religious loyalties and obligations, as well as propaganda specifically directed at inducing recruitment.

War: Children do not go looking for conflicts in which to participate; war comes to them. War involves the militarisation of society, making participation in military activities seem the norm. War exacerbates already existing problems, such as the lack of educational and economic opportunities. Family life is disrupted. Children experience and witness acts of violence. War gives rise to feelings of vulnerability and helplessness among children. Membership of an armed force or group may be seen as the best of a series of bad alternatives. Volunteering at least provides some security and a subsistence wage. This is particularly the case with street children, orphans, refugees and displaced children. Children living in zones of conflict, according to Rachel Brett and Margaret McCallin, are most likely to

[32] *Ibid.*

[33] Brett and McCallin, *op. cit.* note 16, p. 103.

[34] Rachel Brett and Irma Specht, *Young Soldiers – Why They Choose to Fight*, Geneva/New York: ILO/Lynne Rienner, forthcoming 2004; summary in 'Child Soldiers: Why Adolescents Volunteer: Statement by Friends World Committee for Consultation (Quakers) to the 28th International Conference of the Red Cross and Red Crescent', Geneva, 5 December 2003.

have the direct experience of abuse by government armed forces that they identify as the main reason for their volunteering for armed opposition groups. However, although children do not going looking for war, Rachel Brett and Irma Specht also state that: 'for adolescents war can also be an opportunity: for employment (formal or informal); for escape from an oppressive family situation or humiliation at school; for adventure in serving "the cause" or emulating real or fictional military role models'.[35]

Poverty: Poor children have the strongest economic and social incentives to volunteer. Poverty is the single most easily identifiable common characteristic of child soldiers. It is rare for children not living in poverty to become child soldiers.

Education: School is one of the institutions at the centre of children's lives. War often disrupts children's schooling, leaving them at a loss as to what to do and thus vulnerable to the blandishments of armed forces and groups. In Afghanistan, with approximately 90 per cent of children having no access to schooling, the Machel report noted a rise in the proportion of child soldiers from 30 per cent to at least 45 per cent.[36]

Employment: Lack of education restricts children's choice of employment; while lack of employment can make enlistment into an armed force or group appear an attractive option. Armed forces recruit most easily during times of high unemployment and in areas in economic difficulties. Indeed, Brett and Specht see child soldiering as a form of child labour, and argue that eliminating child soldiering without providing adequate alternatives will simply lead to a rise in other forms of child labour.

Family: As with school, family is at the centre in a child's life. It is well documented that the loss or absence of family frequently leads to children joining armed forces or groups, hence the high level of recruitment among orphans and children who have been separated from their families. In Uganda, as a result of the 1983–5 anti-insurgency campaign by the Obote government, thousands of children were orphaned or separated from their families. Many fled to the rebel National Resistance Army (NRA), which absorbed some 3,000 children under 16 into its ranks.[37] Although originally used in auxiliary roles, by 1985 the NRA was pressing every available soldier into action, and many of the child soldiers were highly motivated, seeking to avenge the atrocities committed against their families by government forces.[38] Conversely, many adolescents who volunteer are running away from abusive or exploitative domestic situations. In particular, there seems to be a high correlation between domestic exploitation, physical and/or sexual abuse and girls' decisions to volunteer.

Societal attitudes and propaganda: Although Brett and Specht argue that addressing 'the stereotyping which encourages or pressurizes boys into taking up

[35] *Ibid.*, p. 1.
[36] Machel report, para. 40.
[37] Cohn and Goodwin-Gill, *op. cit.* note 5, p. 34.
[38] Dodge, *op. cit.* note 23, pp. 51–4.

arms would have a major impact on child soldiering',[39] they do not specifically emphasize children's ecologies as a major factor in their joining armed forces and groups. Other writers have looked at matters differently. For Cohn and Goodwin-Gill, the factors influencing children's decision to volunteer can be divided into two groups: objective features of children's war-related experiences and children's subjective appraisals of those experiences.[40] In deciding how to cope with their experiences and the emotions engendered by them, children are heavily influenced by social, community and family values, and by peer pressure. Societal attitudes, as advanced by community leaders, teachers and parents, and their peers can direct children to the conclusion that the best way of overcoming their personal difficulties, displaying maturity and becoming a full member of the collective is to join the struggle. Such pressures are peculiarly potent because children are in the process of identity formation.

Girls' motives for volunteering: Brett and McCallin identified the main contrast between government armed forces and armed opposition groups as being that whereas the former are overwhelmingly male, the latter tend to involve both men and women. To a large extent this is because everyone in a guerrilla camp is self-identified as a member of the group, whereas the same does not apply to the civilian population within which government armed forces live. However, even taking this into account, it does appear that women and girls are more in evidence in armed opposition groups, and, in particular, are more likely to serve as combatants. It has often been assumed that all child soldiers are boys, or that girls are only associated with armed forces and groups as 'camp followers': cooks, domestic servants, nurses, porters, and concubines and 'wives' of adult combatants. It is now better recognised that both girls and boys serve in combatant roles. However, girls' motives for volunteering are distinct and their particular situation needs to be taken into account when developing strategies to eliminate volunteerism.

A recent survey has looked at the experiences of girl child soldiers in armed opposition groups.[41] It found that becoming a child soldier was very dependent on a combination of the local environment and the personal circumstances surrounding the girl's life.

> Girls who volunteered were usually influenced to join by a significant person in their life or because they believed the movement's propaganda that promised them a better life. They saw themselves as having food, a uniform that would give them status and a group to which they could belong. On a personal level they had either dropped out of school or found going to school problematic, were poor and lived in abusive or separated families. They also wanted to participate in the important decisions that were going to affect their life. For, example they did not want to accept an arranged marriage planned by their family or be hired out as a domestic

[39] *Ibid.*, p. 3.

[40] *Op. cit.* note 5, pp. 31–43.

[41] Yvonne E. Keairns, *The Voices of Girl Child Soldiers*, Geneva: Quaker United Nations Office/Coalition to Stop the Use of Child Soldiers, 2002.

> servant for low pay, cruel treatment and separation from the significant people in their life. Generally speaking the girls who volunteered had some notion that their life would be improved by joining.[42]

Factors influencing girls' decisions to volunteer included poverty, which was a key determinant; exploitation and/or abuse within the family; propaganda by the group (although recruits were attached not so much by the cause as by the chance to do something exciting, purposeful and capable of leading to change); and because significant others (boyfriends, brothers, girlfriends) in their life had already joined the movement. Girls interviewed from the Philippines and Colombia felt that the groups to which they had belonged had provided them with opportunities which they otherwise would not have achieved and, if not for the fighting, they would have preferred life in the group to civilian life.[43] It may not be coincidental that the groups of which these girls were members are highly ideological, and, as adherents of Marxist ideologies, at least nominally committed to social change and sexual equality. Girls who had been forcibly recruited were, unsurprisingly, less positive about their experiences.

Conclusions: Brett and Specht concluded their survey by arguing that 'any activities which (1) end wars, (2) reduce poverty, (3) provide access to relevant and good quality education for all children, and (5) improve family solidarity and parenting skills' will have an effect on reduc, the incidence of child volunteering. Twelve years previously, Cohn and Goodwin-Gill's conclusions did not much differ. They wrote that child volunteers' motivation: 'lies in the very root of the conflicts, in the predominant macro social, economic and political issues defining their lives. Overwhelming as it may seem, confronting these larger concerns may be the only realistic road to preventing youth participation in otherwise unavoidable hostilities'.[44] The only method liable to ensure a permanent reduction of children's volunteering is to address the root causes of such behaviour. This has been the mantra reiterated by virtually all persons active in addressing the issue. It suggests, however, that the child-soldier phenomenon is likely to continue to be with us for the foreseeable future.

What are the effects of children's membership of armed forces and groups?

Child soldiers generally receive much the same treatment as adult recruits. However, in both government armed forces and armed opposition groups, the treatment accorded to recruits of all ages is often inhuman and degrading. Although children usually receive the same training and health care as their adult comrades,

[42] *Ibid.*, p. 3.
[43] *Ibid.*, p. 4.
[44] *Op. cit.* note 5, p. 23.

this may mean little or nothing. Training is hard and discipline harsh. The food is often poor and the medical care available inadequate. Such treatment and conditions often impact more seriously on child recruits, as they are less physically and psychologically equipped to withstand it.

Moreover, child soldiers are often victimised by their adult comrades, who require them to act as servants and perform personal services. Recruits may face brutal initiation rituals. Girl child soldiers, in particular, are often subjected to sexual abuse. A girl soldier from Honduras recounted that: 'I found out that girls were obliged to have sexual relations "to alleviate the sadness of the combatants". And who alleviated our sadness after going with someone we hardly knew? At my young age I experienced abortion. It was not my decision. There is a great pain in my being when I recall all these things'.[45] Several armed opposition groups practise sexual slavery, forcibly recruiting girls for sexual purposes. Girls are forced to 'entertain' the troops or serve as 'wives' to adult combatants. In Angola, girls were forced to dance, sing and respond to the sexual demands of the troops. They were forbidden to talk about their former lives. If they refused the men's advances, they were tied to trees and beaten with sticks. Some were killed.[46] In the RUF in Sierra Leone, girl child abductees were considered to belong to the soldier who kidnapped them, becoming his 'wife'.[47] Many of them were forced to bear their captor's children. However, not all girl child soldiers are sexually abused. Among the Tamil Tigers in Sri Lanka, love affairs or sexual relations were considered offences subject to severe disciplinary action if discovered. In an armed group in the Philippines, female and male members of the group were segregated and approval had to be obtained from the group's authorities for any relationship.

Child soldiers are subject to military discipline. Severe physical abuse is often the penalty for infractions such as failing military training, falling asleep on guard duty, disobeying orders or attempting to desert. Some armed opposition groups mete out especially brutal treatment to children. The LRA in Uganda, for example, 'initiates' all children a day or two after their abduction, giving them a severe beating, purportedly to 'harden' them to life as soldiers, and smearing them with shea nut oil. The children are told they will be killed if they attempt to leave the group. They are beaten by LRA commanders and soldiers for any disobedience and to encourage them to march faster.[48] Many case studies report children being shot for attempted desertion or attempting to evade enrolment. Children in armed opposition groups who cannot keep up or who try to escape are often routinely killed so as to prevent them revealing the group's secrets or simply *pour encourager les autres*. There are also numerous reports of children being given drugs and/or alcohol, particularly before battle. A former RUF child soldier reported how before attacks every combatant, including the children, was given cocaine and marijuana.

[45] Quoted in the Machel report, para. 46.
[46] Keairns, *op. cit.* note 41, pp. 7–8.
[47] *Op. cit.* note 25, at p. 9.
[48] *Op. cit.* note 27, at pp. 8–9.

He said: 'After sniffing cocaine, I was not afraid of anything. I became bloody'.[49] When child soldiers refused to take drugs they were beaten and, in some cases, killed.[50] When child soldiers in armed opposition groups are well treated it is usually because everyone in the group is similarly well treated.

Child soldier's experiences lead to certain consequences. Being a child soldier is hazardous, and child soldiers are frequently killed or wounded. Even if they escape physical injury, child soldiers may suffer psychological damage. In addition, they may suffer from lack of education and skills training and be stigmatised as a result of their membership of an armed force or group. Girl child soldiers face particular problems.

Physical injury: Child soldiers suffer both at the hands of the enemy and from the treatment meted out to them by their own side. Many are killed, others wounded. Because of their lack of physical maturity and smaller size, children are at greater risk of injury than their adult comrades. Frequently reported injuries are loss of hearing (caused by using heavy weaponry without ear protectors), loss of limbs and blindness. In addition, the strenuous tasks they are required to perform and the lack of proper food and medical treatment they often suffer, can lead to illness and disability. Reporting on children who had been abducted by the LRA in Uganda:

> A nurse at World Vision identified gunshot wounds, skin problems from walking long distances, and sexually transmitted diseases as the major physical problems affecting returnees. She estimates that about fifteen percent return with gunshot wounds and another five percent have injuries from bomb fragments. Fifteen children assisted by the [World Vision rehabilitation] center [in Gulu] since 1996 have had limbs amputated.[51]

Psychological consequences: Even if child soldiers escape physical injury, they frequently suffer psychological trauma. The move from the care of one's family to the closed environment of an armed force or group is disturbing, particularly when it is accompanied by physical abuse, bullying and harassment. Child soldiers are often the victims, perpetrators and/or witnesses of atrocious acts: killing, maiming, rape, torture, wounding, the destruction of property and the displacement of people. They may develop a dependency relationship with their commanders and become inured to killing. A Liberian psychiatrist described the typical child soldier in the Liberia's civil war as follows.

> He is 15 years and may be a young as 9. He carries a gun that is sometimes heavier than his body weight. ... He is very *deadly*. He has been *programmed* to carry out orders without question. He is too immature to differentiate what is good from what is evil. He has been catapulted from childhood to adulthood. He has been taught to get everything he desires forcibly. Patience, perseverance, respect for elders are not part of the make-up of his thinking faculty ... He enjoys the cracking

[49] *Op. cit.* note 25, at p. 4.
[50] *Ibid.*, at p. 7.
[51] Quoted, *op. cit.* note 27, p. 18.

> of his gun and the sound of a gun going off, the menacing noise of an RPG [rocket-propelled grenade] while oblivious to the destruction and taking of life it may cause.[52]

Child soldiers can develop post-traumatic stress disorder, as well as experiencing feelings of fear, impotence, guilt and depression. The World Vision nurse also said of returnees from the LRA that: 'Almost all of them suffer from nightmares and flashbacks, especially those that were long in the bush. Some are quiet, withdrawn and don't want to talk'.[53] The psychological consequences may continue long after child soldiers have recovered from their physical injuries. It may, however, be that the extent to which a child soldier suffers psychological difficulties depends on how he views himself. Volunteers may be less prone to such problems than those who were compulsorily or forcibly recruited.

Loss of education: Serving as a soldier in almost all cases disrupts the child soldier's education and prevents him or her accessing vocational training opportunities. In addition, child soldiers grows up in a closed military environment, which often prizes prompt obedience at the expense of individual initiative. Their lack of education and skills makes them less employable, while they are unused to taking responsibility for their own actions. As a result, former child soldiers frequently find reintegration into civilian life difficult and are often unable to find any but the most menial employment.

Stigmatisation: Former child soldiers are also often stigmatised because of their past membership of the armed force or group with which they were associated. Because of child soldiers' participation in atrocities, even if often coerced, communities may be unwilling to permit them to return home. In other cases, the locality might be controlled or populated by opponents of the group, whose aims and opinions they impute to the former child soldier. In addition, former child soldiers are often stereotyped as violent and disturbed.

Consequences for the girl child soldier: These can include sexually transmitted diseases and fertility problems (particularly as a result of inexpert abortions). They may have borne, and now have responsibility for, their captors' children. Participation in an armed force or group is frequently seen as especially stigmatising for girls: shaming their families (who may, as a result, be unwilling to accept them home), damaging their marriage prospects, and rendering them purportedly unfit for respectable employment.

More broadly, families, communities and entire societies can suffer repercussions from children's participation in armed forces and groups, ranging from collective punishment for permitting their children to be recruited, to juvenile delinquency and discipline problems, to having to care for the homeless, orphaned

[52] Quoted in Stephen Ellis, *The Mask of Anarchy: The Destruction of Liberia and the Religious Dimension of an African Civil* War, London: Hurst & Co, 1999, p. 131 (emphasis in original).

[53] Quoted, *ibid.*, at p. 18.

and disabled. Occasionally, children's participation in armed forces and groups is argued to have various positive effects. These include the opportunity to better oneself and learn useful skills, greater political awareness and group identity. These, however, have not been emphasised in the literature.

Children in armed forces in peacetime

The foregoing survey is, however, a partial one. International concern has concentrated on the recruitment and use of child soldiers in times of war. Yet many children serve in armed forces in peacetime. Indeed, taking such children into account could double our estimate of how many child soldiers there are in the world today.

National armed forces accepting the voluntary enlistment of under-18s include those of Angola, Australia, Bangladesh, Brazil, Canada, France, Germany, Iran, Israel, India, Italy, Mexico, Poland, Serbia-Montenegro, Tanzania, the UK and the USA.[54] For example, the US armed forces permit the recruitment of 17-year-olds with parental consent and some 50,000 such children are recruited into the US military each year,[55] although only a small proportion (no more than 2,500) of these recruits complete training prior to turning 18.[56] The British army recruits 16-year-olds into the Army Foundation College, while 17-year-olds can join the 'man's service', although parental consent is still required.[57] Under-18s were deployed during the first Gulf War, where nearly 500 British soldiers were aged under 18, and in Kosovo.[58]

In the USA, the UK and elsewhere, the age of recruitment for voluntary enlistment is linked to the school leaving age. Recruiting soldiers young ensures that individuals considering a military career have that option as soon as they finish education, ensuring that they do not have to obtain other employment until they are old enough, which might lead them to abandon their original ambition, or get into trouble before they have the opportunity to enlist. It is also thought that soldiers who are recruited young stay in the military longer. The position of the UK Ministry of Defence is that the recruitment of 16- to 18-year-olds with their parents' consent is fundamentally different from 'the abusive, compulsory, or coercive involvement of children as members of militia or para-military groups'.[59] Indeed, it has been argued that the campaign to raise the minimum age of recruitment to 18 has been

[54] For a list, see p. 80.

[55] Michael J. Dennis, 'Newly Adopted Protocols to the Convention on the Rights of the Child' (2000) 94 AJIL 798, at p. 791.

[56] *Ibid.*, at p. 792.

[57] Michael Smith, 'Britain Bans Boy Soldiers Going to War', *Daily Telegraph*, 29 March 2002.

[58] *Op. cit.* note 4.

[59] Quoted in Smith, *op. cit.* note 57.

supported by some states not so much for humanitarian reasons as because they do not rely on volunteers to fill their armed forces. Michael J. Dennis, on of the US negotiators of the Optional Protocol to the Convention on the Rights of the Child on the Involvement of Children in Armed Conflict, has written that:

> Governments that meet their national armed forces' recruitment needs through compulsory or forced recruitment have insisted on raising the minimum age standard to eighteen, whereas other governments, like the United States and the United Kingdom, maintain all-volunteer armed forces and have professed the need for flexibility to recruit individuals during the time they are finishing their secondary education.[60]

Although human rights groups have condemned the peacetime recruitment of under-18-year-olds, their focus has remained on the participation of children in armed conflict. However, in 2000 Amnesty International produced a report on the treatment of child soldiers in the British army. The report concluded that the recruitment of under-18s and their training in military establishments puts their mental and physical integrity at risk; that training using live ammunition and endurance exercises aimed at pushing recruits to their limits endangered the mental and physical health of under-18s; and that allegations of ill-treatment and bullying in the armed forces, coupled with the inadequacy of the complaints procedure, might amount to cruel, inhuman or degrading treatment of recruits.[61] Amnesty International's policy is that no child should be permitted to serve in an armed force or group.[62]

A number of these issues have been taken up elsewhere.[63] In 1991, Jack Ashley MP proposed the establishment of a military ombudsman to protect soldiers' interests. This suggestion was echoed in the recent report of Surrey Police into the deaths of four young recruits at Deepcut Barracks.[64] All four died of gunshot wounds and although their families have suggested that they were murdered, all investigations undertaken into the circumstances of the recruits' deaths have concluded that each took his or her own life. The final report by Surrey Police stated that:

> Training can be considered a significant point in soldiers' vulnerability, as it marks the transition at which recruits, some as young as 16 years old, move from civilian to service life, and the time when the Army knows least about them. At this point recruits may be in barracks up to 24 hours-a-day, away from the immediate support of families and friends. They are contained in a training environment, which is in itself demanding and turbulent.[65]

[60] Michael J. Dennis, 'The ILO Convention on the Worst Forms of Child Labor' (1999) 93 AJIL 943, at p. 945.

[61] Amnesty International, *United Kingdom: U-18s: Child Soldiers at risk*, AI Index EUR 45/56/00, 2000, at p. 20.

[62] *Ibid.*, pp. 1–2.

[63] For an outline of developments, see Surrey Police, *The Deepcut Investigation: Final Report* (2004).

[64] *Ibid.*, para. 2.22.

[65] *Ibid.*, para. 4.0.

The report found that the Army had been slow to respond to the deaths or to learn any lessons from them, and that this failure derived in part from 'the Army's inability to consider the possible relationships between the Army care regime, the training regime and episodes of undetermined death, suicide and self-harm'.[66] However, the report also considered that a 'fundamental change' had occurred in the Army's response from August 2002, following the involvement of the deceased soldiers' families, the start of Surrey Police's investigation and increasing public scrutiny.[67] Although the Ministry of Defence's decision not to hold a public inquiry into the deaths has been criticised,[68] what is interesting is how little stress has been placed on the fact that two out of the four deceased recruits were under 18 at the time of their deaths. Instead, the emphasis on the British Army's responsibility to all young soldiers in its care. Perhaps unsurprisingly, the voluntary recruitment of 16- and 17-year-olds with their parents' consent is not seen by the British public in the same way as the forced or compulsory recruitment of pre-pubescent children. To the extent that Article 1 of the Convention on the Rights of the Child (CRC) defines childhood as an undifferentiated state, it differs from popular perceptions of what childhood is, when it ends and how it is divided into different stages.

Indeed, later provisions of the CRC itself take a more nuanced approach, Article 12(1) providing that: 'States Parties shall assure to the child who is capable of forming his or her own views the right to express those views freely in all matters affecting the child, the views of the child being given due weight in accordance with the age and maturity of the child'. The best interests of the children are to be determined by taking account of the child's wishes, although these may not be conclusive. In English law this has meant, in the words of Lord Denning, that: 'the legal right of a parent to the custody of a child ends at the eighteenth birthday and even up till then, it is a dwindling right which the courts will hesitate to enforce against the wishes of the child, the older he is. It starts with a right of control and ends with little more than advice'.[69] Lord Denning contrasted this view with the attitude of the courts in the Victorian period, which saw absolute paternal authority continuing until a child attained majority. His insight was that views of what childhood is and what it entails develop over time. The next chapter will consider the issue of how perceptions of childhood and children's rights have changed, and how this has affected the ways in which child soldiers have been viewed. It will be shown that viewing the child-soldier phenomenon through a child rights prism in no way simplifies the issue.

[66] *Ibid.*, para. 4.4.

[67] *Ibid.*, para. 4.12.

[68] See, e.g. 'Out of order', leader, *Guardian*, 25 May 2004.

[69] *Hewer* v. *Bryant* [1970] 1 QB 357 at 369. See also *Gillick* v. *West Norfolk and Wisbech Area Health Authority* [1986] 1 AC 112. However, even the options of a child viewed as being '*Gillick* competent' are subordinate to the child's best interests as determined by the courts.

2

Childhood and children's rights: changing perceptions

Introduction

Perceptions of childhood vary across time and space. Whereas it seems to be the case that few, if any cultures, do not consider that children should be protected against the ravages of war, views as to the extent to which children should be involved in conflict have varied. Indeed, in many cases, what would now be condemned as child soldiering was seen as nothing of the sort. The 'child soldiers' were considered to be appropriately behaving adults and perceived themselves as such. Although NGOs have campaigned for a 'straight 18' ban on all recruitment of children, as we have already seen, such views continue to persist.

One recent change in how children are perceived is the view that children have rights which they can oppose against adults, in particular their parents, and which permit them to make various claims against society in general. It will be seen, however, that applying ideas of children's rights to child recruitment is by no means unproblematic. Indeed, it has been argued that, at least with older children, it should lead to the conclusion that although forced and compulsory recruitment should be prohibited, voluntary recruitment should be permitted.

One criticism that can be made about viewing the issue through a children's rights prism, however, is that it obscures the fact that children and adults frequently face the same pressures and act for the same reasons. As shown in Chapter 1, children are recruited alongside adults; are actuated to join armed forces and groups by much the same motives as adults; and, once within the military, are often treated in much the same ways. Accordingly, looking at child recruitment might also lead us to reconsider our views about adults' participation in the armed forces.

The history of childhood

In his 1960 book *L'Enfant et la vie familiale sous l'ancien régime*,[1] Philippe Ariès claimed that prior to the seventeenth century the idea of childhood did not exist.

[1] Translated into English as *Centuries of Childhood*, New York: Vintage, 1962.

There was no recognition of childhood as a particular state distinct from adulthood. From age 7 onwards, a child was seen as an adult. From then onwards, children lived with adults, played with adults and worked alongside adults. Children under 7, on the other hand, were hardly seen as persons at all. Given the high rate of infant morality, the death of a young child was largely a matter of indifference to his or her parents. A little later, Lloyd deMause equally famously proclaimed that: 'The history of childhood is a nightmare from which we have only recently begun to awaken'.[2] Only from the eighteenth century had parents any true empathy with their children. Prior to that, the history of childhood was a history of abuse; the further back in history, the worse the abuse. In this deMause differed from Ariès, as Ariès did not consider that the lack of recognition of the idea of childhood necessarily meant that children were treated worse in the Middle Ages than they were later. Nevertheless, Ariès and deMause's views, taken together, have greatly influenced children's rights advocates.[3]

Children's rights advocates have viewed the history of childhood teleologically; as progressing from widespread abuse and neglect towards an ever-greater recognition of childhood and of children's rights. This development is thought to be self-evidently a good thing. However, from the time of their publication Ariès and deMause's conclusions have been controversial. To a large extent, they have been discredited. Two things seem clear. First, to use David Archard's terminology,[4] it is necessary to make a distinction between the 'concept' of childhood and 'conceptions' of childhood. For there to be a concept of childhood children must be seen as distinguishable from adults in respect of an unspecified set of attributes. A conception of childhood, on the other hand, specifies what those distinguishing attributes are. One has a concept of childhood if one views and treats children differently from adults. How one views and treats them differently, however, depends upon one's conception of childhood.[5] Contrary to Ariès's conclusions, it seems that all societies at all times have had the concept of childhood. It is their conceptions of childhood that have differed.

Archard suggests three basic ways in which conceptions of childhood can differ: in their boundaries, dimensions and divisions.[6] First, childhood is a relational concept. What a child is can only be understood in relation to what an adult is. The boundary of childhood is when it is deemed to end; that is, when a child becomes an adult. Even today this is not an uncontentious matter, as can be seem from the text of Article 1 of the CRC, which states that: 'For the purposes of the

[2] Lloyd deMause, 'The Evolution of Childhood', in Lloyd deMause (ed.), *The History of Childhood*, New York: Harper, 1976, p. 1.

[3] See Vivian C. Fox, 'Historical Perspectives on Children's Rights', in E. Verhellen and F. Spiesschaert (eds), *Ombudswork for Children: A Way of Improving the Position of Children in Society*, Leuven/Amersfoort: F. Acco, 1989, pp. 297–300; and David Archard, *Children: Rights and Childhood*, London: Routledge, 1993, pp. 15–17.

[4] Taken in turn from John Rawls, see Archard, *ibid.*, pp. 21–2.

[5] *Ibid.*, p. 22.

[6] *Ibid.*, p. 24.

present Convention, a child means every human being below the age of eighteen years unless, under the law applicable to the child, majority is attained earlier'. Article 1 CRC was the result of a compromise between advocates of a universal conception of childhood, defined wholly by age, and thus immunised from cultural differences, and those who considered that local conceptions of where childhood ended and adulthood begin should be recognised. Second, the dimensions of childhood originate in the different perspectives from which childhood is viewed. What a society sees as the significant differences between childhood and adulthood determines how it thinks children should be treated and when it considers childhood ends. Third, the divisions of childhood are how a society sub-divides childhood into periods, such as infancy (which nearly all societies recognise) and adolescence (a rather more contentious category). The manner in which the boundaries, dimensions and divisions of childhood are perceived determines how a society thinks about the extent, nature and significance of childhood.[7] However, to say that past societies had different conceptions of childhood from those held today is not to say that they had no concept of childhood.

The second criticism, of deMause in particular, is based on the work of historians who have found copious evidence of the affection parents had for their children in the past.[8] Much of what has been condemned as child abuse resulted either from economic necessity (child labour, the use of wet nurses) or from misplaced beliefs that the suffering inflicted on children was for their own good (swaddling, corporal punishment, some medical remedies). Indeed, a major problem with both Ariès and deMause's work is its failure to see the past in its own terms. Both authors saw past attitudes to childhood through the prism of present attitudes and found the former wanting. Although purporting to write history, their perspective was fundamentally ahistorical. Indeed, one might speculate that it was precisely this perspective that rendered their conclusions so attractive to some children's rights advocates.

One of the problems when studying the global history of childhood is the paucity of work on the subject. Although the past thirty years have seen an explosion in the literature, it remains concentrated on the history of childhood in Europe and North America. Historians of childhood in South America, Africa and Asia are thin on the ground. Nevertheless, it might be thought that looking at how European and North American societies have conceived childhood and treated children – and how children have responded to the treatment meted out to them – provides a useful perspective by which to view current debates on the status of children in the South. There exist numerous parallels between past and present economic and social developments. Until well into the nineteenth century, most children in the West were brought up in rural environments. The history of

[7] *Ibid.*, p. 27.

[8] See, in particular, Linda Pollock, *Forgotten Children: Parent–Child Relations from 1500 to 1900*, Cambridge: Cambridge University Press, 1983, although Pollock's conclusions, in their turn, have been criticised for idealising the parent–child relationship.

childhood in Europe saw a movement from agrarian, rural societies to industrialised, urban societies, accompanied by the establishment of increasing private and state surveillance over the activities of families and children. Although large differences in cultural and religious traditions exist, similar developments are currently occurring in the South.

Perhaps most importantly, the role of the family has changed in the West. Until the mid-nineteenth century, the family had several functions: '[i]t had to provide for the subsistence of its members, plus their education, vocational training, health, entertainment and old age'.[9] Families were economic as well as emotional units. Indeed, in many cases, sending children to work was necessary for the family's survival, as the parents' wages alone were insufficient for the family to live on.[10] Even if they were not sent out to work, children might perform useful roles in the household and deputise for absent parents. Families were not so child centred. Children worked to support adults as well as vice versa. Today, by contrast, at least in the West, children are seen as economically 'worthless' but emotionally 'priceless'.[11]

Childhood was shorter and less well defined. Children were expected to take on adult roles earlier. There was not the modern idea that an individual's working life only begins when his or her schooling ends. From around 7 years old, children were expected to help around the house, the farm or the workshop. Their tasks would not be the same as those of adults, but increasing responsibilities would be placed upon children as they grew older, ending with them working alongside adults by their early teens. By then they might even have left home to go into service or take up an apprenticeship. Education and employment were not alternatives. A child might be sent to school or receive instruction at home, but education often took second place to children's work at home, on the farm or in the factory. As a result, the move from childhood into adulthood was less of a break and more of a continuum.

Nor were children always anxious to remain in school. Studies of children's responses to schooling in the nineteenth and twentieth centuries show that for many children school was a chore to be avoided. Classes were large, teachers barely trained, lessons based on rote learning and discipline maintained by the copious application of corporal punishment. There was often little of interest for the bright child, and no support for the slow student. Studies show that these conditions are frequently replicated in many schools in the developing world today.[12] One might see a certain irony in the fact that the child's right to education has been implemented by making schooling compulsory.

[9] Colin Heywood, *A History of Childhood: Children and Childhood in the West from Medieval to Modern Times*, Cambridge: Polity, 2001, p. 88.

[10] *Ibid*., pp. 134–5.

[11] See Viviana A. Zelizer, *Pricing the Priceless Child: The Changing Social Value of Children*, Princeton, Princeton University Press, 1986, p. 2.

[12] An interesting study, from a children's rights perspective, is Human Rights Watch, *Spare the Child: Corporal Punishment in Kenyan Schools*, New York: HRW, 1999.

Appreciating that conceptions of childhood have differed across time and space helps us understand why child soldiers continue to be recruited and how child soldiers themselves might view their experiences. Although there is no reason to disagree with the Secretary-General's view that: 'historically most societies have recognized the fundamental obligation to protection children from harm, even in times of conflict',[13] the scope and content of those obligations seem to vary from place to place, depending not least upon how a society perceives the boundaries, dimensions and divisions of childhood. Many of the reasons why we are concerned about children, rather than adults, serving as soldiers arise out of our conceptions of what a child is and what childhood should involve. The present view of childhood in the North is that it is a discrete period in which children are largely segregated from adults other than their parents and teachers. Children dress differently from adults; have different pastimes; and spend their days at school or play rather than work. Childhood is also a 'long' process and is generally seen as ending only with the attainment of voting rights, most usually at age 18. Children are seen as 'innocent incompetents', their innocence, frailty and vulnerability requiring protection from adults and adult life.

Indeed, it has been argued that the standards embodied in the CRC are the result of the institutionalisation and globalisation of these Western conceptions of childhood. Vanessa Pupavac writes that: 'the Convention requires the universal attainment of a modern Western childhood without the industrialization and development that was considered a prerequisite to this modern construction of childhood as a period of dependency and protection'.[14] Pupavac continues by arguing that: 'Southern societies are judged as having violated their children because the lives of the children do not conform to the image of childhood held by the West'.[15] What are in fact patterns of inequality in North–South relations are redefined as patterns of inequality within societies in the South. Child soldiers, indeed war-affected children generally, are seen as victims of child abuse or neglect for which the adults in their country are responsible, rather than victims of conflicts which may have a variety of causes, not all of which are endogenous. Children's strategies for coping with such conflicts, such as volunteerism, are defined as proscribed behaviour, but no alternatives are provided for them.

There are few areas of study more perilous than discussion of culture and tradition. It is important not to be essentialist. Cultural traditions are not static. They serve as repertories of themes and practices from which social actors can borrow in attempts to justify their actions. Those who recruit child soldiers can call on tradition to justify their behaviour. Child soldiers themselves can do so to

[13] Report of the Secretary-General: Children and Armed Conflict, 19 July 2000 (A/55/163-S/2000/712), para. 11.

[14] V. Pupavac, 'The Infantilization of the South and the UN Convention on the Rights of the Child', (1998) 3(2) *University of Nottingham Human Rights Law Review* 3, available at: www.nottingham.ac.uk/law/hrlc/hrlc_studentsnewsletter.htm.

[15] *Ibid.*, p. 5.

explain their condition. Such justifications and explanations will not necessarily be accepted by the wider community. However, to ignore the potential power of such arguments, simply plays into the hands of the purveyors of the 'new barbarism', which sees conflict in the developing world as fundamentally apolitical and irrational.[16] In addition, unless one understands how the various actors in a particular situation perceive themselves, one is unlikely to be able successfully to influence their behaviour.

The idea of children's rights

The idea that children have rights, and that those rights operate to oblige their parents and other adults to do or refrain from doing certain things to them, is new. Nevertheless, it is argued that it is an idea whose time has come. The CRC, with 192 states parties, is the most widely ratified human rights treaty. This 'paper' adherence to children's rights, however, has to be seen in the context not only of widespread disregard of the rights guaranteed by the CRC but also of continuing uncertainty over how children's rights can be justified and the nature, content and implications of the rights to which children are entitled.

Traditionally, the view was that an individual had rights because he or she was able to choose to exercise them. The right-holder was an autonomous individual able to make rational choices for him or herself. Possession of rights secured individuals from interference in a sphere of autonomy within which they could make those decisions. In this scenario, children, by virtue of their lack of capacity and their dependence upon adults, could not be rights-holders. Some child liberationists have argued that children's lack of capacity and dependency on adults is taught behaviour and that if children were granted rights they would learn how to exercise them.[17] There may be some truth in this argument as regards adolescents but it is difficult to imagine how infants could manage their own affairs. Taken on its own terms, the capacity theory excludes the majority of children from being rights-holders.

Instead, children's rights advocates have largely based their arguments on an interest theory of rights. The interest theory of rights argues that an individual has rights if their interests justify having rules requiring other persons to behave in a particular way. As Joseph Raz expains: 'a law creates a right if it is based on and expresses the view that someone has an interest which is sufficient ground for holding another to be subject to a duty'; and that 'to be a rule conferring a right

[16] The term the 'new barbarism' was coined by Paul Richards. See Paul Richards, *Fighting for the Rainforest: War, Youth and Resources in Sierra Leone*, James Currey: Oxford, 1996, pp. xiii–xv. The most prominent exponent of the thesis is James Kaplan. See, in particular, James Kaplan, 'The Coming Anarchy', *Atlantic Monthly*, February 1994.

[17] See Richard Farson, *Birthrights*, New York: Macmillan, 1974; and John Holt, *Escape from Childhood: The Needs and Rights of Children*, New York: E.P. Dutton, 1975.

it has to be motivated by a belief in the fact that somebody (the rightholder's) interest should be protected by the imposition of duties on others'.[18] On this view, a child can have rights if his or her interests require the imposition of duties on others to protect those interests. There is no requirement that the child should be aware of his or her interests or be able to act to vindicate them.

John Ekeelaar has classified children's interests as basic, developmental and autonomy interests.[19] Basic interests are children's claims to general physical, emotional and intellectual care within the social capabilities of their immediate care-givers. Developmental interests are what children may expect from the wider community. Children may expect society, as well as their parents, to ensure that they are no worse off than other children in opportunities to realise their life chances. Autonomy interests involve children's freedom to choose their own lifestyle and enter social relations unconstrained by adult views. It can immediately be seen that there is a potential for conflict between children's basic and developmental interests, on the one hand, and their autonomy interests, on the other. A child might choose to play truant. His or her decision not to attend school, however, could put him or her at a disadvantage in adulthood. However, where there is a clash between children's autonomy interests and their basic and development interests the latter will prevail.

What this means in practice is that in many cases adults will act on behalf of children; what has been called the 'caretaker' thesis.[20] Children's rights can be categorised as 'self-determination' or 'welfare' rights. Self-determination rights are rights that children themselves can exercise. In such cases, adults' views are immaterial. The decision is the child's. Welfare rights, on the other hand, are children's rights to various forms of treatment considered to be beneficial to their welfare. It is not the child's decision whether or not to benefit from such treatment. Decision-making is delegated to adult 'caretakers', usually the child's parents. The right, however, remains the child's, and the caregiver is required to act in his or her best interests. To take an example used by Eekelaar, although a parent may think it best that he or she decides what medical treatment his or her child receives, the child has the right to the best possible treatment, not necessarily the parent's chosen treatment, although the two often coincide as the parent's choice is likely to be the treatment he or she considers to be best for the child. The parent is merely the caretaker of the child's best interests. If parents act contrary to a child's welfare rights, the state can step in to exercise those rights for the child, up to and including taking the child away from his or her parents if that is necessary to ensure that his or her best interests are served. If the parent refuses to permit the child to have necessary medical treatment – a blood transfusion, for

[18] 'Legal Rights' (1984) 4 OJLS 1, pp. 13–14.

[19] John Eekelaar, 'The Emergence of Children's Rights' (1986) 6 OJLS 161, pp. 170–1.

[20] See Archard, *op. cit.* note 3, p. 52.

example – then the state might have the child made a ward of court so that the treatment can be carried out regardless of the parent's wishes.[21]

The cynic might say that the right is the child's only as a matter of form, what the thesis really does is to empower one set of adults (state functionaries) over another set (parents).[22] Such a conclusion, however, may be too simple. The care-giver is required to determine what the child's interests are by making an 'imaginative leap'[23] and looking at what the child would want were he or she an adult looking at his or her childhood retrospectively. For example, one might consider that in hindsight an adult would rather have gone to school while a child even though when a child he or she preferred to play truant. Accordingly, in cases of conflict basic and developmental interests trump autonomy interests, although this is not to say that the child's opinions should not be taken into account when determining what his or her basic and developmental interests are. In addition, the care-giver should be afforded a margin of discretion, on the grounds, first, that as he or she best knows the child he or she can be taken to know best what the child's best interests are, and, second, that as he or she is likely to be the person with the greatest affection for the child, he or she can best be counted on to act in furtherance of the child's best interests.

Children's rights and child soldiers

Children are compulsorily and forcibly recruited into armed forces and groups, but they also enlist voluntarily. International law, as will be seen, is moving towards prohibiting all compulsory or forcible recruitment of children. As the law currently exists, however, it does permit children aged 15 years or above to volunteer for military service. This is opposed by children's rights advocates, who argue for a 'straight-18' ban on all recruitment and use of child soldiers.

Adults can both enlist voluntarily and be conscripted into national armed forces. An adult's decision to enlist in an armed force or group is recognised because adults are deemed to be sufficiently mature to make such choices. In addition, however, adults' full participation in the national community is argued to impose responsibilities as well as rights, including the responsibility to help to defend their country. There is no right in international law to avoid military service because of one's conscientious objections, whether based on one's religious, ethical or political beliefs. Although several treaties prohibit slavery, servitude and forced or compulsory labour, compulsory military service is excepted from the definition

[21] See, for example, *Re A (A Minor) (Blood Transfusion)* [1993] 2 FLR 757.

[22] Transposed to the international level, this is very much Pupavac's view. For her, a focus on children rights provides a pretext for First World interventions in the Third World. Outside agencies are empowered as against the adult population of the South. See *op. cit.* note 13, p. 5.

[23] Archard, *op. cit.* note 3, p. 170.

of those terms. For example, Article 4(3) of the European Convention on Human Rights on the prohibition of slavery and forced labour provides that:

> For the purposes of this article, the term 'forced or compulsory labour' shall not include:
> [...]
> b. any service of a military character or, in case of conscientious objectors in countries where they are recognised, service enacted instead of compulsory military service.

Similar provisions appear in the International Covenant on Civil and Political Rights[24] and the American Convention on Human Rights.[25] In addition, punishment for refusal to undertake military service is not generally considered to be persecution for the purposes of the Refugee Convention and cannot found a claim for asylum.[26] The United Nations High Commissioner for Refugees' Handbook states that: 'it is open to Contracting States to grant refugee status to persons who object to performing military service for genuine reasons of conscience'.[27] The decision whether to recognise a right to conscientious objection is within each state's discretion. Such a right may be emerging[28] but it is not yet *lex lata*. Adults can be forced to fight.

Adults, save in exceptional cases, do not have caretakers. Nor do they always act in their own best interests. Adults frequently act in ways we consider to be wrong, and in many cases, although we do not agree with them, we consider it is their right to do so. Indeed, the classic liberal view is that an adult may act as irrationally or self-destructively as he or she likes providing that in so doing he or she avoids harming others. The argument for preventing a child from behaving in a particular way, however, is that we, as adults, know better than the child what his or her best interests are. If children have a right not to be recruited into an armed force or group, the right is a welfare right based on a view that military service, even if voluntary, is contrary to children's best interests. The interests that the right serves trump any autonomy interests which might be served by permitting

[24] Article 8(3), International Covenant on Civil and Political Rights (ICCPR) (1966) 999 UNTS 171.

[25] Article 6(3), American Convention on Human Rights (1969) 1144 UNTS 133.

[26] There are exceptions: if the penalties for draft evasion are excessive or disproportionate (which ground is in itself an implicit admission that states are allowed to punish draft evaders); if conscription is administered in a discriminatory manner; or if conscription would result in having to participate in illegal activities.

[27] UNHCR, *Handbook on Procedures and Criteria for Determining Refugee Status* (1979), para. 173.

[28] See, e.g., Article 10(2), European Charter of Fundamental Rights. It also appears that if alternatives to military service are permitted, then any differences in treatment of conscientious objectors and military conscripts, such as the length of service required, must be based on reasonable and objective criteria and are not within the unfettered discretion of the state: see *Foin* v. *France*, Communication No. 66/1995, UN Doc. CCPR/C/67/D/666/1995, views of the Human Rights Committee, 9 November 1999.

children the choice whether or not to volunteer. Accordingly, two issues arise. First, is a child's membership of an armed force or group ever in his or her best interests? Second, leaving aside the issue of whether it is in his or her best interests, should we not respect the child's decision anyway?

It might be argued that in some situations a child's decision to join an armed force or group is rational. One of the more disturbing developments in warfare over the last century has been the change in who constitute the casualties of war.[29] Modern warfare frequently sees soldiers preying on civilians rather than engaging in combat with each other. Statistically, it might be safer to be a soldier than a civilian. And, in addition, possession of a gun means access to other goods. In situations of scarcity, it is the men with guns (and their families) that get fed. As John Ryle has written:

> In Africa, where there is no state to protect you, a gun may be the only way to ensure that you and your family have food – and that someone else doesn't take it away from you. If I were a 17-year-old in Southern Sudan or Somalia today I would get myself a gun as soon as I could – I'd join a guerrilla force or a government militia – whatever it took.
>
> If I were the responsible adult in my family – and a 15-year-old can be, perforce, an adult – it would be my obligation to acquire the means to defend myself and my weaker relatives. If a foreigner, or anyone else, told me that I was a child and had to be protected from military service, I'd laugh.[30]

No one would consider the situation to be ideal, but joining an armed group can be situationally rational: the best option when faced with a bad choice.

This argument dovetails into the second issue to be considered: that children's choices should be respected. It is the child who is in the situation requiring him or her to make the choice. We, on the other hand, are thousands of miles away, and do not have to live with the consequences of our decision. The argument made by campaigners is that children lack the psychological maturity to make a meaningful decision to enlist into an armed force or group. Children are too easily swayed by extraneous factors: peer pressure, parental and societal attitudes, and media propaganda. However, objective factors – poverty, lack of security, absence of educational or employment opportunities – also weigh heavily on children's decisions to volunteer. Indeed, the factors driving child volunteering are also those that cause young adults to enlist as soldiers as well.[31] We may not agree with their decision or consider the conditions under which it was made ideal for making a

[29] See p. 6.

[30] John Ryle, 'Why Must a Child be Forced to Kill?', *Guardian*, 25 January 1999.

[31] This argument, of course, cuts both ways. On the one hand, we might argue that children's decisions to enlist should be viewed as being a valid as those of adults. On the other, we might say that we should examine adults' decisions to enlist very carefully to ensure that they are not vitiated for the reasons that we argue invalidate children's decisions to do the same.

considered choice, but we do not see such enlistments as coerced or constituting a violation of those individuals' rights. Indeed, the argument that children would decide not to volunteer if asked retrospectively whether they would have wished to do so might be thought to lose some of its force when we see that young adults in similar situations make the same decisions for much the same reasons.[32]

Both issues arise in any situation when a child might wish to enlist as a soldier, not just in the extreme circumstances already posited. For example, we might wish to consider their relevance to the question whether children should be permitted to enlist voluntarily in peacetime. Whether one considers a child's decision to enlist a rational one or not depends largely on one's view of what military service entails and a weighting of its benefits and detriments against the other alternatives open to the decision-maker. Service in the armed forces can open opportunities for education, vocational training, professional and social advancement, and inculcates qualities such as courage, discipline and responsibility; at least these are the arguments put forward by armed forces which do recruit individuals before their eighteen birthday. One might ask whether it is a lack of sympathy for military life and values that has led to the refusal to accept such arguments as having any cogency. Instead, we might wish to respect what the recruits themselves and their parents think, as they might be thought to be the persons best placed to know what is in each child's best interests.

The most recent international treaty on the subject, the Optional Protocol to the Convention on the Rights on the Involvement of Children in Armed Conflict largely reflects such a position. It permits the voluntary enlistment of children aged 16 or above, but only if such recruitment is truly voluntary, fully informed and consented to by the recruit's parents. States parties are, moreover, required to use all feasible measures to ensure that such child soldiers do not participate directly in hostilities. Both the Optional Protocol and ILO Convention 182 on the Worst Forms of Child Labour prohibit the forced and compulsory recruitment of under-18s. Such a position, one might consider, acknowledges that childhood is not an undifferentiated state and that adolescents are moving towards full maturity, while maintaining a distinction between childhood and adulthood.

With regard to younger children, the argument that their development right not to be recruited trumps their autonomy right to make their own decisions seems much simpler. Younger children are less able to take decisions for themselves, while being less suited to military life owing to their lack of physical and psychological maturity. In addition, it might be said that the issue is as much about public order as it is about children's rights. René Provost has argued that the provisions in the two Additional Protocols and in the CRC prohibiting the recruitment and use of children under 15 to participate, or participate directly, in hostilities, do not confer rights upon children falling within their terms. Instead, for Provost: 'the

[32] Although adults looking back might still say that they would not have wished to volunteer when they did but only later when they had reached adulthood.

Convention on the Rights of the Child echoes the conclusion ... that humanitarian law standards, although grounded in the principle of humanity, are not directly attached to the human person, but instead stem from international public order requirements'.[33] Indeed, one argument for such standards stresses not the children's but others' interests. Young children are too immature to be counted upon to comply with international humanitarian law, as all combatants are required, under threat of incurring individual criminal responsibility, to do. Their lack of inhibitions and suggestibility means they are less disciplined and more likely to commit atrocities. Indeed, there have been numerous cases of child soldiers being used to do so. Although all persons are under an obligation to comply with international humanitarian law, in general, it is combatants who are in the best position to violate its tenets. Accordingly, young children are banned from the battlefield for the protection of others, as well as for their own benefit.

The irony is that when an individual reaches 18 not only can he or she decide to enlist and fight but he or she can be forced to do so. Many adult soldiers are compulsorily or forcibly recruited, or enlist 'voluntarily' for the same reasons as motivate child volunteers. Adult soldiers often face the same hardships and harsh treatment as do their child comrades.[34] By their concentration on the child soldier phenomenon, however, human rights activists have ignored the plight of adult soldiers. It might be preferable, instead, to follow John Ryle, who has argued that: 'it is conscription that is the issue, not chronological age ... The right that has to be asserted is the right not to fight'.[35]

One may doubt whether such considerations were always at the front of the participants' minds during the negotiations of the various recent treaties in which provisions regarding child soldiers appear. Nevertheless, it is clear that the child soldier phenomenon itself has moved up the international agenda in recent years. In the next chapter we will examine the results of this growth of concern within the United Nations and how the organisation has responded.

[33] René Provost, *International Human Rights and Humanitarian Law*, Oxford: Oxford University Press, 2002, p. 34.

[34] Although they may be better able to endure it.

[35] *Op. cit.* note 18.

3

The UN and child soldiers

Introduction

In his third report to the Security Council on children and armed conflict,[1] the UN Secretary-General stated that:

> Since 1998, when the issue of war-affected children was formally placed on the agenda of the Security Council, the progressive engagement of the Council has yielded significant gains for children. These include four resolutions devoted to the issue … an annual debate and review, an annual report submitted by the Secretary-General, the incorporation of child-specific concerns into the briefs of Security Council fact-finding missions, an important contribution to monitoring and accountability through the listing of parties to conflict that violate the rights of children and the stipulation for the systematic inclusion of children in country-specific reports.[2]

The Secretary-General also noted that: 'Child protection has been integrated into the mandates and reports of peacekeeping missions and the training of personnel'.[3]

This chapter will give a brief description of those developments, highlighting a number of issues which will be dealt with in greater detail in subsequent chapters. The intention is to provide readers with a narrative account so that they can situate the later, more analytical, chapters in the context of events. It should be noted, however, that matters will be looked at with a fair degree of selectivity. The United Nations (UN) has tended to consider the issue of child soldiers as a part of the broader issue of war-affected children. Here, the latter issue will be dealt with only insofar as it illuminates the former.

[1] Report of the Secretary-General: Children and Armed Conflict, UN Doc. A/58/ 546-S/2003/1053* (10 November 2003).

[2] *Ibid.*, para. 4.

[3] *Ibid.*, para. 5.

The beginnings of UN involvement

All the advances highlighted by the Secretary-General have been made in a comparatively short time. Following the coming into force of the CRC, the Committee on the Rights of the Child was established to monitor and supervise states' compliance with their obligations under the Convention. The Committee was quick to look at the issue of children and armed conflict. At the Committee's second session in 1992, a proposal was made that an optional protocol to the CRC be developed to further restrict children's participation in hostilities.[4] At its third session in 1993, the Committee recommended to the United Nations General Assembly that the Secretary-General should undertake a study of the ways and means of improving the protection of children from the adverse effects of armed conflicts.

Both initiatives were supported by the 1993 World Conference on Human Rights. The Conference devoted a entire section of its Vienna Declaration and Programme of Action[5] to the rights of the child, going much further and dealing far more specifically with the situation of children than did the previous UN World Conference on Human Rights, which in its Tehran Proclamation of 1968 merely stated that the protection of the child was the concern of the international community and that '[t]he aspirations of the younger generation for a younger world ... must be given the highest encouragement'.[6] By contrast, the Vienna Declaration stated that:

> The World Conference on Human Rights strongly supports the proposal that the Secretary-General initiate a study into means of improving the protection of children in armed conflicts. Humanitarian norms should be implemented and measures taken in order to protect and facilitate assistance to children in war zones. Measures should include protection for children against indiscriminate use of all weapons of war, especially antipersonnel mines. The need for after-care and rehabilitation of children traumatized by war must be addressed urgently. The Conference calls on the Committee on the Rights of the Child to study the question of raising the minimum age of recruitment into armed forces.[7]

The Conference also recommended that 'matters relating to human rights and the situation of children be regularly reviewed and monitored by all relevant organs and mechanisms of the United Nations system'.[8]

[4] UN Doc. CRC/C/10, paras 61–77.

[5] UN Doc. A/CONF.157/24 (adopted 25 June 1993).

[6] United Nations World Conference on Human Rights, Proclamation of Tehran (1968), reproduced in P.R. Ghandhi (ed.), *Blackstone's International Human Rights Instruments*, Oxford: Oxford University Press, 3rd edn, 2002, p. 414.

[7] *Op. cit.* note 2 (Part I, ch. III, s. II), para. 50.

[8] *Ibid.*, para. 51.

The General Assembly becomes involved

The Vienna Conference and the Committee of the Rights of the Child's proposals were noted by the United Nations General Assembly in its Resolution 48/157 of 20 December 1993 on the protection of children affected by armed conflict. The resolution, among other things, stated that the General Assembly:

> Takes note with appreciation of the report of the Committee on the Rights of the Child on its third session and the recommendations contained therein concerning the situation of children affected by armed conflict; Requests the Secretary-General to appoint an expert, working in collaboration with the Centre for Human Rights of the Secretariat and the Untied Nations Children's Fund, to undertake a comprehensive study of this question, including the participation of children in armed conflict, as well as the relevance and adequacy of existing standards, and to make specific recommendations on ways and means of preventing children from being affected by armed conflicts and of improving the protection of children in armed conflict and on measures to ensure effective protection of these children ... and to promote their physical and psychological recovery and social reintegration ... taking into account the recommendations by the World Conference on Human Rights and the Committee on the Rights of the Child.[9]

Resolution 48/157 marked the first time that the General Assembly had considered the issue of children affected by armed conflict in any specific way. In Resolution 44/25 it had adopted the text of the Convention on the Rights of the Child, and in Resolution 3318(XXIX) it had proclaimed the Declaration on the Protection of Women and Children in Emergency and Armed Conflict, which was largely concerned with emphasising the need to provide special protection to women and children belonging to the civilian population.[10] However, neither resolution had resulted in any sustained engagement with the issue. Resolution 48/157, by contrast, went into detail, set out a plan of action and proved to be the beginning of a continuing commitment by the political organs of the UN to the issue of children's involvement in armed conflict.

The Secretary-General followed the General Assembly's recommendation, appointing Ms Graça Machel of Mozambique to conduct the study. Ms Machel took two years to produce her report, consulting widely before reporting on 26 August 1996.[11] A programme of research into issues of particular concern was undertaken through the preparation of thematic papers and case studies[12] and

[9] GA Res. 48/157 of 20 December 1993: Protection of Children Affected by Armed Conflict, paras 6 and 7 (paragraph numbers omitted).

[10] This was later reflected in Articles 76 and 77 of AP I, when women and children were declared to be objects of special respect.

[11] Impact of Armed Conflict on Children: Report of the Expert of the Secretary-General, Ms. Graça Machel, submitted pursuant to GA Res. 48/157, UN Doc. A/51/306 (26 August 1996).

[12] *Ibid.*, para. 10.

a number of regional consultations were held.[13] Ms Machel also conducted field trips to several areas affected by armed conflicts[14] and received guidance from a group of eminent persons coming from a variety of political, religious and cultural backgrounds.[15] The report remains a point of reference to those considering the impact of armed conflict on children.

One of the most serious ways in which armed conflict affected children was found to be their participation as soldiers. This was identified as '[o]ne of the most alarming trends in armed conflicts'.[16] The report examined how child soldiers were recruited, how they were used, their demobilisation and reintegration into society, and how future recruitment might be prevented. With regard to the last issue, it made a number of proposals. In particular:

> Governments must pay much closer attention to their methods of recruitment, and, in particular, they must renounce the practice of forced recruitment. They should ensure that all children are registered at birth and receive documentation of age. To be certain that these measures succeed, Governments must establish effective monitoring systems and back them up with legal remedies and institutions that are sufficiently strong to tackle abuses.

These are not minor matters; they go to the very effectiveness of states' administrative and judicial systems. The report also made a number of specific recommendations with regard to the problem of child soldiers generally.

> (a) … a global campaign should be launched … aimed at eradicating the use of children under the age of 18 years from the armed forces …
> (b) United Nations bodies, specialized agencies and international civil society actors should begin to pursue quiet diplomacy with Government and non-state forces and their international supporters to encourage the immediate demobilization of child soldiers and adherence to the Convention on the Rights of the Child;
> (c) All peace agreements should include specific measures to demobilize and reintegrate child soldiers into society …
> (d) States should ensure the early and successful conclusion of the drafting of the optional protocol to the Convention on the Rights of the Child on involvement of children in armed conflicts, raising the age of recruitment and participation in the armed forces to 18 years.

These recommendations have been followed up throughout the UN's continuing engagement with the issue.

The General Assembly welcomed the Machel report and took note of its recommendations.[17] The General Assembly also recommended that the

[13] In Addis Ababa, Cairo, Abidjan, Manila, Bogotá and Florence. See Promotion and Protection of the Rights of Children: Impact of Armed Conflict on Children: Note by the Secretary-General: Addendum, UN Doc. A/51/306/Add.1 (9 September 1996).

[14] *Op. cit.* note 8, para. 14.

[15] *Ibid.*, para. 15.

[16] *Ibid.*, para. 34.

[17] GA Res. 51/77 (12 December 1996), para. 13.

Secretary-General appoint a special representative on the impact of armed conflict on children, and set out the Special Representative's mandate.[18] The Special Representative should:

(a) Assess progress achieved, steps taken and difficulties encountered in strengthening the protection of children in situations of armed conflict;
(b) Raise awareness and promote the collection of information about the plight of children affected by armed conflict and encourage the development of networking;
(c) Work closely with the Committee on the Rights of the Child, relevant United Nations bodies, the specialized agencies and other competent bodies, as well as non-governmental organizations;
(d) Foster international cooperation to ensure respect for children's rights in these situations and contribute to the coordination of efforts by Governments, relevant United Nations bodies, notably the office of the United Nations High Commissioner for Human Rights/Centre for Human Rights, the Office of the United Nations High Commissioner for Refugees, the United Nations Children's Fund, the specialized agencies and the Committee on the Rights of the Child, relevant special rapporteurs and working groups, as well as United Nations field operations, regional and subregional organizations, other competent bodies and non-governmental organizations.

The Special Representative was also to submit an annual report to the General Assembly and the Commission on Human Rights.[19] In September 1997, the Secretary-General appointed Mr Olara Otunnu of Uganda to the position, which he has held ever since.[20]

The General Assembly has continued to pass resolutions dealing with the protection of children in armed conflict,[21] to support efforts to end the use of children as soldiers in armed conflict, and to raise the minimum age for recruitment and participation in armed conflicts. The General Assembly has also condemned specific instances of the recruitment and use of child soldiers by parties to conflict. For example, in a series of resolutions it has condemned the Burmese Government and other parties to conflict in Burma, and urged the government to put an end to the practice and ensure the child soldiers' disarmament, demobilisation and reintegration.[22]

[18] *Ibid.*, paras 35–6.

[19] *Ibid.*, para. 37.

[20] Although originally only for a three-year term (*ibid.*, para. 35), Mr Otunnu's mandate has been twice renewed. See GA Res. 54/149 of 17 December 1999: The Rights of the Child, section II, para. 2; and GA Res. 57/190 of 18 December 2002: The Rights of the Child, section V, para. 2.

[21] See GA Res. 52/107 of 12 December 1999: The Rights of the Child; GA Res. 53/128 of 9 December 1998: The Rights of the Child; GA Res. 54/149 of 17 December 1999: The Rights of the Child; GA Res. 55/79 of 4 December 2000: The Rights of the Child; GA Res. 56/138 of 19 December 2002; and GA Res. 58/157 of 22 December 2002: The Rights of the Child. See also GA Res. S-27/2 of 10 May 2002: A World Fit for Children.

[22] See GA Res. 55/122 of 4 December 2000: Situation of Human Rights in Myanmar, para. 18; GA Res. 56/231 of 24 December 2001: Situation of Human Rights in Myanmar,

The Special Representative in action

The Special Representative published his first report on 12 October 1998.[23] In it, he set out his aims.

> A serious and systematic effort by all concerned parties – from Governments to the United Nations system to civil society organizations to private citizens – is needed to address the abominations being committed against children in the context of armed conflict. As an advocate on behalf of these children, the Special Representative is working to spearhead that effort. He is seeking to combine normative, political and humanitarian strategies in efforts to promote prevention, protection and rehabilitation for the benefit of children.[24]

More specifically, he announced three major activities to achieve his objectives: protection through public advocacy; the promotion of concrete initiatives in the midst of ongoing conflicts; and mobilisation of concerted responses to post-conflict needs. The Special Representative selected certain themes from the wide range of issues highlighted in the Machel report where he considered his advocacy efforts would have particular impact.[25] These themes included the participation of children in armed conflict and a number of issues linked to it, such as encouraging the incorporation of human rights and humanitarian law standards protecting children affected by armed conflict into UN policies, procedures and operations.[26] In particular, the Special Representative stated that he would strongly support efforts to raise the legal age for recruitment and participation in hostilities to eighteen years.[27]

The Special Representative has engaged in a number of activities in pursuit of his mandate. He has been indefatigable in seeking to gain media attention for the issue of war-affected children. He has forged close links with NGOs working on the issue. He lobbied vigorously and successfully for the adoption of an optional protocol to the CRC on the involvement of children in armed conflict, and has continued to lobby states to sign and ratify it, and to designate 18 years as the minimum age for voluntary recruitment into their armed forces. He also, with UNICEF and several NGOs, successfully campaigned for a war crime of conscripting or enlisting children under the age of 15 into armed forces or groups, or

para. 22; GA Res. 57/231 of 18 December 2002, para. 5(e); and GA Res. 58/247 of 23 December 2003: Situation of Human Rights in Myanmar, para. 6(c). The resolutions vary in their terms. Earlier resolutions on the situation do not mention the issue specifically.

23 *Protection of Children Affected by Armed Conflict*: Report of the Special Representative of the Secretary-General for Children and Armed Conflict, annexed to Protection of Children Affected by Armed Conflict: Note by the Secretary-General, UN Doc. A/53/482 (12 October 1999).

24 *Ibid.*, para. 13.

25 *Ibid.*, paras 14–17.

26 *Ibid.*, para. 40.

27 *Ibid.*, para. 21.

using them to participate actively in hostilities to be included within the Rome Statute of the International Criminal Court (ICC). In addition, the Special Representative has been active in visiting countries affected by conflict, seeking commitments for child protection from parties to conflict and proposing child-friendly provisions in peace agreements. And he has served as an advocate within the UN system to promote a child-centred approach in peacemaking, peacekeeping and peace-building operations.

The Special Representative and parties to armed conflict

The Special Representative has been an advocate for children in a number of recent and ongoing armed conflicts. In his first report, the Special Representative reported that on visits to Sierra Leone in 1998 he had obtained commitments from the government, the CDF (Civil Defence Forces – Kamajors) and ECOMOG (the Economic Community of West African States' Monitoring Group). The CDF agreed to stop the recruitment and initiation of children under the age of 18 and to begin demobilising child combatants currently in their ranks. ECOMOG and the CDF agreed to provide special protection to Armed Forces Revolutionary Council (AFRC) and Revolutionary United Front (RUF) child combatants who fell into their hands. It was agreed that a joint taskforce should be constituted, comprising senior representatives from ECOMOG, the CDF, the Ministry of Social Welfare, Gender and Children's Affairs and international humanitarian agencies, in order to establish and oversee a systematic procedure for the demobilisation and reintegration of child combatants. The Sierra Leone Government agreed not to recruit children under 18 into the new national army which it proposed establishing under the aegis of ECOMOG. Visits to Sri Lanka and Sudan also bore fruit. In Sri Lanka, the Special Representative elicited an undertaking from the Tamil Tigers in Sri Lanka that they would not use children under the age of 18 in combat or recruit children under the age of 17, and from the Sri Lankan Government a reiteration of its commitment not to recruit children under the age of 18.[28] In Sudan, the Government confirmed to the Special Representative its commitment not to recruit or deploy children under the age of 18.[29]

In his second report, the Special Representative reported that he had secured a commitment from the principal Congolese insurgent group, the *Rassemblement congolais pour la démocratie*, to cooperate with UN agencies and NGOs in ensuring the demobilisation and reintegration of child soldiers in its ranks. In Burundi, the Government undertook to raise the minimum age of recruitment from 16 to 18. In Sudan, the Government reaffirmed its pledge to help facilitate the release and repatriation of children abducted from northern Uganda by the LRA. In Colombia, following discussions with the Special Representative, the Government announced

[28] *Ibid.*, para. 65.
[29] *Ibid.*, para. 77.

a new policy not to enlist persons below the age of 18 into the armed forces. On 27 December 1999, the Government discharged the final contingent of 950 soldiers under the age of 18.[30] The principal Colombian rebel group, the *Fuerzas Armadas de Colombia* (FARC), agreed to end recruitment of children below 15 years of age and expressed a willingness to explore with the UN and relevant NGOs a framework for the demobilisation of children already within its ranks. The FARC, however, did not comply with its commitment, although following another appeal by the Special Representative, it said it had 'committed an error' in recruiting under-15s into its forces and had repudiated the practice.[31] On another visit to Sierra Leone in September 1999, the Special Representative obtained a commitment from the RUF not to recruit children under 18 and to release those already in its ranks. In all, during his first mandate the Special Representative elicited thirty-six commitments for the protection of children (not all concerning the recruitment or use of child soldiers) from parties to armed conflicts. Only nine of them, however, were fully met.[32]

In 2001, following discussions between the Special Representative and the Head of the United Nations Peace-building Support Office in Guinea-Bissau (UNOGBIS), the latter was successful in persuading the Government of Guinea-Bissau to release 603 children under 18 years of age who were serving in the national army. The Office of the Special Representative worked with the United Nations Children's Fund (UNICEF) and the Department of Political Affairs providing advice to UNOGBIS and the UNICEF country office on their demobilisation and reintegration. Also in 2001, several parties to the conflict in the Democratic Republic of Congo made commitments to the Special Representative to refrain from recruiting children into their armed forces or groups.[33] Following the making of this commitment, both the Government and the *Rassemblement congolais pour la démocratie–Goma* developed action plans for the demobilisation of child soldiers.[34] In his sixth and most recent report, the Special Representative stated that altogether he has received sixty commitments from fifteen parties to armed conflicts.[35] However, although they all have been significant as advocacy benchmarks, not all of them have been observed.

[30] Report of the Special Representative of the Secretary-General for Children and Armed Conflict: Protection of Children Affected by Armed Conflict, 3 October 2000 (A/55/442), at para. 76.

[31] *Ibid.*

[32] *Ibid.*, at para. 110.

[33] Report of the Secretary-General: Children and Armed Conflict, 26 November 2002 (S/20002/1299), at para. 36.

[34] Report of the Secretary-General: Children and Armed Conflict, 10 November 2003 (A/58/546-S/2003/1053*), at para. 48.

[35] Report of the Special Representative of the Secretary-General for Children and Armed Conflict: Protection of Children Affected by Armed Conflict, 29 August 2003 (A/58/328), at para. 22.

The Special Representative has also worked to incorporate children's concerns into peace negotiations, proposing specific provisions for inclusion into peace agreements. The Special Representative had a sustained engagement with the parties to the conflict in Sierra Leone, and his proposals for children were included in the 1999 Lomé peace agreement, the first peace accord to stipulate that particular attention be paid to the special needs of child soldiers in disarmament, demobilisation and reintegration programmes.[36] Working with Julius Nyerere, the facilitator of the Burundi peace negotiations, the Special Representative proposed several child-specific provisions that were included in the 2000 Arusha peace accords. More recently, the Special Representative worked with the Special Representative of the Secretary-General for West Africa, ECOWAS and UNICEF to ensure the incorporation of provisions for the protection and rehabilitation of children in the 2003 Liberian peace agreement.[37] The Special Representative has also elicited commitments from governments and insurgent groups in Colombia, Sudan and Sri Lanka to place the rights and protection of children on the agenda of their ongoing peace processes and continues to work towards their fulfilment.[38]

The Special Representative has been active in undertaking humanitarian diplomacy and acting as an advocate for war-affected children. In pursuit of his mandate, however, he has been considerably aided by the increasing interest the Security Council has taken in the issue and the support it has given to his activities.

The Security Council intervenes

From the late 1990s, Security Council resolutions began to make reference to conflict-affected children. At first, the references were specific to situations with which the Council was seised. In two resolutions in 1996 on the situation in Liberia, the Council condemned the practice 'of recruiting, training and deploying children for combat'.[39] In Resolution 1071, the Council requested the Secretary-General to include in a report on what assistance the UN could provide in support of the Liberian peace process, details on the 'inhuman and abhorrent practice', while in Resolution 1083 it called upon the parties to the conflict to release child soldiers in their ranks for demobilisation. These calls, however, had little impact in practice.[40]

In 1998, in Resolution 1181 on the situation in Sierra Leone, the Council welcomed:

[36] Report of the Secretary-General: Children and Armed Conflict, 19 July 2000 (A/55/163-S/2000/712), at para. 41.

[37] *Op. cit.* note 35, at para. 24.

[38] See *op. cit.* note 36, at para. 49; and *op. cit.* note 34, at para. 9.

[39] SC Res. 1071 of 30 August 1996 On the Situation in Liberia, para. 9; and SC Res. 1083 of 27 November 1996 On the Situation in Liberia, para. 6.

[40] See Chapter 7, p. 112.

> the efforts of the Government of Sierra Leone to coordinate an effective national response to the needs of children affected by armed conflict, and the recommendation of the Special Representative of the Secretary-General for Children in Armed Conflict that Sierra Leone be made one of the pilot projects for a more concerted and effective response to the needs of children in the context of post-conflict peace building.[41]

In 1999, in another resolution on Sierra Leone, the Council deplored 'all violations of human rights and international humanitarian law … including the recruitment of children as soldiers' which had occurred in the recent upsurge of violence in the country, and urged the prosecution and punishment of those responsible for such violations.[42]

On 29 June 1998, the President of the Security Council made a statement on its behalf in connection with its consideration of an agenda item entitled 'Children and armed conflict'.[43] The statement followed a public debate held at the request of the Special Representative.[44] It expressed the Security Council's grave concern at the harmful impact of armed conflict on children. The Council condemned the targeting of children in armed conflict, as well as their recruitment and use in hostilities 'in violation of international law', and called upon parties to conflict to put an end to such activities. The Council also called upon all parties to comply with their international legal obligations and stressed the obligation on all states to prosecute those responsible for 'grave breaches of international humanitarian law'. It continued by stating that:

> The Security Council recognizes the importance of the mandate of the Special Representative of the Secretary-General on Children and Armed Conflict, supports his activities and welcomes his cooperation with all relevant programmes, funds and agencies of the United Nations system which he deems appropriate.
>
> The Security Council expresses its intention to pay serious attention to the situation of children affected by armed conflicts and, to this end, to maintain contact, as appropriate, with the Special Representative of the Secretary-General and with the relevant programmes, funds and agencies of the United Nations system.

The Special Representative described the Security Council's debate and the adoption of the statement as marking its recognition 'that the situation of children affected by armed conflict is a matter of grave and continuing concern for the Council'.[45]

[41] SC Res. 1181 of 13 July 1998 On the Situation in Sierra Leone, para. 14.

[42] SC Res. 1231 of 11 March 1999 on the situation in Sierra Leone, para. 3.

[43] Statement by the President of the Security Council of 29 July 1998 (S/PRST/1998/18).

[44] See Report of the Special Representative of the Secretary-General on Children and Armed Conflict, 12 October 1998 (A/53/482), at para. 104.

[45] *Ibid.*, at para. 106.

The Security Council made further references to the harmful impact of armed conflict on children in a number of other subsequent presidential statements.[46] However, on 30 August 1999 the Security Council intensified its engagement with the issue. Resolution 1261, passed by the Security Council on that day, was its first resolution specifically concerned with the situation of children in armed conflict.[47] The preamble to the resolution noted the recent efforts to bring to an end 'the use of children as soldiers in violation of international law', in particular the adoption of International Labour Organisation (ILO) Convention 182 on the Prohibition and Immediate Action for the Elimination of the Worst Forms of Child Labour and the provisions of the Rome Statute of the International Criminal Court characterising as a war crime the recruitment or use to participate actively in hostilities of children under the age 15. In the resolution's operative part, the Council condemned the targeting of children in armed conflict, including their recruitment and use in violation of international law, and called on all parties concerned to put an end to such practices. The Council also called upon parties to armed conflict to comply with their international legal obligations, including states' obligation to prosecute those responsible for grave breaches of international humanitarian law. Resolution 1261 also expressed the Council's support for the work of the Secretary-General's Special Representative for Children and Armed Conflict, and for that of the working group of the Commission on Human Rights on the draft optional protocol to the CRC on the involvement of children in armed conflict.

The similarity of the resolution's provisions to the terms of previous presidential statements is apparent. However, the resolution also made a number of recommendations. It urged parties to armed conflicts to ensure that the protection, welfare and rights of children are given due importance in peace negotiations and processes; to undertake feasible measures during armed conflicts to minimise the harm suffered by children, and to promote, implement and respect such measures; to abide by concrete commitments made to ensure the protection of children in armed conflict; and to take special measures to protect children, in particular girls, from rape and other forms of sexual abuse and gender-based violence in situations of armed conflict. States and all relevant parts of the UN system were urged to intensify their efforts to ensure an end to the recruitment and use of children in armed conflict in violation of international law, and to facilitate the disarmament, demobilisation, rehabilitation and reintegration of children used as soldiers in

[46] Statement by the President of the Security Council of 12 February 1999 (S/PRST/1999/6): Children and Armed Conflict: Statement by the President of the Security Council of 23 March 2000 (S/PRST/2000/10): Maintenance of Peace and Security and Post-conflict Peace Building; Statement by the President of the Security Council of 31 August 2001 (S/PRST/2001/21*): Small Arms: Statement by the President of the Security Council of 15 March 2002 (S/PRST/2002/6): Protection of Civilians in Armed Conflict; Statement by the President of the Security Council of 7 May 2002 (S/PRST/2002/12): Children and Armed Conflict.

[47] SC Res. 1261 (25 August 1999).

violation of international law. The Council itself undertook, when taking action to promote peace and security, to give special attention to the protection, welfare and rights of children, and requested the Secretary-General to ensure that personnel involved in UN peacemaking, peacekeeping and peace-building activities had appropriate training on the protection, rights and welfare of children. Finally, the Council requested the Secretary-General to submit a report on the implementation of the resolution by 31 July 2000.

It was as much the passage of the resolution as its content that was significant. The Security Council, as the UN organ with primary responsibility for the maintenance of international peace and security,[48] has traditionally left to the General Assembly 'softer' subjects such as 'assisting in the realization of human rights and fundamental freedoms'[49] on the ground that they were irrelevant to the fulfilment of its responsibilities. By passing a resolution on children and armed conflict, the Council was implicitly stating that children's protection, welfare and rights in situations of armed conflict were issues affecting international peace and security. This, in its turn, implied that peace, for the Council, was more than simply the absence of war: it encompasses the presence of a variety of goods also. The report of the Secretary-General on the implementation of Resolution 1261[50] started by stating that:

> The present resolution is submitted pursuant to paragraph 29 of Security Council Resolution 1261 (1999), which represents a veritable landmark in the cause of children affected by armed conflict. The adoption of the resolution has finally given full legitimacy to the protection of children exposed to conflict as an issue that properly belongs to the agenda of the Council. The Council has now clearly acknowledged in several resolutions and presidential statements that the harmful impact of conflict on children has implications for peace and security.[51]

Since then, the Security Council has passed a number of further resolutions dealing specifically with children and armed conflict. Security Council Resolution 1314 of 11 August 2000 responded to the Secretary-General's report on the implementation of Resolution 1261. The Council welcomed the adoption of the Optional Protocol to the CRC and urged UN Member States to sign and ratify it. It reiterated many of the concerns expressed and recommendations made in its earlier resolution but also set out specific action-orientated measures directed at the various actors. It also noted that:

> The deliberate targeting of civilian populations or other protected persons, including children, and the committing of systematic, flagrant and widespread violations of international humanitarian and human rights law, including that relating to children,

[48] Charter of the United Nations, Article 24(1).

[49] *Ibid.*, Article 13(1)(b).

[50] Children and Armed Conflict: Report of the Secretary-General, UN Doc. A/55/613-S/2000/712 (19 July 2000).

[51] *Ibid.*, para. 1.

> in situations of armed conflict may constitute a threat to international peace and security and in this regard *reaffirms* its readiness to consider such situations and, where necessary to adopt appropriate steps.[52]

Again, the Council requested the Secretary-General to submit a report on the implementation of the resolution and of Resolution 1261.

Having considered the Secretary-General's second report,[53] the Security Council responded with Resolution 1379 of 20 November 2001. The resolution strengthened the measures provided for in Resolution 1314, making them more targeted. The Council expressed its determination to give the fullest attention to the question of the protection of children in armed conflict when considering the matters of which it is seised, and its readiness explicitly to include provisions for the protection of children when considering the mandates of peacekeeping operations. It urged a variety of recommendations on parties to armed conflict and UN Member States and made a number of requests to the Secretary-General and the agencies, funds and programmes of the UN. These included a suggestion that Member States consider taking appropriate measures to ensure that parties to armed conflict respect international norms for the protection of children.[54] Again, it requested the Secretary-General to submit a report on the implementation of the resolution and its predecessors. Most significantly, however, the Council requested the Secretary-General:

> To attach to his report a list of parties to armed conflict that recruit or use children in violation of the international obligations applicable to them, in situations that are on the Security Council's agenda or may be brought to the attention of the Security Council by the Secretary-General, in accordance with Article 99 of the Charter of the United Nations, which in his opinion may threaten the maintenance of international peace and security.[55]

In the resulting report,[56] the Secretary-General described the list produced as 'an important step forward in our efforts to induce compliance with international child protection obligations by parties to conflict'.[57] Twenty-three parties to conflict were found to be engaged in recruiting and/or using children in violation of their international obligations in five conflicts – in Afghanistan, Burundi, the DRC, Liberia and Somalia – of which the Security Council was seised and were included in a list annexed to the report. Other situations of concern mentioned with regard to the recruitment and use of children soldiers were Burma, Colombia, Nepal, the

[52] SC Res. 1314 of 11 August 2000 On Children and Armed Conflict, para. 9.

[53] Report of the Secretary-General: Children and Armed Conflict, 7 September 2001 (A/56/342-S/2001/852).

[54] See SC Res. 1379 of 20 November 2001 On Children and Armed Conflict, para. 9.

[55] *Ibid.*, para. 16.

[56] Report of the Secretary-General: Children and Armed Conflict, 26 November 2002 (S/2000/1299).

[57] *Ibid.*, at para. 28.

Philippines, Sudan, northern Uganda and Sri Lanka. The Secretary-General's report was particularly enlightening with regard to the legal standards applicable to the recruitment practices of non-state parties to armed conflicts.[58]

In Resolution 1460 of 30 January 2003, the Security Council expressed its concern about what the list revealed. The Council called upon all parties to armed conflict recruiting or using child soldiers in violation of their international obligations immediately to halt such recruitment. In particular, it called upon all parties identified in the list to provide information to the Special Representative on the steps taken to halt their recruitment or use of child soldiers. They were asked to do so 'bearing in mind paragraph 9' of Resolution 1379, a rather oblique way of warning them that adverse consequences could attach to their failure to take such steps. The Council requested the Secretary-General to prepare another report including information on the progress made by the parties listed in the annex of his previous report in ending the recruitment or use of child soldiers in violation of their international obligations. It expressed its intention to consider taking 'appropriate steps' to further address the issue if it deemed that insufficient progress had been made following a review of the report.

The Secretary-General reported on 10 November 2003.[59] Two lists were annexed to the report: one containing an updated list of parties annexed to the previous report; the other containing a list of parties named in the body of the previous report. Both lists included new parties that the Secretary-General had found to be recruiting or using children in armed conflict. The Secretary-General assessed progress made by the parties listed in his previous report by reference to whether they had engaged in dialogue with the Secretary-General's representatives in the field, ended the recruitment or use of child soldiers, developed action plans for the demobilisation of child soldiers, and had begun to demobilize child soldiers. However, despite some progress, all parties listed had continued to use or recruit children in armed conflict and, in a new development, all the parties to the conflict in Côte d'Ivoire were recruiting or using child soldiers. The situation with parties merely mentioned in the previous report was similar.

In Resolution 1460, the Security Council had supported the Secretary-General's call for an 'era of application'[60] and asked the Secretary-General to provide: 'Specific proposals on ways to ensure monitoring and reporting in a more effective and efficient way within the existing United Nations system on the application of the international norms and standards for the protection of children in situations of armed conflict in all its various aspects'.[61] In his fourth report, the Secretary-General put forward a number of proposals to that end. The Secretary-General noted that although any credible monitoring and reporting system must

[58] See Chapter 6, p. 94.

[59] Report of the Secretary-General: Children and Armed Conflict, *op. cit.* note 1.

[60] SC Res. 1460 of 30 January 2003 On Children and Armed Conflict, para. 1.

[61] *Ibid.*, para. 14(c).

be based on specific and clear standards, such standards already existed in international law. He considered that a number of especially egregious violations against children, including the recruitment and use of child soldiers, should receive priority attention in monitoring operations, and that a monitoring network of various bodies and actors, each of which could bring its specific expertise to the process, should be developed. These would include the Security Council itself, the UN field presence, the UN human rights regime, the International Criminal Court and the Office of the Special Representative but would also engage participants outside the UN system. The Secretary-General proposed that the development of these proposals constitute a particular priority for his Special Representative. More immediately, and following recommendations made by the Special Representative,[62] the Secretary-General proposed a number of measures necessary to deepen and render sustainable progress achieved so far and to lay the foundations for an 'era of application'. One proposal was that the Security Council should take concrete steps where insufficient or no progress made by parties in accordance with Resolutions 1379 and 1460. Such measures, the Secretary-General suggested, could include the imposition of travel restrictions on leaders and their exclusion from any governance structures and amnesty provisions; a ban on the export or supply of small arms; a ban on military assistance; and restrictions on the flow of financial resources to the parties concerned. In addition, specific steps should be taken to ensure that persons responsible for crimes against children be among the first to be prosecuted in the ICC,[63] and that the listing of parties recruiting or using children in armed conflict be updated annually and include all situations where such practices persisted.

Recently, in Resolution 1539 of 22 April 2004, the Security Council has responded to the Secretary-General's suggestions. The Council stated that it remained 'deeply concerned over the lack of overall progress on the ground, where parties to conflict continue to violate with impunity the relevant provisions of applicable international law relating to the rights and protection of children in armed conflict'.[64] The Council requested the Secretary-General, as a matter of urgency and preferably within three months, to devise an action plan for a systematic and comprehensive reporting mechanism, as sketched in his report: 'to provide timely, objective, accurate and reliable information on the recruitment and use of child soldiers in violation of applicable international law and on other violations and abuses committed against children affected by armed conflict, for consideration in taking appropriate action'.[65] Those parties mentioned in the Secretary-General's report as remaining in violation of their international obligations were called upon by the Security Council to prepare within three months 'concrete time-bound action plans' to halt their illegal practices in collaboration with the

[62] See *op. cit.* note 35, at para. 72.
[63] It appears that this may well be the case: see Chapter 8, pp. 119–20.
[64] SC Res. 1539 of 22 April 2004 On Children and Armed Conflict, pre. para. 3.
[65] *Ibid.*, at para. 2.

relevant UN peacekeeping missions and UN country teams. In addition, the resolution announced that the Council would consider the imposition of: 'targeted and graduated measures, through country-specific resolutions, such as, inter alia, a ban on the export or supply of small arms and light weapons and of other military equipment and on military assistance, against these parties if they refuse to enter into dialogue, fail to develop an action plan or fail to meet the commitments included in their action plan'.[66] The Council also called upon the parties in the other situations of armed conflict mentioned in the Secretary-General's report immediately to halt their illegal recruitment or use of children, and expressed its intention to consider taking appropriate steps to further address their activities.

At the time of writing, the Secretary-General has yet to publish his report and we cannot know what action the Security Council will take in the not unlikely event of at least some parties' failure to comply with its demands. Even so, it is clear that Resolution 1539 marks another landmark in the Council's involvement in the issue of the recruitment and use of child soldiers. Although the Council has restricted the threat to impose sanctions to those situations of which it is already seised, indicating that it does not consider the recruitment or use of children in armed conflict to be in itself a threat to international peace and security, the threat itself is a weighty indication of how seriously it now views the practice and how high up the Security Council's agenda the issue has risen in recent years.

Child soldiers and UN activities

Security Council interest and the advocacy of the Special Representative have also resulted in the issue of the rights and welfare of conflict-affected children being mainstreamed in UN policy-making and activities. Child protection has been incorporated into peacekeeping mandates, training and reports.

In his second report, the Special Representative proposed that child welfare and protection be an explicit priority in the mandate of every UN peace operation. He also suggested that, in order to ensure implementation of those elements of a mission, there should be a senior officer explicitly responsible for ensuring their coordination.[67] This proposal was the germ of the concept of the child protection adviser, a number of whom have been appointed to UN peace missions. Both elements were adopted by the Security Council into the mandates and staffing of UN missions to Sierra Leone and the DRC, starting even before the its groundbreaking resolutions on children and armed conflict. Security Council Resolution 1260 of 20 August 1999 on the situation in Sierra Leone authorised 'the strengthening of the political, civil affairs, information, human rights and child protection

[66] *Ibid.*, at para. 6(c).

[67] Report of the Special Representative of the Secretary-General for Children and Armed Conflict, 1 October 1999 (A/54/430), at para. 173.

elements' of the United Nations Observer Mission in Sierra Leone (UNOMSIL).[68] The resolution went on to state that the Council welcomed:

> The commitment of the Government of Sierra Leone to work with the United Nations Children's Fund and the Office of the Special Representative of the Secretary-General for Children and Armed Conflict and other international agencies to give particular attention to the long-term rehabilitation of child combatants in Sierra Leone, and [encouraged] those involved also to address the special needs of all children affected by the conflict in Sierra Leone, including through the disarmament, demobilization and reintegration programme and the Truth and Reconciliation Commission, and through support to child victims of mutilation, sexual exploitation and abduction, to the rehabilitation of health and education services, and to the recovery of traumatized children and the protection of unaccompanied children.[69]

In Resolution 1279 of 30 November 1999 on the situation concerning the DRC, in establishing the United Nations Organization Mission to the Democratic Republic of the Congo (MONUC), the Security Council included in its mandate the task of assisting in 'the protection of human rights, including the rights of children'.[70] Child protection advisers were appointed to both missions.

The importance of the deployment of child protection advisers was also stressed by the Secretary-General in his report to the Economic and Social Council on strengthening the coordination of emergency humanitarian assistance of the UN.[71] And in Resolution 1314, the Security Council expressed its readiness to deploy child protection officers as appropriate in future peacekeeping operations.[72] Terms of reference for child protection advisers were drawn up by the Department of Peacekeeping Operations (DPKO), the Office of the Special Representative and UNICEF.[73] Since then, in addition to Sierra Leone and the DRC, child protection advisers have also been deployed in UN peace missions in Angola[74] and Côte d'Ivoire.

Further Security Council resolutions concerning the DRC referred specifically to the recruitment and use of child soldiers by the parties to the conflict there. Resolution 1332 expressed the Council's grave concern at the continued recruitment and use of child soldiers, called on all armed forces and groups immediately to cease such practices, and demanded that immediate steps be taken, with the assistance of relevant UN and other agencies and organisations, to disarm, demobilise, return and rehabilitate all such children.[75] Resolution 1341 reiterated the

[68] SC Res. 1260 of 20 August 1999 On the Situation in Sierra Leone, at para. 6.

[69] *Ibid.*, para. 16.

[70] SC Res. 1279 of 30 November 1999 On the Situation Concerning the Democratic Republic of the Congo, at para. 5(e).

[71] UN Doc. A/55/82-E/2000/61.

[72] *Op. cit.* note 48, para. 12.

[73] See *op. cit.* note 36, Box 5.

[74] See SC Res. 1433 of 15 August 2002 On the Situation in Angola, para. 5.

[75] SC Res. 1332 of 14 December 2000 On the Situation Concerning the Democratic Republic of the Congo, pre. para. 16 and para. 14.

Council's concern but also, acting under Chapter VII of the Charter, demanded that: 'all armed forces and groups concerned bring an effective end to the recruitment, training and use of children in their armed forces'; called upon them to extend full cooperation to MONUC, UNICEF and humanitarian organisations for the demobilisation, return and rehabilitation of such children; and requested the Secretary-General to task his Special Representative with overseeing compliance with its demands.[76] Resolution 1355, also passed by the Security Council acting under Chapter VII, repeated these demands.[77] It also incorporated a number of child protection elements into MONUC's renewed mandate. In particular, the Security Council called upon the Secretary-General to: 'ensure sufficient child protection advisers to ensure consistent and systematic monitoring and reporting of the conduct of the parties to the conflict as concerns their child protection obligations under humanitarian and human rights law and the commitments they have made to the Special Representative of the Secretary-General for Children and Armed Conflict'.[78]

Reports by the Secretary-General on both country-specific situations and thematic issues have regularly included information on the protection of conflict-affected children. And in Resolution 1460, the Security Council requested that the Secretary-General include sections on the protection of children in armed conflict in all his reports on country-specific situations.[79] Child-specific concerns have also been incorporated into the briefs of Security Council fact-finding missions.

Following the Secretary-General's submission to the Security Council of a report on the protection of civilians in armed conflict,[80] the Council asked the Secretary-General to produce an aide memoire listing the issues pertaining to the protection of civilians relevant to its deliberations of peacekeeping mandates.[81] The Secretary-General duly produced such a document, and by a presidential statement of 15 March 2002 the Security Council adopted it 'as a means to facilitate its consideration of issues pertaining to the protection of civilians'.[82] Although not intended as a blueprint, the aide memoire lists specific issues for the Council to consider when pursuing various objectives. One of the primary objectives mentioned is a mission's effect on children: to address the specific needs of children for assistance and protection. Issues for consideration listed include preventing the recruitment of child soldiers in violation of international law; taking

[76] SC Res. 1341 of 22 February 2001 On the Situation Concerning the Democratic Republic of the Congo, pre. para. 8 and para. 10.

[77] SC Res. 1355 of 15 June 2001 On the Situation Concerning the Democratic Republic of the Congo, para. 18.

[78] *Ibid.*, para. 35.

[79] *Op. cit.* note 52, para. 15.

[80] UN Doc. S/2001/1331 (30 March 2001).

[81] Letter from the President of the Security Council to the Secretary-General dated 21 June 2001.

[82] Statement by the President of the Security Council (S/PRST/2002/6) of 15 March 2002.

effective measures to disarm, demobilise, reintegrate and rehabilitate child soldiers; securing the negotiated release of children abducted in situations of armed conflict; and including specific provisions for the protection of children in peace missions' mandates, including, where appropriate, the integration of child protection advisers in peace operations. The aide memoire is a guide for the Security Council. As such, it should ensure that issues of children's rights, welfare and protection are considered whenever the Council decides whether to establish, renew or end a peace operation's mandate.

In several resolutions in 1999 and 2000, the Security Council requested the Secretary-General to ensure that personnel involved in UN peace operations received appropriate training in child-related provisions of international humanitarian, human rights and refugee law.[83] In August 1999, the Secretary-General issued a bulletin on the observance by UN forces of international humanitarian law.[84] With regard to children, however, it simply provides that children shall be the object of special respect and be protected against any form of indecent assault, and that children under 16 who take a direct part in hostilities and are detained or interned by UN forces shall continue to benefit from this special protection. As the Secretary-General himself stated, it would also be useful: 'Within a peacekeeping and post-conflict environment ... to provide guidance on appropriate modes of response when confronted by child soldiers in the field, the protections due to detained combatants and child civilians, and recommended procedures for responding to sexual abuse'.[85] Since then inter-agency working groups have produced guidelines on the integration of child protection into peacemaking, peacekeeping and peace-building,[86] and materials for training military, police and civilian personnel in child protection issues adaptable to the mandate of any peace operation.[87]

Concern for children has also influenced who the UN considers should represent it in peace operations as well as what training they should receive. On 29 October 1998, the Secretary-General announced that Member States contributing to UN peacekeeping operations should not send civilian police and military observers under the age of 25, and that troops should, ideally, be over 21 and never younger than 18 years of age.[88]

To conclude, over the past few years child protection considerations have been integrated into the mandates, training, staffing, practices and reporting of UN peace operations. This development is only one facet of the UN's growing concern for

[83] See *op. cit.* note 43, para. 19; SC Res. 1265 of 25 August 1999 On the Protection of Civilians in Armed Conflict, para. 14; and SC Res. 1296 of 19 April 2000 On the Protection of Civilians in Armed Conflict, para. 19.

[84] Secretary-General's Bulletin on the Observance by United Nations Forces of International Humanitarian Law, UN Doc. ST/SGB/1999/12; reproduced in (1999) 38 ILM 1656.

[85] *Op. cit.* note 36, at para. 57.

[86] *Op. cit.* note 52, at para. 8.

[87] *Ibid.*, para. 11.

[88] See *op. cit.* note 36, at para. 40.

war-affected children. In a little over a decade the issue has gone from nowhere to high on the agendas of both the General Assembly and the Security Council and seems likely to remain there for the foreseeable future. The next few chapters will show how this growth in concern has influenced the international law on child soldiers. It will be seen, however, that when imposing commitments upon themselves, states have been unwilling to move as far as the various UN actors have recommended.

4

The legal regulation of the recruitment and use of children in hostilities: international humanitarian law

Introduction

Although children have always participated in armed conflicts, international law has only recently attempted to regulate their participation. Indeed, although the four Geneva Conventions of 1949 (the GCs) contain a number of provisions dealing with children as civilians, the first treaties including provisions about children's recruitment and use in hostilities were the two Additional Protocols of 1977 (the APs). This chapter will examine those provisions. The next chapter (Chapter 5) will go on to look at how the subject has been covered in a number of subsequent human rights treaties: the Convention on the Rights of the Child (the CRC) and its Optional Protocol on the Involvement of Children in Armed Conflict (the OP), ILO Convention 182 Concerning the Prohibition and Immediate Action for the Elimination of the Worst Forms of Child Labour, and the African Charter on the Rights and Welfare of the Child. Chapter 6 will then consider what customary international law exists, taking account, in particular, of the wide variety of conference declarations and General Assembly and Security Council resolutions that have been promulgated in recent years; and the extent to which international law requires non-state entities to refrain from recruiting or using child soldiers.

The 1949 Geneva Conventions

That the drafters of the GCs did not include any provisions specifically dealing with children's recruitment and use to participate in hostilities was neither surprising nor unusual. In the immediate circumstances of the 1949 Diplomatic Conference, the major influences on the participants' thinking were the events of the Second World War, only recently ended. This was particularly the case with the Geneva Convention Relative to the Protection of the Civilian Population in Time of War (GC IV), the only one of the Conventions that dealt with the situation of children in armed conflicts. Mass deportations, starvation, forced labour and massacre, whether as reprisal or for ideological reasons, were the situations from which the drafters of the GCs sought to protect civilians. Regulating the recruitment of children as soldiers was not a priority. The Second World War had been fought largely by mass conscript armies and only in extremis, such as in Germany in 1945, had any of the major powers conscripted children into their armed forces. Where children had participated in hostilities it had been as irregulars – partisans or resisters. Such participation was consequently seen by the Allied powers as voluntary and heroic or (at best) an unfortunate necessity. It was seen as something exceptional and not, consequently, requiring legal regulation; being unlikely to be repeated.

Second, and more profoundly, the regulation of children's participation in hostilities was perceived as being primarily an internal matter. It was for each state to determine the age from which it recruited its nationals into its armed forces. Developments in international law whereby individuals have gained rights against their own states have been largely a post-war phenomenon and were not very far advanced in 1948–49 when the GCs were being negotiated.[1] Such issues were still considered to be matters within a state's domestic jurisdiction. International humanitarian law traditionally sought to protect individuals from the acts of states other than their own.[2]

GC IV was intended primarily to protect two classes of persons against the acts of enemy powers: enemy nationals living within the territory of a belligerent state and the inhabitants of territories occupied by an enemy power (but excluding nationals of the occupying state). Accordingly, Article 4(1) of the GC IV defined 'protected persons' for the purposes of the Convention as 'those who, at any given moment and in any manner whatsoever, find themselves, in the case of a conflict or occupation, in the hands of a Party to the conflict or occupying power of which they are not nationals'. As Pictet's *Commentary on the Geneva Conventions* stated: 'The definition [of protected persons in Article 4(1)] has been put in a negative form; as it is intended to cover anyone who is *not* a national of the Party to the conflict or occupying Power in whose hands he is. The Convention thus remains faithful to a recognised principle of international law: it does not interfere in a State's relations with its own nationals'.[3] Part II of GC IV applies to the whole of the populations of countries in conflict.[4] However, the Convention marks a breach of that 'recognised principle' only to the extent of binding states to certain general obligations in respect of categories of persons (women, children, old people, the

[1] Of the major international and regional human rights instruments, only the Genocide Convention and the Universal Declaration of Human Rights of 1948 had been adopted.

[2] For a restatement of the traditional view, see *Prosecutor* v. *Tadić*, Case No. IT-94-1-T, Trial Chamber, ICTY, judgment of 7 May 1997, reproduced in (1997) 36 ILR 908. For a civilian to have the status of a 'protected person' under GC IV, he must be in the hands of a party to the conflict or an occupying power of which he is not a national. This element of the decision was, however, overturned on appeal: see *Prosecutor* v. *Tadić*, Case No. IT-94-1-A, Appeals Chamber, ICTY, judgment of 15 July 1999. For a critical account, see M. Sassoli and L.M. Olson, 'The Judgment of the ICTY Appeals Chamber on the Merits in the *Tadić* case' (2000) IRRC No. 839, p. 737.

[3] J. Pictet (ed.), *Commentary on the Geneva Conventions of 12 August 1949*, Geneva: ICRC, 1955, vol. IV p. 46. Emphasis in the original.

[4] Article 13 GC IV.

sick and wounded) who, by their nature, were seen as taking no part in hostilities. Again, as Pictet's *Commentary* stated: 'These various categories [in Article 14 of GC IV][5] among the civilian population are based on a very simply criterion: they are persons who are taking no part in hostilities and whose weakness makes them incapable of contributing to the war potential of their country'.[6]

A number of articles in the Convention make special provision for children.[7] No definition of 'child' or 'children' is given. However, in a number of articles an age limit of 15 is specified[8] and the implication seems to be that for the purposes of GC IV a child is a person under 15 years of age. Two provisions in Part III of the Convention are, however, of interest. Article 50(1) states that: 'The Occupying Power shall take all necessary steps to facilitate the identification of children and the registration of their parentage. It may not, in any case, change their personal status, nor enlist them in formations or organisations subordinate to it'. This provision is not concerned with prohibiting the enlistment of children who are not nationals of the occupying power into its armed forces. It refers to the enrolment of children into youth movements of an ideological character, such as those established in a number of countries under German occupation during the Second World War. The recruitment of protected persons is covered in Article 51, which prohibits the conscription of protected persons into an occupying power's armed forces and any pressure or propaganda aimed at securing the voluntary enlistment of such persons. As Article 51 refers to all protected persons, children are included in its scope but, owing to its general nature, the article cannot be seen as aimed specifically at their protection. Indeed, Article 51 cannot be seen as solely concerned with individuals who are protected persons. It is also concerned with the duties that those individuals have to the states of which they are nationals. As Pictet wrote: 'The prohibition in paragraph 1 [of Article 51] is not new, since a basic principle, universally recognised in the law of war, strictly prohibits belligerents from forcing enemy subjects to take up arms against their own country'. The principle might be seen, from one point of view, as an 'anti-poaching agreement', a pact between states that they will not trespass on each others' sovereign right to their nationals' allegiance. Indeed, both Articles 50 and 51 can be seen as a reaffirmation of the rule in the 1907 Hague Regulations[9] that: 'It is forbidden to compel the inhabitants of occupied territory to swear allegiance to the hostile power'.[10]

[5] Article 14 GC IV refers to wounded, sick and aged persons, children under 15, expectant mothers and mothers of children under 7.

[6] *Op. cit.* note 3, p. 126.

[7] See articles 14, 16, 23, 24, 38, 50, 51 and 68 GC IV. For an examination of the rights of children as civilians, see J. Kuper, *International Law Concerning Child Civilians in Armed Conflict*, Oxford: Oxford University Press, 1997.

[8] See Articles 14, 23, 24, 38 and 50 GC IV.

[9] Regulations Respecting the Laws and Customs of War on Land annexed to the 1907 Hague Convention IV Respecting the Laws and Customs of War on Land.

[10] Article 45, *ibid.*

GC IV was a minor influence on the provisions regulating the recruitment of children in the two APs. The Convention concerns itself with the protection of children in situations of occupation or armed conflict and sets an age of 15 as the end of childhood, but it only restricts the recruitment of children into states' armed forces if they are protected persons. It says nothing about the conditions under which a state can recruit children of its own nationality into its armed forces. Indeed, the view of children purveyed in GC IV is one that sees them as essentially civilians and non-combatants.

Additional Protocol I

Only with the two APs of 1977 did the international community lay down rules regulating the participation in hostilities of children *qua* children. The two APs were negotiated together during the 1974–77 Diplomatic Conference on the Reaffirmation and Development of International Humanitarian Law Applicable in Armed Conflicts. The impetus for their negotiation arose out of two perceptions, not always very well distinguished. First, that the four GCs had a number of lacunae which required filling. Second, that international humanitarian law was in need of progressive development, either for specifically humanitarian reasons or because it was seen as the product of developed nations, favouring their interests over those of the developing nations and their allies, particularly 'national liberation movements'.[11]

The provisions dealing with the participation of children in armed conflict in AP I appear in Section III, on the treatment of persons in the power of a party to the conflict. Article 72, which sets out the field of application of the section, describes its provisions as being additional to GC IV and any 'other applicable rules of international law, relating to the protection of fundamental rights during international armed conflict'. Article 77 contains the provisions relating to the protection of children in international armed conflicts. It reads as follows:

Article 77 – Protection of children

1. Children shall be the object of special respect and shall be protected against any form of indecent assault. The Parties to the conflict shall provide them with the care and aid they require, whether because of their age or for any other reason.
2. The Parties to the conflict shall take all feasible measures in order that children who have not attained the age of fifteen years do not take a direct part in hostilities and, in particular, they shall refrain from recruiting them into their armed forces. In recruiting among those persons who have not attained the age of eighteen years, the Parties to the conflict shall endeavour to give priority to those who are oldest.

[11] For the background to the Diplomatic Conference, see G. Best, *War and Law Since 1945*, Oxford: Oxford University Press, 1994, pp. 341–7.

3. If, in exceptional cases, despite the protection of paragraph 2, children who have not attained the age of fifteen take a direct part in hostilities and fall into the power of an adverse Party, they shall continue to benefit from the special protection accorded by this Article, whether or not they are prisoners of war.
4. If arrested, detained or interned for reasons related to the armed conflict, children shall be held in quarters separate from the quarters of adults, unless where families are accommodated as family units as provided in Article 75, paragraph 5.
5. The death penalty for an offence related to the armed conflict shall not be executed on persons who had not attained the age of eighteen years at the time the offence was committed.

Article 77(1) is a general provision. It complements Article 76(1) AP I, which declares women to be the object of special respect. The two provisions are simply an exercising in gap-filling; remedying an omission in GC IV, where the wounded and sick, the infirm and expectant mothers, but not women or children *per se*, were declared to be objects of 'particular protection and respect'.[12] Article 77(2) deals with children's participation in hostilities. Before dealing specifically with paragraph 2, however, three general points should be made about the class of persons protected by Article 77 and the scope of the protection given to them.

The definition of 'children'

The word 'children' is nowhere defined in Article 77. This was intentional.[13] In paragraphs 2 and 5 reference is made to persons under 18 years old. Given the location of these references in an article on the protection of children, it might be argued that they peg the upper limit of childhood at 18 years of age. However, it might also be argued, on the basis of the references in paragraphs 2 and 3 to 'children who have not attained the age of fifteen years', that childhood ends on attainment of an individual's fifteenth birthday. This would render the provision consistent with the corresponding provisions of GV IV. However, although paragraphs 2, 3 and 5 state to whom they apply, this is not the case with paragraphs 1 and 4. Those two provisions simply refer to 'children'.[14] In consequence, it might be argued that the reference is simply to persons under 15 years old. If this is the case, then childhood ends rather earlier for the purposes of AP I than it does for those of the CRC, where a child is defined as a person below the age of 18 years. There are two reasons, however, for considering that this is not a necessary conclusion. In the first place, the references to 'children who have not attained the age of fifteen years' in Article 77(2) and (3) might serve to indicate that there can be children

[12] See Article 16, GC IV. H. Mann, in his article 'International Law and the Child Soldier' (1987) 36 ICLQ 32, at p. 34, refers to the original omission as a 'strange lacuna' in GC IV.

[13] See Official Records (OR) XV, p. 465; CDDH/407/Rev. 1, para. 63.

[14] As do the provisions on the evacuation of children in Article 78 AP I.

above that age. The text of Article 77 does not prevent a reading of the term 'children' as meaning persons under 18 years old. In the second place, we might consider it appropriate, if at all possible, to read the earlier treaty in conformity with the latter, given that all parties to AP I are also parties to the CRC.

The scope of the definition

In addition, the references to children in Article 77 are blanket ones. They do not refer, as in GC IV, only to persons who are not nationals of the state into whose hands they have fallen. It was the International Committee of the Red Cross's stated intent that Article 77 should apply to state parties' own nationals. Mr Surbeck of the International Committee of the Red Cross (ICRC), introducing draft article 68 (which formed the basis of Article 77) to Committee III of the Diplomatic Conference, stated that the article was intended to operate: 'for the benefit of all children who were in the territories of the Parties to the conflict, whether the territory was occupied or not, and whether or not the children fell within the definition of protected persons in Article 4 of the fourth Geneva Convention of 1949'.[15] No objections to this characterisation of Article 77 appear on the record and the amendments to the draft article did not affect its blanket character.[16]

The scope of the provision

AP I is applicable in the same situations as the four GCs, as set out in common Article 2 of the GCs,[17] that is, in cases of armed conflict between two or more of the 'High Contracting Parties' (the states parties to the treaties) and in cases of partial or total occupation of the territory of a high contracting party.[18] Common Article 2 of the GCs, however, commences by stating: 'In addition to the provisions which shall be implemented in peacetime, the present Convention shall apply …'.

It is arguable that the prohibition on the recruitment of children aged under 15 years into a state's armed forces under Article 77(2) is a provision of AP I which should be implemented in peacetime. Although the paragraph is worded to refer to a conflict from which children should be protected, to permit states to recruit children into their armed forces when not engaged in armed conflict might be thought to permit the circumvention of the fundamental purpose of the paragraph.

15 OR XV, p. 68; CDDH/III/SR.45.

16 Obviously, Article 77(3), as it expressly states, only imposes obligations on an adverse party.

17 See Article 1(3), AP I.

18 Under Article 1(4), the Protocol is also stated to apply in conflicts 'in which peoples are fighting against colonial domination and alien occupation and against racist regimes in the exercise of their right of self-determination'. This provision has been the subject of much controversy. It is, however, no longer of much practical significance.

A state which had recruited children in peacetime might be unwilling to discharge them on the outbreak of war, or one state launching an attack on another might kill or injure child soldiers in the second state's army before they could be demobilised. On the other hand, Article 77(2) specifically refers to 'Parties to the conflict', which would seem to imply that a conflict must exist for the provision to apply. We will return to this issue when we consider the corresponding provision in the CRC.

The ICRC draft article

Article 77(2) was much amended from the ICRC's original draft,[19] which stated: 'The parties to the conflict shall take all necessary measures in order that children aged fifteen or under shall not take any part in hostilities and, in particular they shall refrain from recruiting them in their armed forces or accepting their voluntary enlistment'. However, although paragraph 2 was extensively amended during the Diplomatic Conference, no record exists of the deliberations leading to the amendments. Committee III, to whom the draft article was assigned, referred it to its Working Group.[20] Meetings of the Working Group were held in private.[21] Consequently, the only explanations given for the changes made by the Working Group appear in the report to Committee III on the work of the Working Group submitted by the Rapporteur, Ambassador George Aldrich of the USA.

In relation to draft article 68, Ambassador Aldrich stated: 'This Article was the subject of discussion in the Working Group for the period of a week. The final product was a compromise in many respects and was not completely satisfactory to a number of representatives'.[22] On adoption of the article by Committee III, a number of representatives took the opportunity to give explanations of their votes, but these are not, by and large, particularly enlightening. No explanations of votes were given on the adoption of the article by the Conference in plenary session.

As a result, whereas it is clear that the form of Article 77(2) was the subject of controversy and of extensive discussion, the reasons for the amendments made to the original draft are obscure. Common sense suggests that they were made with the intention of weakening the contents of the paragraph, but nowhere in the Conference's record is this made wholly explicit. Consequently, a number of issues as to the meaning of the text arise both out of the text itself and out of its relationship with the previous draft.

[19] Draft article 68(2). See OR I, Part Three, for the text of the draft Additional Protocol.

[20] After amendment by the Working Group, the article was adopted by consensus, first by Committee III and then by the Conference in plenary session. See OR XV, p. 218; CDDH/III/SR.59 and OR IV, p. 251; CDDH/SR.43.

[21] See the Conference's Rules of Procedure at OR II, p. 15; CDDH/2/Rev.3.

[22] OR XV, p. 521; CDDH/III/391.

What are 'all feasible measures'?

Similar formulae appear elsewhere in AP I. In particular, the term is used in relation to precautionary measures in the conduct of military operations.[23] The meaning of the words 'everything feasible' in Article 57(2)[24] was extensively discussed during the negotiations. According to the ICRC commentary, the expression should be understood by reference to its dictionary meaning: 'feasible' meaning 'capable of being done, accomplished or carried out, possible or practicable'.[25] One might comment that the definition is itself not wholly clear. There is a distinction between something being possible and something being practicable. Whether something is possible is a question of whether it can be done at all. Whether something is practicable is a question referring to whether, in the particular circumstances of the moment, the efforts required to do it are not disproportionate to the result obtained on having done so. This distinction seems to have been reflected in statements made by some delegations on Article 57's adoption by the Diplomatic Conference that they understood the words to mean everything that was practicable or practically possible, taking into account all the circumstances at the time.[26] However, in relation to some delegations' claims that all relevant circumstances included 'those relevant to the success of military operations',[27] the ICRC commentary cautions that a focus on the success of military operations should not serve as an excuse for neglecting the humanitarian obligations prescribed in the provision. One might say the same with regard to Article 77(2). The exigencies of the situation, such as shortages in the number of personnel, cannot be used to circumvent parties' duties under the provision.

Consequently, it can be seen that Article 77(2) imposes two related obligations on states parties to the Protocol. First, there is an obligation not to recruit children under 15 into their armed forces. The wording of the paragraph indicates that this is something that it is always feasible for states to do.[28] In most cases this must be right. Governments can legislate as to the minimum age of recruitment into a state's

[23] Articles 57 and 58 AP I. See also Article 76(3).

[24] '(2)With respect to attacks, the following precautions shall be taken:
(a) those who plan or decide upon an attack shall:
(i) do everything feasible to …'

[25] Y. Sandoz, C. Swinarski and B. Zimmermann (eds), *Commentary on the Additional Protocols of 8 June 1977 to the Geneva Conventions of 12 August 1949*, Geneva: ICRC, 1987, pp. 681–2.

[26] Statements in such or similar terms were made by Algeria, Belgium, Canada, Italy, the Netherlands and Spain. See L.S. Boudreault, 'Les réserves apportées au Protocole de Genève sur le droit humanitaire' (1989–90) 6 Revue québécois de droit international 105. See also Part (b) of the Schedule to the Geneva Conventions Act (First Protocol) Order (SI 1998 No. 1754).

[27] Sandoz, Swinarski and Zimmermann (eds), *op. cit.* note 25.

[28] The French text of the paragraph is slightly different. It states: 'Les parties au conflit prendront toutes les mesures possibles dans la pratique pour que les enfants de moins de quinze ans ne participent pas directement aux hostilités, notamment en s'abstenant de les recruter dans les forces armées …'. Unlike the English version, which contains two

armed forces and, having control over the armed forces, can ensure compliance with the legislation by ensuring that individuals aged under 15, or (in cases where proof of age is lacking) who appear to be such, are not recruited. Second, states must take all feasible measures to ensure that children under 15 do not by any other means take a direct part in hostilities. Such circumstances might arise in relation to the pupils of military schools or the members of paramilitary youth organisations, or due to recruitment by military forces not under direct governmental control (pro-government guerrillas and partisans, *levées en masse*, and so on). In all cases, however, the obligation is the same, although it is a far weaker and more subjective one than the ICRC had originally intended. The concept of 'necessary measures' makes reference only to the aim contemplated; the concept of 'feasible measures' also refers to the circumstances in which the measures are to be taken. As Paul Tavernier observed: 'Article 77, Protocol I, imposed on contracting states only an obligation of means and not an obligation of result'.[29]

What are a state's 'armed forces'?

States parties to AP I are prohibited from recruiting children below the age of 15 into their armed forces. But what constitutes a state's armed forces? The 1949 GCs are of little use, as they simply contrast 'members of the armed forces of a Party to the conflict as well as members of militias or volunteer corps forming part of such armed forces' with '[m]embers of other militias and members of other volunteer corps, including those of organized resistance movements, belonging to a Party to the conflict'[30] without defining either category. However, Article 43(1) of AP I is more helpful, providing that:

> The armed forces of a Party to a conflict consist of all organized armed forces, groups and units which are under a command responsible to that Party for the conduct of its subordinates, even if that Party is represented by a government or an authority not recognized by an adverse Party. Such armed forces shall be subject to an internal disciplinary system which, *inter alia*, shall enforce compliance with the rules of international law applicable in armed conflict.

There is no requirement that such persons wear uniform, although failure to do so can have consequences for the individuals themselves when captured by the forces

prepositions coordinated by the word 'and', the French text contains one principal and one subordinate preposition, so that the restriction 'toutes les mesures possibles' applies throughout the sentence. See P. Tavernier, 'Combatants and Non-Combatants', in I.F. Dekker and H.H.G. Post (eds), *The Gulf War of 1980–88: The Iran–Iraq War in International Legal Perspective*, Dordrecht: Martinus Nijhof, 1992, pp. 141–2. Under Article 102 of AP I, the English and French texts have equal status. However, for the reasons given above, this difference in emphasis probably has no practical effect.

[29] *Op. cit.* note 21, at p. 142.

[30] See Article 13 GC I and Article 4 GC III.

of an adverse party. Article 43(3) is also of interest, as it states that: 'Whenever a Party to a conflict incorporates a paramilitary or armed force law enforcement agency into its armed forces it shall so notify the other Parties to the conflict'. This would seem to suggest that recruitment of children who have not yet attained 15 years of age into such organisations, unless they fall within Article 43(1), does not *per se* breach the prohibition on the recruitment of children under 15. It will only do so if the party does not take all feasible measures to ensure that any children under 15 so recruited do not take a direct part in hostilities. The same might be said with regard to the militias, volunteer corps and organised resistance movements not forming a part of a party's armed forces referred to in GC I and III.[31] Although AP I does not use the term child soldier, its provisions reflect a narrower understanding of the concept than the Cape Town Principles,[32] which view children's use in various auxiliary roles as putting them within the definition regardless of whether they have been enrolled into the armed forces. AP I takes a more formal approach. A child soldier is either a member of a state's armed forces or a combatant of some other kind. Indeed, it would be more accurate to say that AP I concerns itself with child combatants rather than child soldiers.

What is a 'direct part in hostilities'?

Article 43(2) of AP I attributes the right to participate directly in hostilities to members of the armed forces of a party to a conflict. The phrase also appears in Article 51, dealing with the protection of the civilian population against the effects of hostilities, paragraph 3 of which provides that: 'Civilians shall enjoy the protection afforded in this section, unless of until and for such time as they take a direct part in hostilities'. In relation to its use in Article 77(2), the phrase can be contrasted with the prohibition in Article 4(3)(c) of children taking a part in hostilities at all. One is a more limited prohibition than the other. Commenting on Article 51(3), the ICRC commentary states: 'In general the immunity afforded to civilians is subject to a very stringent condition: that they do not participate directly in hostilities, i.e., that they do not become combatants on pain of losing their protection. Thus, "direct" participation means acts of war which by their nature or purpose are likely to cause actual harm to the personnel and equipment of the enemy armed forces'.[33]

Putting matters more concretely, taking a direct part in hostilities means: 'that the person in question performs warlike acts which by their nature or purpose are designed to strike enemy combatants or materiel; acts, therefore, such as firing at enemy soldiers, throwing a Molotov-cocktail at an enemy tank, blowing up a bridge

[31] *Ibid.*
[32] See pp. 5–6.
[33] Sandoz, Swinarski and Zimmermann, *op. cit.* note 25, p. 619.

carrying enemy war materiel, and so on'.[34] Taking a direct part in hostilities means taking part in combat. It does not include such activities as the gathering or transmission of military information, the transportation of arms and munitions or the provision of supplies. The use of children in such activities is not prohibited in AP I, another way in which it differs from the Cape Town Principles, which demand that: 'A minimum age of 18 years should be established for any person participating in hostilities or for recruitment in all forms into any armed force or armed group'.

It is doubtful whether the prohibition is broad enough to provide children under 15 with effective protection from the acts of the forces of an adverse party. First, the use of children for the gathering and transmission of military information can place them in danger, if they fall into enemy hands, of being accused of espionage and treated as spies.[35] It appears that children are commonly used for such tasks.[36] Second, despite Article 51 of AP I's insistence that civilians should not be objects of attack unless and for such time as they take a direct part in hostilities,[37] a number of instances spring to mind where for adverse forces not to target civilians who were taking a part, but not a direct part, in hostilities, would be highly improbable, for example if civilians were being used to transport munitions up to the front line for use by the troops fighting there.

What does 'refrain from recruiting' mean?

The original draft of paragraph 2 referred to states refraining from recruiting children under 15 or 'accepting their voluntary enlistment'. It is difficult to do more than speculate as to the reasons behind the deletion of the latter phrase. The only comment on it in the Official Record was made by the representative of Italy, Mr Barile, who stated that his delegation would have preferred the phrase to have been completed in conformity with the ICRC draft.[38] It seems likely that the intention of the deletion was to weaken the provision. The question is whether it succeeded.

The issue has been raised recently. In his dissenting opinion in the Appeals Chamber of the Special Court for Sierra Leone's interlocutory decision in *Prosecutor* v. *Norman*,[39] Justice Robertson stated that: '"Recruitment" is a term

[34] F. Kalshoven, *Constraints on the Waging of War*, Geneva: ICRC, 1987, p. 91.

[35] See Article 46, AP I.

[36] As Cohn and Goodwin-Gill state: 'A Zimbabwean officer who fought against the Smith regime explained it simply: children can move freely and are not instantly suspected of spying and supplying'. I. Cohn and G.S. Goodwin-Gill, *Child Soldiers: The Role of Children in Armed Conflicts*, Oxford: Clarendon Press, 1994, p. 96.

[37] Article 51(2) and (3), AP I.

[38] OR XV, p. 220; CDDH/III/SR.59. The comment was made during the explanation of votes, after the adoption of the article by Committee III.

[39] *Prosecutor* v. *Samuel Hinga Norman*, Case No. SCSL-2004-14-AR729E, Special Court for Sierra Leone (Appeals Chamber), decision on preliminary motion based on lack of jurisdiction (child recruitment), 31 May 2004.

which implies some active soliciting of "recruits", i.e. to pressure or induce them to enlist: it is not synonymous with "enlistment"'.[40] Justice Robertson's comments were with regard to Article 4(3)(a) of AP II, but would seem to apply equally to Article 77(2), the corresponding provision of AP I. Such an interpretation would seem to imply that children under 15 can serve in armed forces and a group, providing that their enrolment is not actively solicited.

In Article 31(1) of the Vienna Convention on the Law of Treaties, generally accepted as reflecting customary international law, it is stated that: 'a treaty shall be interpreted in good faith in accordance with the ordinary meaning to be given to the terms of the treaty in their context and in the light of its object and purpose'. In English usage the word 'recruitment' is broader than the word 'conscription'. It covers both voluntary enlistment and conscription into a state's armed forces.[41] In the context of the paragraph, the prohibition is part of a broader obligation on states to take all feasible measures to prevent children from taking a direct part in hostilities. Plainly, it is as feasible for a state to refuse to accept the voluntary enrolment of children into its armed forces as it is to refrain from conscripting them. Finally, the object and purpose of AP I, as its preamble makes clear, is to protect civilians from the effects of armed conflict. As does GC IV, the Protocol views women and children as quintessential civilians and non-combatants. Accordingly, it is immaterial whether a child's recruitment is voluntary or coerced. It is interesting that Justice Robertson, elsewhere in his opinion, stated that international law prohibits the enlistment of under-15-year-olds, not just their recruitment.[42]

Finally, paragraph 2 stipulates that in recruiting among persons who have attained the age of 15 years but who have not yet attained the age of 18, states shall endeavour to give priority to those who are oldest. This provision is fairly self-explanatory. It was inserted into the paragraph as a sop to those states who wanted a higher minimum age for recruitment and participation in hostilities than 15.[43] Two points about the provision can, however, be made. First, it is an indication that (under the age of 18) the younger a person is, the more undesirable is his or her participation in hostilities. Second, it imposes an obligation on states, if only a weak one, to regulate such participation. Although a number of states do recruit persons under 18, few recruit 15- or 16-year-olds.

[40] *Ibid.*, Dissenting Opinion of Justice Robertson, para. 27.

[41] Under Article 102 of AP I, the Arabic, Chinese, English, French, Russian and Spanish texts of the Protocol are all equally authentic. I am unable to comment on the Arabic, Chinese, Russian or Spanish texts. The equivalent word in the French text, however, is *recruter*, which can apply to both forcible and voluntary recruitment and also (as with its English equivalent) refer to the recruitment of employees in civilian life.

[42] *Op. cit.* note 40, para. 33.

[43] OR III, p. 301; CDDH/III/325; and Sandoz, Swinarski and Zimmermann, *op. cit.* note 25, p. 901.

Additional Protocol II

AP II departed further from the traditional norms of international humanitarian law than did AP I in that it is concerned with the regulation of non-international armed conflicts. Although AP II sets out a code regulating the conduct of internal conflicts,[44] the code is in far more general terms than the very specific provisions in the four GCs and AP I. It is concerned with setting minimum standards of conduct, rather than laying down detailed regulations; it is prohibitive, rather than prescriptive. The provisions governing the special status of children and regulating their participation in hostilities are somewhat briefer, forming part of Article 4, which lists a number of fundamental guarantees for persons affected by internal conflicts.

However, not only are the provisions in AP II governing the participation of children in hostilities briefer than those in AP I, to a large extent they are at variance with them. The relevant provisions of Article 4(3) are as follows:

> Children shall be provided with the care and aid they require, and in particular:
> […]
> (c) children who have not attained the age of fifteen years shall neither be recruited in the armed forces or groups nor allowed to take part in hostilities;
> (d) the special protection provided by this Article to children who have not attained the age of fifteen years shall remain applicable to them if they take a direct part in hostilities despite the provisions of sub-paragraph (c) and are captured.

Article 4(3)(c) mirrors Article 77(2) of AP I in that both only impose restrictions on the participation in hostilities of persons under the age of 15 years. However, the restrictions imposed in respect of the use of children in hostilities in internal armed conflicts by the provisions of Article 4(3)(c) are far broader than those imposed on the use of children in international armed conflicts by Article 77(2). This is the case in two respects in particular.

The absolute nature of the prohibition

The obligation is an absolute one. It is an obligation of result, not of means and is, consequently, more onerous than that imposed by AP I.

The wider scope of the prohibition

In AP I, children under 15 are not to take a 'direct part' in hostilities; in AP II, they are not to take part in hostilities at all. Consequently, not only must they not take part in combat, they must also not take part in such activities as the obtaining

[44] Or, at least, internal conflicts above a certain level of intensity: see Article 1(1), AP II.

and communication of militarily sensitive information and the transportation of munitions or other materiel, nor act as sentries or spies.[45]

Both of these distinctions might be seen as to the credit of the drafters of AP II. Making the obligation upon states to prevent children taking part in hostilities subject to a condition of feasibility allowed scope for abuse, as what, in any particular circumstances, is 'feasible' is often a somewhat subjective judgement. Similarly, permitting children to take part in hostilities at all, even if not a direct part, allows their use in situations often as dangerous as those arising from direct participation. However, it appears that the differences between the two Protocols did not arise out of arguments of principle but were the result of inadvertence.

Examination of the records of the Diplomatic Conference reveals that the provisions protecting children in internal armed conflicts (article 32 of the ICRC draft)[46] were originally distinct from the list of fundamental guarantees for persons in internal armed conflicts (draft article 6).[47] Draft article 32 was assigned to Committee III and its history there followed that of draft article 68 of AP I.[48] Neither the rapporteur's report to Committee III on the work of the Working Group,[49] nor the Committee's own report[50] are at all enlightening as to the circumstances of the amendment of the articles by the Working Group. It is merely stated that the article 'proved relatively easy to adopt'.[51] Why this was is fairly obvious: the argument had already taken place in relation to article 68 of AP I. Article 32, as adopted by Committee III, simply mirrored its terms, stating that:

> (2) … the Parties to the conflict shall, *inter alia* …
> (f) Take all feasible measures in order that children who have not reached fifteen years of age do not take a direct part in hostilities and, in particular, to refrain from recruiting them in their armed forces.[52]

45 See Sandoz, Swinerski and Zimmermann, *op. cit.* note 25, p. 1380.

46 The relevant parts of which stated:

(1) Children shall be the object of privileged treatment; they shall be especially protected against any form of indecent assault. The parties to the conflict shall provide them with the care and aid their age and situation require.

(2) To this end, the parties to the conflict shall, *inter alia*:

[…]

(e) Take the necessary measures in order that children under fifteen shall not take part in hostilities and, in particular, they shall refrain from recruiting them in armed forces or accepting their voluntary enrolment.

47 See OR I, Part III: Draft Additional Protocols to the Geneva Conventions of 12 August 1949.

48 The article was referred to the Working Group. After consideration by the Working Group, it was adopted by Committee III by consensus. See OR XV, pp. 77ff.; CDDH/III/SR.46; and OR XV, pp. 209ff.: CDDH/III/SR.59.

49 OR XV, pp. 517ff.; CDDH/III/407/Rev.1.

50 OR XV, pp. 445ff.; CDDH/III/407/Rev.1.

51 OR XV, p. 524; CDDH/III/407/Rev.1.

52 OR XV, p. 508; CDDH/III/407/Rev.1.

This was not, however, the text that became Article 4(3)(c) of AP II. A different text[53] was put before the Conference by Judge Hussain of Pakistan at its 53rd plenary session of 6 July 1977 and was adopted by consensus.[54] The introduction of the new text was part of an initiative designed to save the Protocol from rejection and no explanation for the changes to the provision were given. Aldrich has commented that:

> I don't know if anyone noticed the change in the text on child combatants; certainly no-one commented on it. In all probability, the revision was designed by Judge Hussain simply to avoid any reference to 'Parties to the conflict', a phrase he excised from all article of Protocol II in order to eliminate any suggestion that a rebellious party was being recognized as having rights under the Treaty.[55]

Consequently, an initiative designed to render the Protocol less onerous (and, hence, more acceptable) to the negotiating states resulted, in this one instance, in the imposition of more stringent obligations than had been intended.[56]

It has been argued that, given this negotiating history, it cannot be said that Article 4(3)(c) does impose more stringent obligations on states than does its counterpart article in AP I. Such an argument has little credibility. The terms of Article 4(3)(c) are clear, so there is no occasion to look to any supplementary means of interpretation to ascertain their meaning.[57]

Conclusions

The two APs marked the beginning of the legal regulation of children's participation in hostilities. It has been seen that the two treaties differed in a number of respects. However, although the divergences already highlighted may have been the respect of inadvertence, another difference between the two protocols was intentional. When AP I speaks of 'Parties to the conflict' it refers to state parties to the Protocol, to national liberation movements who have made a unilateral declaration undertaking to apply the GCs and AP I,[58] and possibly to the forces of other recognised and already existing subjects of international law, such as governments in exile.[59] AP II, by contrast, does not address itself to anyone. It was

[53] OR IV, p. 20: CDDH/427.

[54] OR IV, pp. 141ff.; CDDH/SR.53.

[55] G.H. Aldrich, 'Comments on Tavernier's "Combatants and Non-Combatants"', in Dekker and Post, *op. cit.* note 28, p. 149.

[56] Aldrich's comments would also provide an explanation for the discrepancy between Articles 4(3)(c) and 4(3)(d), the latter of which covers under-15-year-olds taking 'a direct part', rather than simply a part, in hostilities.

[57] See Article 32, Vienna Convention on the Law of Treaties, (1969) 1115 UNTS 331.

[58] See also Articles 1(3) and 96(3) AP I.

[59] See Sandoz, Swinarski and Zimmermann, *op. cit.* note 25, p. 507.

deliberately drafted in an impersonal manner. The only clue in the text as to whom AP II applies is in Article 1 on its material field of application.

> This Protocol ... shall apply to all armed conflicts which are not covered by Article 1 of the Protocol Additional to the Geneva Conventions of 12 August 1949, and relating to the Protection of Victims of International Armed Conflicts (Protocol I) and which take place in the territory of a High Contracting party between its armed forces and dissident armed forces or other organized armed groups which, under responsible command, exercise such control over a part of its territory as to enable them to carry out sustained and concerted military operations and to implement this Protocol.

To put it another way, AP II binds not only states which have ratified or acceded to it, but also armed opposition groups fighting against the governments of such states. This is clear from the drafting history and is highlighted in the ICRC Commentary.[60] Precisely how AP II binds armed opposition groups is less clear. This result has generally been founded upon states' right to prescribe for their nationals or regarding activities taking place in their territory.[61] However, rebels are by definition persons who have forsworn allegiance to their governments. In addition, AP II was redrafted specifically to avoid referring to insurgent groups so as to avoid any implication that their mention conferred any form of recognition, so one might ask how its provisions can bind such groups as opposed to the individuals composing them. Despite these theoretical problems, however, it is generally accepted that armed opposition groups are bound by AP II, and it has been consistently interpreted in that way. For example, in 1991 the United Nations Observer Mission in El Salvador (ONUSAL) reported that:

> The continuing armed conflict has caused the Mission to also examine recruitment by the FMLN [Farabundo Marti para la Liberacion Nacional]. It has been noted that there are a significant number of children under the age of 15 in the ranks of the guerrillas, in violation of the provisions of Protocol II concerning the protection of children. FMLN leaders have pledged to discontinue the recruitment of children under 15 and to assign other tasks to those already recruited.[62]

Similarly, in its 1999 report on Colombia, the Inter-American Commission on Human Rights stated that: 'when groups of armed dissidents and paramilitary groups induct children under 15 into their units, they are violating the principles of international humanitarian law'.[63] This statement can be read widely, as implying that armed groups are under a customary law obligation, but it should also be noted

[60] Sandoz, Swinarski and Zimmermann, *op. cit.* note 25, p. 1345.

[61] *Ibid.*

[62] Report of the Secretary-General on ONUSAL and report of the ONUSAL Human Rights Division, UN Doc. A/46/658-S/23222 (15 November 1991), para. 167; reproduced in *The United Nations and El Salvador 1990–1995*, pp. 179–80.

[63] Inter-American Commission on Human Rights, Third Report on the Human Rights Situation in Colombia, OEA/Ser.L/V/II. 102 (26 February 1999).

that Colombia was at the time a party to AP II, having ratified the Protocol on 14 August 1995.

AP I, however, does not bind armed opposition groups.[64] This might not be seen as much of an omission, as international armed conflicts are, by definition, conflicts between states.[65] However, at least according to the Appeals Chamber of the International Criminal Tribunal for the former Yugoslavia (ICTY), the test for when an armed conflict is internationalised and when the acts of an armed opposition group can be imputed to a state are not the same. An armed opposition group can fight alongside a state's armed forces in an international armed conflict without that state having either 'effective' or 'overall' control over the group's actions.[66] AP I does not reflect the messy reality of many modern day armed conflicts. There is a normative gap whereby armed opposition groups participating in international armed conflicts are not bound by the provisions of either AP I or AP II. Their state sponsor may be internationally responsible for the group's actions, either because it is a *de facto* agent or organ of the state, or the state has failed to take 'all feasible measures' to prevent the group using children to participate in hostilities or to 'ensure respect' for international humanitarian law. As a matter of treaty law, however, the armed opposition group itself is under no obligation not to recruit or use child soldiers.[67] Fortunately, as will be seen in Chapter 6, customary international law has developed to fill this normative gap.

[64] With the exception of national liberation movements in armed conflicts in 'which peoples are fighting against colonial domination and alien occupation and against racist regimes in the exercise of their right of self-determination': see Articles 1(4) and 96(3) AP I.

[65] Common Article 2 GCs.

[66] See *Prosecutor* v. *Kordić and Čerkez*, Case No. IT-95-14/2 Trial Chamber, ICTY, judgment of 26 February 2001, paras 66 and 79.

[67] The jurisprudence of the ICTY argues that a 'minimum core of mandatory rules', as expressed under Common Article 3 of the GCs, apply regardless of the internal or international nature of a conflict: see *Prosecutor* v. *Delalić et al.*, Case No. IT-96-21-A, Appeals Chamber, ICTY, judgment of 20 February 2001, paras 140–50. This, however, goes to individual criminal responsibility and may not, in any case, catch the war crime of child recruitment (see Chapter 8, pp. 00–00).

5

The legal regulation of the recruitment and use of children in hostilities: international human rights law

Introduction

Following the conclusion of the two APs, the locus of the development of the law relating to the recruitment and use of children in hostilities moved from the arena of international humanitarian law to that of international human rights law. To an extent, this reflected the UN's increasing involvement with the issue, with negotiations taking place under UN auspices rather than those of the ICRC. In addition, however, as the issue primarily concerned how states treat their own nationals, it fitted neatly onto the human rights agenda.

An article regulating the participation of children in hostilities appears in the 1989 Convention on the Rights of the Child (CRC). However, following dissatisfaction with the provisions contained in the CRC, in 2000 an Optional Protocol (OP) to the Convention on the Rights of the Child on the Involvement of Children in Armed Conflict was adopted to cure their defects. Difficulties in the negotiation of the OP, however, meant provisions on child recruitment were also included in a 1999 ILO treaty, ILO Convention 182 on the Worst Forms of Child Labour. The only regional treaty on the rights of the child, the 1989 African Charter on the Rights and Welfare of the Child, also includes provisions on child-soldiering.

The CRC

In contrast to the two APs, the CRC does define what a child is. A child is a 'human being below the age of eighteen years unless, under the law applicable to the child, majority is attained earlier'.[1] The general age of majority is 18. National law has only a subsidiary importance. Article 4 of the CRC provides that: 'States Parties shall undertake all appropriate legislative, administrative, and other measures for the implementation of the rights recognized in the … Convention'. Article 38 deals with the participation of children in hostilities. The article provides:

[1] Article 1 CRC.

1. States Parties undertake to respect and ensure respect for rules of international humanitarian law applicable to them in armed conflicts which are relevant to the child.
2. State Parties shall take all feasible measures to ensure that persons who have not attained the age of fifteen years do not take a direct part in hostilities.
3. State Parties shall refrain from recruiting any person who has not attained the age of fifteen years into their armed forces. In recruiting among those persons who have attained the age of fifteen years but who have not attained the age of eighteen years, States Parties shall take all feasible measures to give priority to those who are oldest.
4. In accordance with their obligations under international humanitarian law to protect the civilian population in armed conflicts, State Parties shall take all feasible measures to ensure protection and care of children who are affected by an armed conflict.

The article marks little advance from the provisions of AP I, although it does confirm that the prohibition on the recruitment of children under 15 is a blanket prohibition applying in times of peace as well as war; the CRC, as a human rights treaty, applying at all times. It is weaker than Article 4(3)(c) of AP II. This was a disappointment to a number of states and NGOs involved in the negotiation of the CRC. Indeed, Article 38 is the only provision in the Convention that includes provisions extending protection only to children under 15 years old, as opposed to all children.

The text of the CRC was negotiated within an open-ended Working Group established by the UN Commission on Human Rights (UNCHR) in 1979.[2] The original draft of the CRC did not include any provision on the protection of children in armed conflicts. This was seen, particularly by NGOs, as a lacuna in the treaty. A number of proposed new articles dealing with the subject were submitted in the 1985 and 1986 sessions of the Working Group and at the 1986 session, after a lengthy debate, a draft article was adopted. The new draft article 20 provided that:

1. The States Parties to the present Convention undertake to respect and ensure respect for rules of international humanitarian law applicable to them in armed conflicts which are relevant to the child.
2. States Parties to the present Convention shall take all feasible measures to ensure that no child takes a direct part in hostilities and they shall refrain in particular from recruiting any child who has not attained the age of fifteen years into their armed forces.

[2] For discussion of the negotiation of the CRC, see S. Detrick (ed.), *The United Nations Convention on the Rights of the Child: A Guide to the 'Travaux Préparatoires'*, Dordrecht: Martinus Nijhof, 1992; and Françoise Krill, 'The Protection of Children in Armed Conflict', in M. Freeman and P. Veerman (eds), *The Ideologies of Children's Rights*, Dordrecht: Martinus Nijhof, 1992.

3. In accordance with their obligations under international humanitarian law to protect the civilian population in armed conflicts, States Parties to this Convention shall take all feasible measures to ensure protection and care of children who are affected by an armed conflict.

The new article was, in its turn, seen as unsatisfactory by a number of states and NGOs, in that it failed to live up to the standards set in international humanitarian law, let alone develop them. In at least one respect (the lack of any provision obliging states to give priority to the oldest when recruiting among persons aged between 15 and 18 years of age), the article was weaker than Article 77(2) of AP I. Following representations made at the 1986 and 1987 sessions, discussion of the article was reopened at the 1988 session of the Working Group.

At the 1988 session, however, the Chairman distinguished two items on the agenda: amendments to the existing text which improved international standards, and the insertion of new text taken from Article 77(2) of AP I. It was agreed to insert the new text (imposing an obligation to give priority to the oldest when recruiting persons between 15 and 18), but to leave the amendments to the existing text to the second reading of the Convention.[3] That took place at the 1989 session, when two texts were placed before the Working Group: the text adopted during the first reading with suggested amendments by UNICEF, and a proposal made by a drafting group of Angola, Australia, Austria, France, Italy, Mozambique, the Netherlands, Norway, Sweden, the USA, the UNHCR, the ICRC, the Friends' Committee for Consultation and Rädda Barnen. In relation to the second text, the drafting group had not attained consensus on all of its contents. There was a lengthy debate regarding which text should be adopted. This debate centred in particular on which of the two versions of paragraph 2 of the second text should be adopted. The choice before the Working Group was as follows:

1. (2) States Parties shall take all feasible measures to ensure that no child takes a direct part in hostilities. With regard to persons who have attained majority before the age of 18 years, States Parties shall endeavour to prevent them from taking a direct part in hostilities. Persons who have not attained the age of 15 years shall not be allowed to take part in hostilities.
   or
2. (2) States Parties shall take all feasible measures to ensure that persons who have not attained the age of 15 years do not take a direct part in hostilities.

The majority of states represented in the Working Group were in favour of the first version, as was the ICRC, although India and the UK said that they supported the consensus with some hesitation. However, the USSR and the USA indicated support for the second version, with the representative of the USA stating his unwillingness to join a consensus in favour of the first. Efforts to agree a compromise text failed, whereupon the Chairman, stating that no participants in the

[3] UN Doc. E/CN.4/1988/28, at p. 26.

Working Group opposed the standards contained in the text of the second version, held that they were the maximum level of protection on which consensus had been reached and that, therefore, the second version of paragraph 2 was adopted.

The decision was the subject of much acrimony. Threats were made to reopen the issue at a higher level, at the Commission on Human Rights or even the General Assembly. In the event, however, doubtless due to fears that any such action would reopen discussion of other provisions of the Convention, the text was adopted unmodified. Accordingly, the restrictions on the recruitment of children and their participation in hostilities in the CRC are (save for their greater scope) identical in content to those in AP I.

In contrast to the APs, which only slowly gained general acceptance, the CRC has been very widely ratified. Indeed, it is the multilateral human rights treaty with the greatest number of parties. As of 9 June 2004, there were 192 states parties to the CRC[4] and only two UN Member States (Somalia and the USA) were not parties. However, unhappiness remained about the level of protection afforded by the CRC to children involved in armed conflicts. A number of state parties to the CRC[5] made declarations that they considered Article 38, by failing to prohibit the use of all persons under 18 in armed conflicts, not to offer children sufficient protection and/or stating that they would apply their own national legislation rather than the principles laid down in the CRC to regulate the recruitment of persons into their national armed forces.

The OP to the CRC on the Involvement of Children in Armed Conflict

Dissatisfaction with Article 38 also manifested itself in the Committee on the Rights of the Child, the body established to supervise states' compliance with their obligations under the CRC.[6] Almost immediately, at its second session in the autumn of 1992, a proposal was made for the development of an Optional Protocol (OP) to the CRC further restricting the participation of children in hostilities.[7] The Committee decided to appoint one of its members to prepare a preliminary draft OP raising the minimum age of recruitment to 18.[8] A short draft was prepared.[9] The substantive provisions appeared in draft articles 1 and 2, which provided that:

[4] Office of the High Commissioner for Human Rights, 'Status of Ratifications of the Principal Human Rights Treaties as of 9 June 2004'. Available at: www.unhchr.ch/html/menu3/b/k2crc.htm.

[5] Andorra, Argentina, Austria, Colombia, Ecuador (upon signature), Germany, the Netherlands, Spain and Uruguay.

[6] Article 43 CRC.

[7] UN Doc. CRC/C/10, paras 61–77.

[8] UN Doc. CRC/C/625, para. 176.

[9] UN Doc. E/CN.4/1994/91.

1. States Parties shall take all feasible measures to ensure that persons who have not attained the age of 18 years do not take part in hostilities.
2. States Parties shall refrain from recruiting any person who has not attained the age of 18 years into their armed forces.

The draft was submitted to the Commission on Human Rights, and in 1994 the Commission established an open-ended Working Group to negotiate an OP.[10] The Committee on the Rights of the Child's text formed the basis upon which negotiations took place within the Working Group.

Negotiating the OP

Negotiation of the OP took some six years. The Working Group first met in late 1994. Divisions were apparent from its first session. A number of participants argued that it was imperative to set a minimum age of recruitment of 18.[11] The view was also expressed that all forms of participation in hostilities should be prohibited, as in practice there was often little difference between direct and indirect participation in hostilities.[12] It was generally felt that any prohibition should be in relation to all armed groups, whether governmental or non-governmental.[13] On the other hand, some states only wanted to prohibit the conscription of under-18-year-olds and their participation (or direct participation) in hostilities. The USA wanted to reduce the proposed minimum age for recruitment from 18 to 17.[14] Other states wanted to permit recruitment into military schools or for educational or training purposes. There was also some dispute over whether the minimum age for recruitment should be 15 or 16.

Matters advanced somewhat at the second session of the Working Group. It was agreed that there should be no conscription of persons under 18.[15] There was the usual dispute over whether the OP should cover non-governmental armed forces or whether doing so would give unwarranted legitimacy to them, but the general feeling was that such a reference should be made.[16] However, there was disagreement over the objective of the OP: should it be drafted so as to encourage the widest participation by states possible or should it be concerned with setting the highest standards achievable?[17] In addition, the session saw the crystallisation of disputes over the minimum age limit for participation in hostilities, with the USA and Pakistan arguing for 17 rather than 18; and whether all participation or only direct participation should be prohibited, with the USA, Japan and South Africa

[10] CHR Res. 1994/91.
[11] UN Doc. E/CN.4/1995/96, para. 17.
[12] *Ibid.*, para. 23.
[13] *Ibid.*, para. 24.
[14] *Ibid.*, para. 77.
[15] *Ibid.*, paras 24 and 117.
[16] *Ibid.*, paras 31–2.
[17] *Ibid.*, para. 46.

arguing for the latter.[18] Despite agreement that the minimum age of recruitment should be higher, there was disagreement as to what age it should be raised.[19]

By the third session of the Working Group, signs of an impasse were beginning to appear. In relation to the minimum age for participation in hostilities, the UK, South Korea and Bangladesh favoured a 17-year age limit but stated that they would not block consensus on 18.[20] The USA, Pakistan and Cuba continued to favour 17.[21] Disagreement also remained over whether the prohibition should be in relation to all forms or only direct participation in hostilities[22] and over the minimum age of recruitment.[23]

At the fourth session, '[a] fundamental difference among States on the question of the minimum age for participation in hostilities was ... noted by the working group'.[24] A 'Chairman's perceptions' paper was circulated, setting out a compromise text.[25] Although the 'vast majority' of states favoured an age limit of 18 for all participation in hostilities and an appeal was made to the dissentient states not to block consensus,[26] no consensus was reached.[27] The representative of the USA indicated that an age limit of 18 rather than 17 was not acceptable to his government, although all other speakers were in favour of or ready to accept it.[28]

The Commission on Human Rights was obliged to step in. It mandated the Chairman of the Working Group to conduct informal consultations, which took place over the next two years.[29] The sixth session of the Working Group finally saw agreement. On 21 January 2000, a draft OP was adopted by consensus. A number of states immediately announced their dissatisfaction with the results achieved. However, the OP was adopted by the General Assembly and opened for signature, ratification and accession on 25 May 2000.[30]

[18] *Ibid.*, paras 93–7.

[19] *Ibid.*, paras 24 and 103–17.

[20] UN Doc. E/CN.4/1997/96, para. 76.

[21] *Ibid.*, para. 78.

[22] *Ibid.*, para. 79.

[23] *Ibid.*, paras 87–97.

[24] UN Doc. E/CN.4/1998/102, para. 23.

[25] *Ibid.*, Annex II. The Chairman's text proposed, first, that States Parties to the Protocol be obliged to take all feasible measures to ensure that under-18-year-olds do not take a direct part in hostilities and, second, that the conscription of persons under 18 and the voluntary recruitment of persons under 17 years of age be prohibited.

[26] *Ibid.*, paras 19–20 and 29.

[27] *Ibid.*, para. 23.

[28] *Ibid.*, para. 69.

[29] The Working Group did meet twice more before agreement was reached but only briefly: in April 1998 it met to elect an new Chairman-Rapporteur: see UN Doc. E/CN.4/1998/102/Add.1; and in January 1999 it met for its fifth session to recommend to the Commission on Human Rights that the Chairman be encouraged to continue her consultations: see UN Doc. E/CN.4/1999/73.

[30] GA Res. 54/263 of 25 May 2000.

The OP

The core of the OP is found in Articles 1, 2 and 3. Article 1 simply provides that: 'States Parties shall take all feasible measures to ensure that members of their armed forces who have not attained the age of 18 years do not take a direct part in hostilities'. As with the corresponding obligations in AP I and the CRC, the obligation is not an absolute one. Given, however, that the OP does not impose a minimum age of recruitment of 18, an absolute obligation might prove impossible to fulfil by states parties which do recruit under-18-year-olds. The fact that under-18s may be recruited into states parties' armed forces renders it likely that such persons will, in situations of armed conflict and whatever precautions are taken, from time to time be attacked by enemy troops, not least because such troops may in many cases be unable to distinguish child soldiers from other enemy forces. However, the UK, in its declaration upon signature of the OP, has read Article 1 rather more widely. The declaration states that:

> The United Kingdom understands that article 1 of the Optional Protocol would not exclude the deployment of members of its armed forces under the age of 18 to take a direct part in hostilities where:
>
> (a) there is a genuine military need to deploy their unit or ship to an area in which hostilities are taking place; and
> (b) by reason of the nature and urgency of the situation:
> (i) it is not practicable to withdraw such persons before deployment; or
> (ii) to do so would undermine the operational effectiveness or their ship or unit, and thereby put at risk the successful completion of the military mission and/or the safety of other personnel.

No other state party has protested this declaration. It might be argued that this suggests that other states parties accept the UK's interpretation, but such a conclusion may be going too far. In a similar vein, however, at the final session of the Working Group the US representative stated that; 'the standard recognize[s] that, in exceptional cases, it might not be feasible for a commander to withhold or remove [child soldiers] from taking a direct part in hostilities'.[31] This seems to go even further than the UK position by permitting commanders to take a positive decision to commit child soldiers to battle if they consider military necessity requires it. The strictures in the ICRC commentary on Article 57(2) of AP I might be profitably recalled; a focus on military needs should not serve as an excuse for neglecting the humanitarian obligations prescribed by the provision.

In addition, Article 1 does not ban all participation by children in hostilities. Children can be used to participate in hostilities; meaning, as with AP I and the CRC, that child soldiers can be employed in a number of roles which are likely to put them in danger from enemy forces. Indeed, this point was made expressly in

[31] UN Doc. E/Cn.4/2000/74, at para. 131.

the USA's declaration on ratification of the OP, which states that the US understanding of the phrase 'direct part in hostilities' is that it: 'does not mean indirect participation in hostilities, such as gathering and transmitting military information, transporting weapons, munitions or other supplies, or forward deployment'.

Article 2, by contrast, does contain an absolute prohibition: 'States Parties shall ensure that persons who have not attained the age of 18 years are not compulsorily recruited into their armed forces'. The conscription of under-18-year-olds is forbidden. Such an obligation seems to be something within states' powers, although difficulties may arise if states have not established proper systems for the registration of births. Consequently, in such cases states must err on the side of caution and not recruit anyone who may be under 18. If a state does so, even inadvertently, it will be in breach of the article.

Article 3 contains the most complex provisions of the OP, a clear sign of its origins in compromise. First, Article 3(1) requires states parties to raise their minimum age for voluntary recruitment 'from that set out in article 38, paragraph 3 of the Convention on the Rights of the Child'. The age set out in Article 38(3) being 15 years, it seems that Article 3 of the OP raises the minimum age of recruitment to 16, if in a rather opaque manner.[32] Second, in raising the minimum age at which they recruit, states parties must do so 'taking into account the principles contained in that article and recognising that under the Convention persons under 18 are entitled to special protection'. The relevant principles in Article 38 of the CRC would appear to be those deriving from its requirement that: 'In recruiting among those persons who have attained the age of fifteen years but who have not attained the age of eighteen years, States parties shall take all feasible measures to give priority to those who are oldest'. In other words, the younger a person is, the more undesirable is his or her recruitment. Invocation of the principles that persons under 18 are entitled to special protection would appear to indicate that all recruitment of under-18-year-olds is undesirable. It is, however, unclear what effect the requirement to take account of these principles is meant to have. If the provision is not simply hortatory, it seems only to impose a weak obligation of states parties to consider whether it is appropriate to recruit under-18-year-olds and to set out criteria which they must take into account when making their decision whether to do so.

Article 3(2) then provides that, upon ratification or accession to the OP, a state party shall deposit a binding declaration setting out the minimum age at which it will permit voluntary recruitment and describing the safeguards it has in place to ensure that such recruitment is truly voluntary. Article 3(4) provides that a state party may, at any time, 'strengthen' its declaration. In consequence, once a state has become a party to the OP it may not later reduce the minimum age from which it recruits but it may increase it, again with binding effect. If a state's

[32] See D. Helle, 'Optional Protocol on the Involvement of Children in Armed Conflict to the Convention on the Rights of the Child' (2000) IRRC No. 839, p. 797.

declaration provides that it will recruit persons aged 17 and upward, it may increase the minimum age to 18, but it may not reduce it to 16, even though that is the minimum age generally permitted under the OP. The provision is akin to a ratchet mechanism. As many states do not, in fact, recruit from 16, the result of the provision may be the establishment of some higher age as the general minimum. As of 29 January 2004, some sixty-nine states had become parties to the OP and had made declarations upon signature or ratification. Three of those states[33] have no armed forces, so their declarations did not set any minimum age for recruitment. Of the others, six set the minimum age at 16; eleven at 17; forty-three at 18; and six at some higher age.

Article 3(3) provides that states which do permit voluntary recruitment of persons under the age of 18 into their armed forces shall maintain a number of safeguards to ensure that such recruitment is genuinely voluntary and not forced or coerced. These shall ensure not only that such recruitment is voluntary but also that it is fully informed and done with the informed consent of the person's parents or legal guardians. States must also only recruit persons who can provide reliable evidence that they are old enough to be recruited. An element of transparency is ensured by requiring states to set out the safeguards employed to ensure that these obligations are met in their declarations upon adherence to the OP.

Finally, Article 3(5) provides that the increase in the minimum age of recruitment from 15 to 16 set out in Article 3(1) does not apply in respect to the enrolment of persons into schools operated by or under the control of states parties' armed forces. The operation of such schools must, however, comply with the relevant provisions of the CRC.[34]

Non-state actors are dealt with in Article 4. Article 4(1) provides that: 'Armed groups that are distinct from the armed forces of a State should not, under any circumstances, recruit or use in hostilities persons under the age of 18 years'. This is an absolute prohibition, in contrast to the earlier, more complex and nuanced provisions regarding recruitment into and use by states parties' armed forces. It appears that such a restriction was more palatable to governments than restrictions on their own recruiting activities. The definition of 'armed groups' is, however, of interest. It does not appear to be limited to armed opposition groups – insurgents in conflict with the governments of states parties – but is wide enough to encompass armed groups allied with a state party's government but not part of or under the control of its armed forces. Such a definition also adds force to the provision in Article 4(2) that states parties shall take all feasible measures to prevent the recruitment and use of under-18-year-olds by armed groups, including by criminalising such practices. States would not appear to have many means to prevent insurgent groups from recruiting or using child soldiers other than

[33] Andorra, Iceland and Panama.

[34] That is, Articles 28 (the child's right to education) and 29 (the developments to which the education of the child shall be directed).

prosecuting and punishing rebels who fall into their hands if they have participated in the recruitment or use of child soldiers, but the situation might be different with regard to armed groups allied to the state's government. There is the usual disclaimer that the application of Article 4 shall not affect the legal status of any parties to an armed conflict.

In some quarters, the adoption of the OP was seen as a triumph for 'international civil society', being the first time that the US had given way on a human rights issue that it regarded as involving its military interests.[35] The contrast was drawn with the Convention on the Use, Stockpiling, Production and Transfer of Anti-Personnel Mines, and the Rome Statute of the ICC, the USA being opposed to the adoption of both.[36] On the other hand, the issue was not one that affected US national security in any major way. At the conclusion of the Working Group's deliberations, President Clinton, as he then was, announced that the text adopted: 'fully protects the military recruitment and readiness requirements of the United States'.[37] Although the US armed forces recruits 17-year-old high school graduates upon graduation rather than waiting for their eighteenth birthday, such recruits total less than half of one percent of the US military and almost all of them reach their eighteenth birthday before completing their training.[38] The USA has not felt it necessary to raise its minimum age of recruitment in order to become a party to the OP.[39]

The OP was the product of a compromise. This is most obvious in the obscurity of the language in a number of its provisions. As a consequence, it has been criticised from both sides. The opposition of a number of states to imposing 18 as the minimum age for all recruitment was premised upon a perception that states' armed forces serve useful functions; that service as a solider can be a worthwhile and fulfilling occupation; and that if states were not allowed to enlist school leavers into their armed forces, then many persons who might otherwise chose a military career would be lost to civilian life.[40] The OP meets these concerns. Recruitment

[35] See 'Optional Protocol adopted by UN General Assembly', *Children of War*, No. 2/00 (July 2000), p. 1.

[36] See P. Malanczuk, 'The International Criminal Court and Landmines: What are the Consequences of Leaving the US Behind?' (2000) 11 EJIL 77.

[37] Statement on the Geneva Protocol on Child Soldiers, 35 Weekly Comp. Pres. Doc. 130 (24 January 2000), cited in M.J. Dennis, 'Newly Adopted Protocols to the Convention on the Rights of the Child' (2000) 94 AJIL 789, p. 792.

[38] See K. Roth, 'Sidelined on Human Rights', *Foreign Affairs* (March–April 1998), p. 2.

[39] Indeed, it appears that the text of Article 3 adopted was based on a US proposal. See Dennis, *op. cit.* note 36, pp. 790–1.

[40] See Dennis, *Ibid.*, p. 790. See also the UK's declaration upon ratification of the OP, which states that: 'The minimum age at which individuals may join the UK Armed Forces is 16 years. This minimum broadly reflects the statutory school leaving age in the United Kingdom, that is the age at which young persons may first be permitted to cease full-time education and enter the full-time employment market'.

from the age of 16 is permitted, providing that recruits and their parents or guardians have given their fully informed consent, although states parties must attempt to ensure that soldiers under 18 years of age do not directly participate in hostilities. At the same time, the OP does increase the minimum age at which recruitment can take place; prohibits the compulsory and (it can be inferred) forcible recruitment of children; and prevents the use of child soldiers to participate directly in hostilities.

However, it may be asked whether the OP will have any real effect on states' behaviour or whether it really augments in any significant manner the protection already given to under-18-year-olds. Most states do not currently recruit from age 15. Some recruit from 16, some from 17, others from 18. When they do conscript, it is generally only from age 18. Few changes will be necessary to comply with the OP. In addition, by permitting the recruitment of under-18s and their participation (if not direct participation) in hostilities, the OP does not give child soldiers effective protection from the effects of armed conflict. As members of a state's armed forces, they remain lawful targets for enemy forces who, in many cases, may be unable to distinguish them from their older comrades. As persons participating in hostilities, they can be put in positions of danger by their own side.

ILO Convention 182 on the Worst Forms of Child Labour

Owing to the impasse in the Working Group on the OP, the issue of child recruitment began to be raised in other fora. In 1998, the International Labour Conference, the annual meeting of the ILO, decided that there should be a legally binding convention obliging states parties to take measures to secure the prohibition and immediate elimination of the worst forms of child labour. It was suggested that the convention should explicitly govern the recruitment and use of children in armed conflict but a decision on the issue was deferred.[41] Consequently, whether provisions on child soldiers and the use of children in armed conflict should be included in the convention became one of the major issues of debate at the Conference's 1999 session.[42]

During the general discussion, a number of government members referred to the issue. Most were in favour of inclusion. The African group had adopted a common position, which proposed that an explicit reference to the recruitment and use of children in armed conflict be included in the definition of the worst forms of child labour.[43] However, the government member of the USA urged

[41] International Labour Conference, 87th Session, Geneva, June 1999, Report of the Committee on Child Labour (Corr.), para. 6.

[42] *Ibid.*, para. 11.

[43] See the statement of the Government member of Ethiopia, speaking on behalf of the members of the African Group on the Committee, *ibid.*, para. 37. See also the comments of the Government members of South Africa (para. 39) and Namibia (para. 45).

caution.[44] The intention of the convention was not to limit traditional military training and voluntary service; its emphasis should be on the coerced or criminal imposition of military activity. The government member of the Russian Federation doubted the advisability of a reference of child soldiers at all, as the issue was being addressed through the consideration of a draft OP to the CRC.[45]

An informal tripartite working group was established to work towards consensus on a number of issues including the explicit inclusion of a provision on the participation of children in armed conflict. Following consultations, the government member of Australia presented a comprehensive proposal to the Committee. An amendment was proposed defining the 'worst forms of child labour' as including 'debt bondage and serfdom and forced or compulsory labour, including forced or compulsory recruitment of children for use in armed conflict'. The proposal was widely supported by government, employer and worker members,[46] and was adopted by consensus.

Not everyone was happy with the new text. The government member of Ethiopia, speaking on behalf of the African Group on the Committee, stated that the proposal did not reflect the views of the members of the Group concerning the participation of children in armed conflict, which they considered the most hazardous and injurious form of child labour.[47] Other states also thought the provision did not go far enough. Several states reiterated their support for a ban on the involvement of all persons under 18 in armed conflicts. The government member of the USA set out his understanding that the Convention did not cover voluntary enlistment in lawful national military service,[48] and that there were no additional obligations related to military service contained in Article 3(d) of the Convention on hazardous work, which included among the worst forms of child labour 'work which, by its nature or the circumstances in which it is carried out, is likely to harm the health, safety or morals of children'. The US Government member specifically noted that no objections had been made to these understandings, and stated that it was only on the basis that the Committee concurred with them that his government was prepared to move forward.[49]

It is clear that the then-stalled negotiations on the OP were much in the minds of the Committee's members. During closing statements in the Committee, the government member of the Netherlands, speaking on behalf of a number of developed states:[50]

44 *Ibid.*, para. 41.

45 *Ibid.*, para. 44.

46 *Ibid.*, para. 130. The ILO is a tripartite organisation made up of representatives of government, labour and business from its Member States.

47 *Ibid.*, para. 132.

48 *Ibid.*, paras 151–2.

49 *Ibid.*, para. 160.

50 Australia, Austria, Belgium, Canada, Denmark, Finland, France, Germany, Greece, Hungary, Ireland, Italy, Japan, Luxembourg, the Netherlands, New Zealand, Norway, Portugal, San Marino, Spain, Sweden, Switzerland, Turkey, the UK and the USA.

> Expressed satisfaction with the work carried out by the Committee in reaching a satisfactory compromise text for a Convention and a Recommendation and considered the major relevant issues were adequately reflected.
>
> The instruments represented a first step towards the setting of international standards on the issue of child soldiers. A basis had been laid for the Working Group on the optional protocol to the United Nations Convention on involvement of children in armed conflict to make further progress.[51]

The Convention and Recommendation were adopted as a whole and without objections by the International Labour Conference. It is clear, however, just as with the OP, that the drive for consensus and to achieve a text that would be widely ratified led to a convention that many delegates would have preferred to have been in stronger terms.

ILO Convention 182 only deals briefly with the issue of child soldiers. Article 1 provides that each ILO Member State which ratifies the Convention 'shall take immediate and effective measures to secure the prohibition and elimination of the worst forms of child labour as a matter of urgency'. Article 2 defines the term 'child' as applying to all persons under the age of 18. Article 3(a) then goes on to define the 'worst forms of child labour' as including, *inter alia*, the 'forced or compulsory recruitment of children for use in armed conflict'. The forced or compulsory recruitment of children for use in armed conflict is also defined as being a form of slavery or a practice similar to slavery. This is of particular interest because slavery and slavery-like practices are already prohibited in international law, both in a number of treaties and as a matter of customary international law.

The provisions on the recruitment of children in ILO Convention 182 corresponded to portions of the text of the draft OP on which there was already general agreement.[52] As a result, the Convention was rapidly and widely ratified, entering into force on 19 November 2000, just eighteen months after its adoption. Indeed, the USA found the treaty so easy to accept that it was only the third state to ratify it.[53] As of 20 April 2004, the Convention had 147 parties.

The African Charter on the Rights and Welfare of the Child

The African Charter on the Rights and Welfare of the Child[54] is the only regional human rights treaty specifically concerned with children's rights. It is also the only regional human rights treaty which deals with children's involvement in armed conflict. The Charter was adopted by the Member States of the Organisation of

[51] *Op. cit.* note 41, paras 395–6.

[52] What is now Article 2 OP.

[53] See M.J. Dennis, 'The ILO Convention on the Worst Forms of Child Labor' (1999) AJIL 943, pp. 947–8.

[54] OAU Doc. CAB/LEG/24.9/49 (1990).

African Unity (OAU) on 11 July 1990. It followed from the Declaration on the Rights and Welfare of the African Child[55] adopted by the Assembly of Heads of States and Government of the OAU in 1979, which did not, however, make any specific reference to children and armed conflict.

To a large extent, the Charter tracks the CRC. However, Article 22 on armed conflicts provides that:

> 1. States Parties to this Charter shall undertake to respect and ensure respect for the rules of international humanitarian law applicable in armed conflicts which affect the child.
> 2. States Parties to the present Charter shall take all necessary measures to ensure that no child shall take a direct part in hostilities and refrain in particular, from recruiting any child.
> 3. States Parties to the present Charter shall, in accordance with their obligations under international humanitarian law, protect the civilian population in armed conflicts and shall take all feasible measures to ensure the protection and care of children who are affected by armed conflicts. Such rules shall also apply to children in situations of internal armed conflicts, tension and strife.

A child is defined in Article 2 of the Charter as 'every human being below the age of 18 years', so the provisions of Article 22 apply to all persons under 18 years of age.

Article 22(1) simply sees the parties to the Charter reaffirming commitments they have already made. Article 22(2), however, is a blanket prohibition of the recruitment of all children into the parties to the Charter's armed forces. The wording on Article 22(2) follows Article 38 of the CRC in confirming that the obligation to refrain from recruiting children is an obligation of result and not simply a sub-set of the obligation that state parties take 'all feasible measures to ensure that no child takes a direct part in hostilities'. Although only the use of children to participate directly in hostilities is prohibited, not their participation *per* se, by prohibiting their recruitment Article 22(2) renders children's participation in hostilities less likely. Although Article 22 is entitled 'Armed Conflicts', the Charter itself is a human rights treaty applying in times of both peace and war, so one should view the obligations set out in Article 22(2) as applying at all times.

Article 22(3) appears to extend considerably states parties' obligations under international humanitarian law. Article 1 of AP II provides that:

> 1. This Protocol ... shall apply to all armed conflicts which are not covered by Article 1 [of AP I] ... and which take place in the territory of a High Contracting Party between its armed forces and dissident armed forces or other organized armed groups which, under responsible command, exercise such control over a part of its territory as to enable them to carry out sustained and concerted military operations and to implement this Protocol.

[55] OAU Doc. AHG/ST.4/Rev.1 (1979).

2. This Protocol shall not apply to situations of internal disturbances and tensions, such as riots, isolated and sporadic acts of violence and other acts of a similar nature, not being armed conflicts …

The final sentence of Article 22(3) seems to extend the ambit of international humanitarian law to precisely the situations from which it is excluded by virtue of Article 1(2) of AP II. Article 22(3) is not wholly clear, however, as to precisely what rules are extended to such situations. At a minimum, one can look to the two APs: children shall be the object of special respect, and be provided with the care and aid they require.[56]

By prohibiting all recruitment of children, the Charter not only went further than the two APs and the CRC but continues to go further than the OP and ILO Convention 182. There is a certain irony in the highest standards having been developed in the continent knowing the greatest use of child soldiers, but one can see the situation as one where the most concerned states are attempting to deal with the problem. Although ratification was slow and the Charter only entered into force on 29 November 1999, some thirty-two of the fifty-three Member States of the OAU are now parties to it. Indeed, the African Charter seems to be the exception to the rule that efforts towards a 'straight-18' ban on the recruitment and use of children to participate in hostilities, despite their gaining considerable support, have been uniformly unsuccessful.

[56] See Article 77(1) AP I and Article 4(3) AP II.

6

The legal regulation of the recruitment and use of children in hostilities: customary international law and non-state actors

Introduction

Over the past two chapters, we have seen that children's participation and use in hostilities is now regulated in a number of treaties: the two APs, the CRC and its OP, ILO Convention 182 on the Worst Forms of Child Labour and the African Charter on the Rights and Welfare of the Child. One result of this is that different states are under different legal obligations according to which treaties they are party. As a consequence, whether there exist any customary rules on the recruitment and use of children in hostilities becomes a very relevant question. General customary international law applies to all states,[1] so any such rules would constitute a minimum standard of behaviour below which states could not fall without being in breach of their international obligations regardless of which treaties they were party. In addition, many of the recruiters of child soldiers are not state governments but non-state groups. Although AP II and the OP attempt to regulate such groups' activities, they do not cover groups operating in states that have not ratified them. Only customary international law can govern their activities.

It might be said that because almost all states are parties to the CRC, there already exists a minimum standard of conduct for states' activities. However, although a rule of customary international law may be identical in content to a treaty obligation,[2] as customary norms exist independently of treaty obligations, states bound by their ratification of a treaty may also be bound under customary law to adhere to the same rule and, consequently, may be unable to terminate their obligations by withdrawal from the treaty. In addition, states may be bound by an obligation in customary law which, by means of reservation, they are not bound

[1] Excluding the possible existence of a 'persistent objector' rule.

[2] See *Paramilitary Activities in and around Nicaragua* (*Nicaragua* v. *USA*) (Merits), ICJ Rep. (1986) 14, p. 96.

by treaty.[3] A number of states have made far-reaching reservations to the CRC.[4] To take one example, the Islamic Republic of Iran has stated that it 'reserves the right not to apply any provisions or articles of the Convention that are incompatible with Islamic laws and the internal legislation in effect'. The reservation is, to say the least, vague. Given Iran's conduct during the Iran–Iraq War, when it enrolled more than 100,000 children under 16 into its armed forces,[5] it is arguable that it is intended to exempt Iran from the obligations contained in Article 38. It is also arguable that such a reservation is incompatible with the object and purpose of the CRC,[6] but the Convention provides no mechanism for determining whether or not a reservation is valid. Similar reservations have been made by Brunei Darussalam, Dijbouti, Oman, Qatar, Saudi Arabia and the Syrian Arab Republic. And to further complicate the matter, various other states have made objections to some or all of these reservations and have declared that they are void and that the CRC remains in force in its entirety between the objecting state and those states to whose reservations objection has been made.[7] If a customary rule existed, it would cut through all this confusion.

Customary international law on the recruitment and use of child soldiers

There is widespread evidence of a state practice restricting the recruitment of children into the armed forces as most states have legislated on the minimum age upon which persons can be recruited into their armed forces.[8] Studies done by the Coalition to Stop the Use of Child Soldiers,[9] augmented by the information in states' declarations on ratifying the OP, give the following data.[10]

[3] For full discussion of these issues, see R.R. Baxter, 'Multilateral Treaties as Evidence of Customary International Law' (1965–66) 41 BYIL 275; and T. Meron, 'The Geneva Conventions as Customary Law' (1987) 81 AJIL 348.

[4] See W.A. Schabas, 'Reservations to the Convention on the Rights of the Child' (1996) HRQ 472; and J. Kuper, 'Reservations, Declarations and Objections to the 1989 Convention on the Rights of the Child', in J.P. Gardner (ed.), *Human Rights as General Norms and a State's Right to Opt Out*, London: BIICL, 1997.

[5] See pp. 106–7.

[6] See Articles 19–21 of the Vienna Convention on the Law of Treaties and Article 51(2) CRC.

[7] See the objections made by Austria, Denmark, Finland, Germany, Ireland, the Netherlands, Norway, Portugal, Slovakia and Sweden.

[8] It is well established that municipal laws can constitute state practice. See M. Akehurst, 'Custom as a Source of International Law' (1974–75) 47 BYIL 1, at pp. 8–10.

[9] Coalition to Stop the Use of Child Soldiers, *Child Soldier Global Report 2001* (2001); and Coalition to Stop the Use of Child Soldiers, *Child Soldier Use 2003: a Briefing for the 4th Security Council Open Debate on Children and Armed Conflict* (2003).

[10] The table is not definitive. The information available is incomplete, out-of-date and often contradictory, and as a result selection was often a matter of judgement. The tendency was, however, to take states at their word, looking at their legislation and statements before international bodies rather than their practice.

Military age	*Voluntary enlistment*	*Names of states*	*Compulsory enlistment*	*Names of states*
15	1	Tanzania		
16	16	Australia, Bangladesh, Belgium, Burundi, Canada, Croatia, El Salvador, India, Iran, North Korea, Libya, Mauritania, Mexico, Rwanda, Singapore, UK	1	Burundi
17	25	Austria, Barbados, Bosnia-Herzegovina, Brazil, Cyprus, Estonia, France, Germany, Greece, Ireland, Israel, Jamaica, Jordan, Luxembourg, Macedonia, New Zealand, Netherlands, Nicaragua, Norway, Serbia-Montenegro, Slovakia, Slovenia, Spain, Switzerland, USA	8	Angola, Croatia, Israel, North Korea, Mauritania, Poland, Slovenia, Sudan
18	77		79	
18+	5		12	
Total	124		100	

The survey shows that state practice tends towards having 18 years as the minimum age of recruitment, at least in law. Most states recruit from age 18 or above. This is particularly the case with regard to compulsory recruitment. Only a few states conscript persons under 18 years of age. However, a substantial minority (some forty-five out of 124 States, over one-third of those surveyed) recruit under-18s. (Although of those forty-five states, only one recruits from age 15.) This second group includes a number of states with significant regional or global military capacities and contains representatives of all regions of the world and of both developing and developed states. Given these differences, it is difficult to see how state practice reflects any consensus on a minimum age of recruitment above 15 or 16. That customary law is moving towards a minimum age for compulsory recruitment of 18, however, seems plausible.[11]

A problem, however, arises. Customary law is the creation of state practice and *opinio juris*, that is, the state practice must have been motivated by a belief

[11] Those few states that still permit the conscription of under-18s might be seen as 'persistent objectors'.

that such conduct was legally obligatory. In cases of issues governed by treaty provisions which have gained widespread acceptance, how can instances of state practice be seen otherwise than signalling states' compliance with their treaty obligations? This problem has become known as the 'Baxter paradox'.[12] Although the survey shows widespread adherence, at least on the legislative level, to the prohibition on the recruitment of children under 15 set out in both APs and the CRC, it is difficult to say that this adherence reflects anything but the states' concerned fulfilment of their treaty obligations.

However, although rules on the recruitment of children and their participation in hostilities were first formulated in the two APs, neither of those two conventions has gained the near universal adherence that the CRC has.[13] During the period 1977–89, before the adoption of the CRC, most states, whether parties to the Protocols or not, did not recruit children under 15 into their armed forces. It might be argued that such state practice was not accompanied by any perception that such conduct was legally obligatory. However, at least two reasons lead to the conclusion that during the later 1970s and early 1980s the provisions contained in Article 77(2) of AP I did become a norm of customary international law.

The first reason is a functioning of the wide participation in the drafting of the two APs.[14] The provisions relating to the participation of children in hostilities were the subject of extensive negotiations and were adopted by consensus both by Committee III and the Conference itself.[15] Although the reasons for the amendments made to the original draft of Article 77(2) are obscure, common sense suggests that they were made with the intention of weakening the contents of the paragraph, and the adoption of the article by consensus further suggests that the text produced by the Working Group was a form of 'lowest common denominator', a version of the article acceptable to all the participants in the negotiations.

Developments following the conclusion of the Conference support this interpretation. Despite the controversial nature of the OPs, it does not appear that any state has stated that its refusal to ratify them is owing to any objection to the provisions regulating the participation of children in hostilities. Quite the reverse, objection seems only to have been taken by states who considered that the provisions were not strong enough. During the Iran–Iraq War, both the ICRC and the UNHCR relied on Article 77(2) in their protests against the belligerents' use

[12] See also *Prosecutor* v. *Delalić et al.*, Case No. IT-96-21-T, Trial Chamber, ICTY, decision of 16 November 1998, paras 302–3.

[13] The number of parties to the two APs has risen significantly in recent years. On 20 November 1989 (the date of the UN General Assembly's adoption of the CRC) 89 states were party to AP I and 81 party to AP II.

[14] 121 states and eleven 'national liberation movements' participated in the Diplomatic Conference. See OR II, p. 25.

[15] See OR XV, p. 218; CDDH/III/SR.59 and OR IV, p. 251: CDDH/SR.43.

of child soldiers,[16] even though the provision itself bound neither state.[17] Indeed, there is evidence that at least one state non-party considered that the restrictions on the participation of children in hostilities in AP I had, or should have customary status. In 1987, Michael J. Matheson, Deputy Legal Adviser at the US State Department, stated that the US Government, although unwilling to ratify AP I, saw a number of its principles as principles that should be observed and, in due course, recognised as customary law, if they had not already achieved that status.[18] In particular, he stated that: 'We [the US Government] support the principle ... that all feasible measures be taken in order that children under fifteen do not take a direct part in hostilities'.[19]

If Article 77(2) of AP I can be seen as the *fons et origo* of a rule of international law which subsequently secured the general consent of states and was thereby transformed into customary law, then Article 38 of the CRC can be seen as incorporating or giving recognition to a rule of customary international law that existed prior to the treaty.[20] Examination of the negotiations of the CRC shows that no state argued that the protection given to children in armed conflict should be less than that imposed by AP I. Although the method by which Article 38 was adopted was the subject of much acrimony, what is of significance is that the underlying dispute was whether the law should be strengthened or not. A number of states involved in the negotiations had not yet ratified AP I,[21] yet its provisions on the recruitment of children were seen as the benchmark from which discussion started.

It has been argued that one should be cautious in identifying treaty provisions which have secured general support during the treaty's negotiations as reflecting rules of customary international law as that support may only reflect the result

[16] See C. Greenwood, 'Customary Law Status of the 1977 Geneva Protocols', in A.J.M. Delissen and G.J. Tanja (eds), *Humanitarian Law of Armed Conflict*, Dordrecht: Martinus Nijhof, 1991.

[17] Iran had only signed, but not ratified AP I, while Iraq had neither signed nor ratified, so the treaty was not in force between them.

[18] In 'The Sixth Annual American Red Cross–Washington College of Law Conference on International Humanitarian Law: a Workshop on Customary International law and the 1977 Protocols additional to the 1949 Geneva Conventions' (1987) 2 *American University Journal of International Law & Policy* 415, p. 421.

[19] *Ibid.*, p. 428. Indeed, as we have seen, the USA, although unwilling to become a party to the APs or the CRC, has ratified both the OP and ILO Convention 182.

[20] According to Judge Baxter, these are the two ways in which a multilateral treaty may be regarded as declaratory of customary international law: Baxter, *op. cit.* note 3, p. 277. See also *North Sea Continental Shelf* cases (*FRG* v. *Denmark*; *FRG* v. *Netherlands*), ICJ Reports 1969, p. 3, at p. 41.

[21] At the time, Australia, the UK and the USSR had signed the Protocol but not yet ratified it. The USA had signed and had announced its intention not to ratify (see the Letter of Transmission from President Ronald Reagan, 'Protocol II Additional to the 1949 Geneva Conventions and Relating to the Protection of Victims of Noninternational Armed Conflict', S. Treaty Doc. No. 2, 100th Cong., 1st Sess., at III (1987), reprinted in (1987) 81 AJIL 910. France and India had neither signed nor ratified.

of a 'package deal' and be the product of a number of mutual and reciprocal agreements struck in relation to the treaty as a whole.[22] However, this argument seems to have less force in relation to treaties of a humanitarian nature, where the beneficiaries are individuals rather than states, than to agreements such as the 1982 UN Convention on the Law of the Sea. Writing of the customary nature of obligations in the GCs, Theodor Meron has stated:

> *Opinio juris* is ... critical for the transformation of treaties into general law. To be sure, it is difficult to demonstrate such *opinio juris*, but this poses a question of proof rather than of principle. The possibility that a party to the Geneva Conventions may be motivated by the belief that a particular course of conduct is required not only contractually but also under the underlying principles of humanity is not farfetched.[23]

Such a conclusion would seem to be particularly apposite to the provisions of regulating the participation of children in hostilities. In relation to the more detailed provisions of the GCs, Meron has cautioned that it is difficult to create a significant layer of customary law alongside them, especially when they are applied only in rare and exceptional circumstances. This caveat would not seem applicable to Article 77(2) of AP I, which although specific, is not excessively detailed, and which is frequently applied. It can be concluded that there does exist a rule of customary international law prohibiting the recruitment of children under 15 into states' armed forces and obliging states to use all feasible efforts to prevent children under 15 from taking a direct part in hostilities.

The opinions of the political organs of the UN

The question needs to be asked, however, whether events since the adoption of the CRC have changed matters. Since 1989, not only has there been a number of new treaties covering children's recruitment and use in hostilities, but the issue has been dealt with extensively by the political organs of the UN. Even if the resolutions of international organisations cannot be seen as having a law-making effect, we might consider them useful in ascertaining what the states participating in their adoption considered the law to be, that is, as expressions of *opinio juris*.

The most that can be said about the series of General Assembly resolutions on the protection of children affected by armed conflict is that the General Assembly considers that the obligation to afford children affected by armed conflict special protection and treatment is a rule of customary international law. In resolution 49/209, the General Assembly called upon states: 'fully to respect the dispositions contained in the Geneva Conventions of 12 August 1949 and the Additional Protocols thereto, of 1977, as well as those in the Convention on the Rights of the

[22] See H. Caminos and M.R. Molitor, 'Progressive Development of International Law and the Package Deal' (1985) 79 AJIL 871.
[23] *Op. cit.* Meron, note 3, p. 367.

Child, which accord children affected by armed conflicts special protection and treatment'.[24] Similar provisions appeared in resolutions 50/153[25] and 51/77.[26] However, in the same or contemporaneous resolutions,[27] the General Assembly called upon states to ratify the CRC and emphasised the importance of states parties to that treaty fully implementing its provisions, indicating that the CRC as a whole was not considered to reflect customary international law. Moreover, in resolution 52/107, the terminology changed and the General Assembly asked:

> All States and other parties to armed conflict to respect international humanitarian law, and, in this regard, calls upon States parties to respect fully the provisions of the Geneva Conventions of 12 August 1949 and the additional protocols thereto of 1977 ... and to respect the provisions of the Convention on the Rights of the Child which accord children affected by armed conflict special protection and treatment.[28]

Similar provisions appear in subsequent resolutions.[29] The General Assembly has confined itself to calling upon all parties to comply with international humanitarian law and states to comply with their treaty obligations; to urge on law-making initiatives; and to applaud their success. The General Assembly has suggested is that: 'the provisions of the Convention [on the Rights of the Child] and other relevant human rights instruments must constitute the standard in the promotion and protection of the rights of the child',[30] but this is a long way from arguing that they reflect customary international law.

Security Council presidential statements and resolutions have been similarly restrained. Statements by the President of the Security Council on its behalf have not distinguished between parties' obligations under international law and their obligations under treaties such as the GCs, the APs and the CRC,[31] but it may be going too far to say that this indicates that the Council considered that the provisions of those treaties reflected customary international law. Indeed, the Council only condemned children's 'recruitment and use in hostilities in violation of international law',[32] which seems a clear indication that it did not consider all recruitment and use of children to participate in hostilities to be unlawful. And

[24] Para. 2, GA Res. 49/209 (23 December 1994).

[25] Para. 7, GA Res. 50/153 (21 December 1995).

[26] Para. 12, GA Res. 51/77 (12 December 1996).

[27] See paras 4 and 5, GA Res. 49/211 (23 December 1994); paras 2 and 3, GA Res. 50/153; and paras 2 and 3, GA Res. 51/77.

[28] Section IV, para. 4, GA Res. 52/107 (13 February 1998).

[29] See section IV, para. 9, GA Res. 53/128 (23 February 1999); section II, para. 6. GA Res. 54/149 (25 February 2000); section V, para. 7, GA Res. 55/79 (22 February 2001); and section V, para. 8, GA Res. 57/190 (19 February 2003).

[30] Preambular para. 2, GA Res. 54/149.

[31] See Statement by the President of the Security Council of 29 June 1998, UN Doc. S/PRST/1998/18; and Statement by the President of the Security Council of 12 February 1999, UN Doc. S/PRST/1999/6.

[32] Statement by the President of the Security Council of 29 June 1998.

the President on behalf of the Council welcomed the adoption of the OP, urged Member States to ratify it and states parties to fully implement its provisions,[33] indicating that only the latter were bound to do so.

The Security Council resolutions on children affected by armed conflict are more precise. Resolution 1261 only condemned the 'recruitment and use of children in armed conflict in violation of international law',[34] and called upon: 'all parties concerned to comply strictly with their obligations under international law, in particular the Geneva Conventions of 12 August 1949 and the obligations applicable to them under the Additional Protocols thereto of 1977 and the United Nations Convention on the Rights of the Child of 1989 …'.[35] This formulation seems to imply that the provisions of the two APs and the CRC, only bind states parties to them, in contrast to the GCs, which apply generally. Similar language appears in resolution 1379.[36] Another resolution, however, merely calls on:

> all parties to armed conflict to respect fully international law applicable to the rights and protection of women and girls, especially as civilians, in particular the obligations applicable to them under the Geneva Conventions of 12 August 1949 and the Additional Protocols thereto of 1977, the Refugee Convention of 1951 and the Protocol thereto of 1967, the Convention on the Elimination of All Forms of Discrimination against Women of 1979 and the Optional Protocol thereto of 1999 and the United Nations Convention on the Rights of the Child of 1989 and the two Optional Protocols thereto of 25 May 2000 …[37]

Perhaps all that can be said, given these differences in terminology, is that neither the General Assembly nor the Security Council has given any clear guidance as to what rules of customary international law govern children's recruitment and use in hostilities. There is one exception to this conclusion. In a letter from the President of the Security Council to the General-Secretary dated 22 December 2000 on the draft Statute of the Special Court for Sierra Leone,[38] it was stated that conscripting or enlisting children under the age of 15 years into armed forces or groups or using them to participate actively in hostilities was a war crime under customary international law and had been since at least 1996.[39] A war crime is simply a violation of the laws and customs of war incurring individual criminal responsibility. Accordingly, the letter would seem to imply that the Council considered the recruitment and use of children under 15 to participate actively in

[33] Statement of the President of the Security Council of 7 May 2002, UN Doc. S/PRST/2002/12.

[34] Para. 2, SC Res. 1261 (30 August 1999). See also para. 3, SC Res. 1460 (30 January 2003).

[35] Para. 3, SC Res. 1261.

[36] Para. 8(a), SC Res. 1379 (20 November 2001).

[37] Para. 9, SC Res. 1325 (31 October 2000).

[38] Letter dated 22 December 2000 from the President of the Security Council addressed to the Secretary-General, UN Doc. S/2000/1234.

[39] For more on this issue, see the discussion in Chapter 7, pp. 128–32.

hostilities to be a violation of international humanitarian law in 1996, or, to put it another way, that customary international law prohibits the recruitment or use of children under 15 to participate actively in hostilities. In addition, when compiling a list, at the request of the Security Council, of 'parties to international armed conflicts that are in violation of the international obligations applicable to them',[40] the Secretary-General stated that his benchmark for states was the obligations contained in the CRC.[41] Included on the Secretary-General's list was the Somali Transitional National Government. Somalia is one of only two states which are not parties to the CRC. Nor is it a party to the two APs, the OP, ILO Convention 182 or the African Charter on the Rights and Welfare of the Child, so any obligations regarding the recruitment and use of child soldiers incumbent on its government can only be customary in nature. The Security Council, on receiving the Secretary-General's report, did not dissent from this conclusion.[42]

This would seem to comply with our earlier conclusions save in one respect. According to the 2000 letter from the Security Council to the Secretary-General, customary international law prohibits the active participation of children under 15 in hostilities, rather than their direct participation. What 'active' might mean in this context is contentious. We will return to this issue later in this chapter (see pp. 97–9).

The Special Court for Sierra Leone

More recently, in *Prosecutor* v. *Samuel Hinga Norman*, the Appeals Chamber of the Special Court for Sierra Leone, while addressing the issue of at what time child recruitment became a war crime, also considered the customary status of the rule prohibiting the recruitment and use of children under 15 to participate actively in hostilities.[43] The majority considered that the prohibition on child recruitment had crystallised as customary law.[44] However, they came to this conclusion on the basis of the wide ratification of the GCs, AP II and the CRC.[45] It has already been argued that such arguments are defective. Adherence to and compliance with the provisions of a treaty cannot of itself show anything more than the parties' commitment to the treaty regime. In addition, the Appeals Chamber also referred to the lack of reservations to Article 38 of the CRC.[46] Again, this shows too little, as

[40] Para. 16, SC Res. 1379 (20 November 2001).

[41] Para. 30, Report of the Secretary-General on Children and Armed Conflict, UN Doc. S/2002/1299 (26 November 2002) (the Secretary-General's third report).

[42] See SC Res. 1460.

[43] *Prosecutor* v. *Samuel Hinga Norman*, Case No. SCSL-2004-14-AR729E, Special Court for Sierra Leone (Appeals Chamber), decision on preliminary motion based on lack of jurisdiction (child recruitment), 31 May 2004.

[44] *Ibid.*, para. 14.

[45] *Ibid.*, paras 18–19.

[46] *Ibid.*, para. 20.

a number of reservations made, although general, might be thought to be sufficiently broadly worded to produce such an effect. Nor did the Appeals Chamber indicate a date by which the customary rule had crystallised, simply stating that it had happened prior to November 1996, the beginning of the Special Court's temporal jurisdiction.[47] Justice Robertson, in his dissenting opinion, agreed with this conclusion.[48] However, although the Special Court's decision leaves the date of the rule's crystallisation unclear, it is unarguable that a rule of customary international law prohibiting the recruitment or use to participate in hostilities of children under 15 years of age presently exists. Certainly, no party to the proceedings argued against its existence.[49]

Customary international law and non-state actors

AP II and the OP purport to bind armed groups, whether in opposition or allied to the government of a state party to the treaty. However, there are gaps in this coverage. Each treaty only binds armed groups within the jurisdiction of States Parties and neither treaty has been universally ratified. In addition, AP II only applies in non-international armed conflicts, and the provisions in AP I and the CRC only bind state parties to those treaties. Any applicable customary rules would, however, apply across the board: to all armed groups and in all armed conflicts.

Both the General Assembly and the Security Council have called on 'all parties concerned' or 'all parties to armed conflict' to comply with their obligations under international humanitarian law. This can be contrasted with calls upon states parties to comply with their obligations under various humanitarian and human rights treaties. Given the context of the resolutions, with most recruitment and use of children taking place in non-international armed conflicts,[50] the terms can only be interpreted to refer to all parties to armed conflicts, states and non-state actors alike. This interpretation is supported by more specific language elsewhere. In Security Council resolution 1379 the Council called on 'all parties to armed conflicts' to: 'Abide by the concrete commitments they have made to the Special Representative of the Secretary-General for Children and Armed Conflict, as well as relevant United Nations bodies, to ensure the protection of children in situations of armed conflict'.[51] The Special Representative has obtained such commitments from both governments and armed opposition groups. Similarly, in resolution 1460 the Security Council noted with concern: 'the list annexed to the Secretary-General's

[47] *Ibid.*, para. 17.

[48] *Op. cit.* note 43, Dissenting Opinion of Justice Robertson, para. 33.

[49] *Op. cit.* note 43, at para. 10.

[50] See also recommendation 4, Children and Armed Conflict: Report of the Secretary-General, UN Doc. A/55/163-S/2000/712 (19 July 2000); and para. 9, Children and Armed Conflict: Report of the Secretary-General, UN Doc. A/56/342-S/2001/852 (7 September 2001).

[51] Para. 8(d), SC Res. 1379 (20 November 2001).

[third] report [on children and armed conflict], and calls on the parties identified in this list to provide information on steps they have taken to halt their recruitment or use of children in armed conflict in violation of the international obligations applicable to them …'.[52] Most of the parties to armed conflict listed in the Secretary-General's report as recruiting or using child soldiers in violation of the international obligations applicable to them were non-state actors.

What the Security Council has not made clear is what it considers these obligations to be. It, however, did endorse the Secretary-General's reports on children and armed conflicts, which have done so. Asked by the Security Council in resolution 1379 to compile a list of parties to conflict that recruited or used children in violation of the international obligations applicable to them,[53] the Secretary-General had to come to a view as to what those obligations were. Explaining how the list was compiled, the Secretary-General wrote that:

> The conduct of non-State armed groups was assessed in accordance with the widely accepted minimum international standard that children under age 15 shall not be conscripted or enlisted into armed forces or groups or used by them to participate actively in hostilities in either international or internal armed conflicts. This standard echoes the Convention on the Rights of the Child, Additional Protocol II to the Geneva Conventions, the Rome Statute of the International Criminal Court, and the Statute of the Special Court of Sierra Leone. In States that have ratified the Optional Protocol to the Convention on the Rights of the Child on the involvement of children in armed conflict, non-State armed groups are held to that higher standard, prohibiting all recruitment and use of children under 18. Commitments made in peace agreements or to my Special Representative were also taken into account.[54]

The Security Council must have agreed with these conclusions because it agreed that the parties on the Secretary-General's list were acting in violation of their international obligations.

It seems clear that the Security Council considers that armed groups distinct from the armed forces of a state have obligations under international law. It also appears that these obligations must, at least in some cases, be customary in nature. In addition to the Transitional National Government, the Secretary-General's list included a number of Somali opposition armed groups. Given that Somalia is not a party to any of the relevant treaties, any obligations that Somali armed opposition groups have not to recruit or use child soldiers can only be customary in nature.

The Appeals Chamber of the Special Court for Sierra Leone in *Prosecutor* v. *Samuel Hinga Norman* considered it 'well-settled that *all* parties to an armed conflict, whether states or non-state actors, are bound by international humanitarian law … Therefore all parties to the conflict in Sierra Leone were bound by the prohibition of child recruitment that exists in international humanitarian law'.[55]

[52] Para. 5, SC Res. 1460 (30 January 2003).

[53] Para. 16, SC Res. 1379 (20 November 2001).

[54] Para. 31, Secretary-General third report, *op. cit.* note 41.

[55] *Op. cit.* note 43, para. 22. Emphasis in original.

Justice Robertson, in his dissenting opinion, was rather clearer as to what customary international law requires, stating that: 'what had emerged, in customary international law, by the end of 1996 was an humanitarian rule that obliged states and armed factions within states, to avoid enlisting under fifteens or involving them in hostilities, whether arising from international or internal armed conflict'.[56]

Direct participation or active participation in hostilities?

Not only did the Secretary-General say that customary international law prohibits the use of children under 15 to participate actively in hostilities but he stated that this was the standard set out in the CRC and AP II.[57] The CRC prohibits children under 15 from direct participation in hostilities. AP II prohibits children under 15 from participation in hostilities. Neither treaty prohibits active participation in hostilities; indeed the term was not used in either of the two APs, nor in the CRC and its OP.

The term has appeared elsewhere. Common Article 3 of the GCs protects: 'Persons taking no active part in hostilities'. General Assembly resolution 2675 of 1970 on the basic principles for the protection of civilian populations in armed conflicts affirms the principle that: 'In the conduct of military operations during armed conflicts, a distinction must be made at all times between persons actively taking part in hostilities and civilian populations'.[58] In the *Tadić* judgment, the Appeals Chamber of the International Criminal Tribunal for the former Yugoslavia stated that resolution 2675 was declaratory of customary international law regarding the protection of civilian populations in armed conflicts of any kind.[59] According to the Appeals Chamber, the customary law relating to internal armed conflicts protects those who do not (or no longer) take an active part in hostilities.[60] Both AP I and AP II, by contrast, distinguish between the civilian population and persons taking a direct part in hostilities. Civilians enjoy general protection against the dangers arising from military operations and are not lawful objects of attack unless and during such time as they take a direct part in hostilities.[61] It might be thought that resolution 2675 pre-dates the two APs and thus has to be read in the light of their provisions; the APs having been meant to develop progressively international humanitarian law. On this reading, active participation and direct participation are synonymous. Indeed, this has been the view of the International Criminal Tribunal for Rwanda. The Trial Chamber in *Akayesu* found that the term

[56] *Op. cit.* note 48, para. 33.

[57] Para. 31, Secretary-General's third report, *op. cit.* note 41.

[58] Para. 2, GA Res. 2675 (XXV) (9 December 1970).

[59] *Prosecutor* v. *Tadić (Jurisdiction)*, decision of 2 October 1995, 105 ILR 453, at p. 513.

[60] *Ibid.*, p. 520.

[61] See Article 50 AP I and Article 13 AP II.

'direct part in hostilities' had evolved from the phrase 'active part in hostilities'.[62] In *Rutaganda*, the Trial Chamber followed the ICRC Commentary,[63] stating that; 'To take a "direct" part in hostilities means acts of war which by their nature or purpose are likely to cause actual harm to the personnel and equipment of the enemy armed forces'.[64]

However, the term also appears in the Rome Staute of the ICC. War crimes within the jurisdiction of the Court include '[c]onscripting or enlisting children under the age of fifteen years into the national armed forces or using them to participate actively in hostilities' during international armed conflicts,[65] and '[c]onscripting or enlisting children under the age of fifteen into armed forces or groups or using them to participate actively in hostilities' during non-international armed conflicts.[66] The question of what active participation in hostilities entailed was raised in the Preparatory Commission for the ICC, convened following the adoption of the Rome Statute to draft the Elements of Crimes defining more precisely the crimes listed in the Statute. Some delegations wanted the term clarified in the Elements of Crimes. Others argued that it was already sufficiently clear; as at the Preparatory Committee that preceded the Diplomatic Conference at Rome a footnote had been inserted explaining what was meant by the term.[67] The footnote provided that:

> The words 'using' and 'participate' have been adopted in order to cover both direct participation in combat and also active participation in military activities linked to combat such as scouting, spying, sabotage and the use of children as decoys, couriers or at military checkpoints. It would not cover activities clearly unrelated to the hostilities such as food deliveries to an airbase or the use of domestic staff in an officer's married accommodation. However, the use of children in a direct support function such as acting as bearers to take supplies to the front line, or activities at the front line itself, would be included in the terminology.[68]

Active participation in hostilities, on this reading, is far broader than direct participation in hostilities. Indeed, it seems identical to participation in hostilities *per se*.[69]

[62] *Prosecutor* v. *Akayesu*, Case No. ICTR-96-4-T, judgment, Trial Chamber, ICTR, 2 September 1998, para. 629.

[63] See pp. 63–4.

[64] *Prosecutor* v. *Rutaganda*, Case No. ICTR-1993-3, judgment, Trial Chamber, ICTR, 6 December 1999, para. 100.

[65] Article 8(b)(xxvi), Rome Statute of the ICC, UN Doc. A/CONF.183/9* (1998).

[66] Article 8(c)(vii), Rome Statute, *ibid.*

[67] K. Dörmann, *Elements of War Crimes under the Rome Statute of the International Criminal Court: Sources and Commentary*, Cambridge: Cambridge University Press, 2002, p. 376.

[68] Draft Statute for the International Criminal Court, Report of the Preparatory Committee on the Establishment of an International Criminal Court, Addendum, Part One, UN Doc. A/CONF.183/2/Add.1, 14 April 1998, at p. 21.

[69] See Y. Sandoz, C. Swinarski and B. Zimmermann (eds), *Commentary on the Additional Protocols of 8 June 1977 to the Geneva Conventions of 12 August 1949*, Geneva: ICRC, 1987, p. 1,380 (commenting on Article 4(3)(c) of AP II).

The Secretary-General's statement that the prohibition of the use of children under 15 to participate actively in hostilities imposed on non-state actors reflects both AP II and the CRC only adds to the confusion given that the obligations imposed by those two treaties differ. As a result, it is difficult to know what customary international law requires. It may be that it is moving towards a prohibition of all use of children under 15 years of age to participate in hostilities; the provisions of the Rome Statute marking the beginning of a shift in the customary law standards to go beyond what is required of states in AP I and the CRC. Even if this is the case, however, the distinction between direct and other participation in hostilities remains a relevant distinction as a matter of treaty law as regards child soldiers aged between 16 and 18 years of age.

Conclusions

Over the past three decades, customary international law has developed to fill the gaps in the protection afforded children by the piecemeal coverage of the various treaties dealing with their recruitment and use to participate in hostilities. Customary law mandates that states refrain from recruiting children below 15 years of age into their armed forces and take all feasible efforts to ensure that they do not take a direct (or possibly any) part in hostilities. The standard imposed on non-state groups is wider: not only are they prohibited from recruiting children under 15 years of age, but their use of them to participate in hostilities at all is also prohibited. There may also be emerging a customary rule, binding both states and non-state actors, prohibiting the compulsory or forced recruitment of children below 18 years of age, but as yet there is little to indicate the existence of a customary, rather than several treaty-based, rules.

7

The legal treatment of child soldiers

Introduction

The last three chapters have shown how international law has sought to prevent or, at least, restrict the participation of children in armed conflict. However, although, as we have seen, the rules restricting the recruitment and use of child soldiers are plentiful and comprehensive, they are by no means always observed. Consequently, the question arises of how international law treats children who do participate in hostilities. The issue can be divided into three aspects. First, what is the status of child soldiers *qua* combatants? Second, how should child soldiers be treated when *hors de combat* and in the hands of an enemy? Finally, at the end of a conflict what obligations exist with regard to the disarmament, demobilisation and reintegration of child soldiers?

Child soldiers as combatants

The prohibitions on the recruitment of children and their participation in hostilities are primarily directed at states and non-state armed groups. More recently, they have been directed at individuals, but at the recruiters of child soldiers, not at the child soldiers themselves.[1] All this has one very direct consequence, not spelled out in AP I but implicit in its provisions; namely, that child combatants in an international conflict, providing they fulfil the relevant criteria,[2] benefit from the same protections as any other lawful combatants. As Article 43 of AP I states, members of the armed forces of a party to a conflict are combatants; they are entitled to participate directly in hostilities.

[1] See M.T. Dutli, 'Captured Child Combatants' (1990) ICRC No. 278, p. 421.

[2] See Article 43 of AP I, Common Article 13/13/4 of GC I/II/III, and Article 4(B) of GC III.

Children under 15 who participate in hostilities are not necessarily 'unprivileged belligerents'.[3] Their status is determined not by their age but by the same criteria as determine whether any other persons are entitled to participate directly in hostilities or not. Children under 15 are not banned from participating directly in hostilities, as are civilians[4] or mercenaries,[5] although, if they fulfil the relevant criteria, children may be civilians or mercenaries or members of some other group of unprivileged belligerents, such as spies, whose activities, although not amounting to direct participation in hostilities, render them liable to punishment under the municipal law of an adverse party. However, a child cannot be penalised simply for having borne arms in an international armed conflict.

It follows from this that when participating in hostilities children are no more privileged that any other combatant. There are no additional rules restricting what the forces of an adverse power may do to them. They may be shot, shelled, bombed or bayoneted just as may any other combatant. The situation is clearly set out in the New Zealand Defence Force Law of Armed Conflict Manual. The Manual defines a child soldier as 'any person taking a direct part in hostilities as part of the armed forces of a state, or as part of an armed group, who is under 18 years of age'.[6] It then provides that:

> Child soldiers who are part of the armed forces of a state or who would, if they were adults, otherwise qualify as combatants:
>
> (a) are entitled to carry out attacks on the adverse party;
> (b) may lawfully be the subject of attack for such time as they take a direct part in hostilities;
> (c) bear no criminal responsibility for killing or injuring members of the opposing force or for causing damage or destruction to property in accordance with the law of armed conflict.[7]

Paragraph (b) is interestingly phrased. It can be contrasted with the corresponding provision on child soldiers not entitled to combatant status, which states that such persons 'may lawfully be the subject of attack *only* during such time as they are taking a direct part in the hostilities'.[8] In general, lawful combatants may be attacked at any time, regardless of whether they are participating in hostilities or not,

[3] For a description of the distinction, see R.R. Baxter, 'So-called "Unprivileged Belligerency": Spies, Guerrillas and Saboteurs' (1951) 28 BYIL 323; but see also G.I.A.D. Draper, 'Status of Combatants and the Question of Guerrilla Warfare' (1971) 45 BYIL 173.

[4] Who lose their protected civilian status if they directly participate in hostilities and who may, subject to the limitations imposed on an occupying power in GC IV, be punished for doing so under that party's municipal law.

[5] Who, under Article 45 of AP I, are not granted POW status on falling into the power of an adverse party and may similarly be punished for their activities. The customary status of this provision has, however, been doubted.

[6] See s. 5.2.11.1, New Zealand Defence Force, Law of Armed Conflict Manual.

[7] S. 5.2.11.2, *ibid.*

[8] Emphasis added.

providing the methods and means of warfare used to do so are legal. There is no reason for thinking this is not the legal position as regards child soldiers. The New Zealand policy seems to have been dictated by humanitarian considerations, as set out in the commentary to the rule, which states that:

> By taking a direct part in hostilities a child soldier loses civilian status and may therefore be the object of lawful attack in the same way as an adult. However NZ recognises that the circumstances under which children are recruited and employed as soldiers renders them victims of armed conflict regardless of their own actions. Where child soldiers are identified as such, and pose no direct threat to NZ forces, combat action against them is to be avoided.

It may frequently be the case, however, that child soldiers cannot be identified as such. They may not be visible to their attackers, as when part of the crew of a military vehicle or vessel, or when situated within a building used for military purposes. They may not be obviously children, in that they may look older than their age, or simply cannot be identified as such because they are being viewed from a distance, in adverse weather conditions or at night. Even when it is obvious that children do form an element of a military formation, they may be interspersed with adult combatants, so that the two groups cannot be separately targeted. Although it has occasionally been argued that child soldiers should not be lawful objects of attack, it is submitted that this would be undesirable and, indeed, pointless. The rule itself would be unlikely to be obeyed. Not only is it, at least some of the time, impossible to identify child soldiers or distinguish them from their adult comrades; it is difficult to stop troops from shooting back when shot at. Indeed, any combatant who did so respond would be able to excuse his conduct by arguing that he had acted in self-defence.[9] Even were compliance possible, the main beneficiaries would be those who recruit child soldiers. Their troops would be able to operate with impunity. Indeed, the existence of such a rule might only serve to fuel the recruitment of children, as the advantages of doing so became apparent.

Child soldiers in the power of an adverse party in international armed conflicts

The provisions governing the treatment of children in the power of an adverse party in an international armed conflict are extensive. Article 77(3) of AP I deals with the treatment of children under 15 who, despite the restrictions imposed in Article 77(2), do take a direct part in hostilities and, whether due to illness, injury or because they have surrendered to that party's forces, fall into the power of an adverse party. Such children fall into three categories: prisoners of war (POWs),

[9] See Article 31(1)(c) of the Rome Statute of the ICC.

who benefit from the provisions of GC III; child combatants who do not have the right to POW status but who are protected persons within the meaning of GV IV; and others, children who have taken a direct part in hostilities and who are neither protected persons nor entitled to POW status but are still entitled to the protection of the fundamental guarantees set out in Article 75 of AP I.

Child soldiers in GC III

GC IIII itself says nothing about child POWs. The Convention provides for the repatriation of POWs prior to the termination of hostilities and requires parties to a conflict to send back to their own country seriously wounded and seriously sick POWs,[10] but there is no requirement that child soldiers be repatriated. Parties to a conflict do, however, remain free to conclude agreements for the repatriation of POWs prior to the cessation of hostilities or for their internment in the territory of some willing neutral country.[11] Given that Article 37 of the CRC requires that the detention of a child shall only be used as a last resort and for the shortest appropriate period of time,[12] it might be argued that there is at least an obligation on parties to a conflict to make good-faith efforts to conclude such agreements in respect of child POWs.[13]

Child soldiers in AP I

Regardless of into what category of detainee a child soldier falls, AP I provides that he is entitled to a number of benefits by virtue of his age. Article 77(3) of AP I states that if children under the age of 15 take a direct part in hostilities and fall into the power of an adverse party they shall continue to benefit from the 'special protection' accorded them by Article 77. What this means is spelled out in Article 77(1), which provides that: 'Children shall be the object of special respect and shall be protected against any form of indecent assault. The Parties to the conflict shall provide them with the care and aid they require, whether because of their age or for any other reason'. The special protection to be accorded to children thus consists of a number of elements, which can be summarised as follows.

[10] Article 109(1) GC III.

[11] Article 109(2) GC III.

[12] It might be argued that Article 37(b) of the CRC only applies in penal matters. However, there is no such qualification expressed in the provision, which is drafted in wide terms, providing that: 'No child shall be deprived of his or her liberty unlawfully or arbitrarily. The arrest, detention or imprisonment of a child shall be in conformity with the law and shall be used only as a measure of last resort and for the shortest appropriate period of time'.

[13] Article 117 GC III provides that no repatriated person may be employed on active military service.

1 'Special respect'. This is a very general obligation. It appears to mean simply that children should be treated with particular consideration in all circumstances.[14]
2 Protection against indecent assault. The party holding the children is obliged to protect them from indecent assault not only from its own forces, but also from the children's own comrades, both adults and children, and anyone else who might wish to cause them such harm. The obligation appears to be an active one. It is not enough simply to prohibit such acts; measures have to be taken to ensure they do not happen. Systems to deter such behaviour should be established (probably including, as a minimum, some segregation of children and adults, on the one hand, and boys and girls, on the other) and to investigate, prosecute and punish such offences if and when they occur.
3 Provision of the aid and care children require for whatever reason. Again, this is a somewhat general provision. It would appear to require that children be provided with medical attention directed towards their particular needs, with appropriate foodstuffs, and with schooling. It has also been argued that the reference to 'any other reason' requires the provision, as appropriate, of psychological help, trauma counselling and other rehabilitation services.[15]

Article 77(3), in distinction from Article 77(1), does not refer to children but to children under the age of 15. One could read this distinction to mean that only children under 15 years of age can benefit from the special protection accorded by Article 77(1) when in the hands of an adverse party. However, Article 77(1) refers to obligations owed by all parties to a conflict; and Article 77(4), which in dealing with children arrested, detained or interned for reasons related to an armed conflict also regulates adverse parties' conduct, refers to all children, not just those under 15 years of age. The better way to read Article 77(3) is to see it as attempting to ensure that children who have participated in hostilities despite the prohibitions in Article 77(2) are not penalised for having done so. The provision is *ex abundanta cautionae*. It is not meant to imply that other, older children do not partake in the same special protection. These benefits accrue to all children, that is, all persons below 18 years of age.[16]

Article 77(4) provides that children arrested or detained for reasons relating to an armed conflict shall be held in quarters separate from those of adults. All child soldiers, not only those under the age of 15, must be accommodated separately

[14] See J. Pictet (ed.), *Commentary on the Geneva Conventions of 12 August 1949*, Geneva: ICRC, 1955, vol. IV, p. 135, for a discussion of the issue.

[15] See I. Cohn and G.S. Goodwin-Gill, *Child Soldiers: The Role of Children in Armed Conflicts*, Oxford: Clarendon Press, 1994, p. 131. The authors cite Article 39 CRC in support of this interpretation.

[16] Article 37(c) of the CRC also requires that: 'every child deprived of liberty shall be separated from adults unless it is considered in the child's best interest not to do so and shall have the right to maintain contact with his or her family through correspondence and visits, save in exceptional circumstances'.

from their adult comrades, although this is not to say that they should all be accommodated together, which might breach the detaining power's obligation to protect them from indecent assault. The only exception to this rule is where families are accommodated as family units. Article 75(5) requires that when families are detained or interned, they shall, whenever possible, be held in the same place and accommodated as family units. Even when not forcibly recruited, child soldiers are frequently posted to locations far away from their families, so one might not consider the provision to be of particular relevance to them. If such circumstances arise, however, the provision applies.

Finally, it should be recalled that when a child falls into the power of an adverse party Article 77(2) continues to apply, preventing that party from recruiting that child into its own armed forces.

Sanctioning child soldiers

Article 77(5) states that the death penalty for offences related to an international armed conflict shall not be executed on persons who had not attained the age of 18 years when they committed the offence. This provision marked an improvement upon Article 68(4) of GC IV, which merely provided that; 'the death penalty may not be pronounced against a protected person who was under eighteen years of age at the time of the offence'. In general, child soldiers are not protected persons under GC IV. However, it should be noted that Article 77(5) prohibits not the imposition of the death penalty but only its execution. It does not prohibit the sentencing of an individual to death for crimes related to an international armed conflict committed before that person's eighteenth birthday; it merely prohibits the carrying out of that sentence. This was deliberate. The ICRC's original draft prohibited the pronouncement of the death penalty. However, in Committee III one delegate argued that his country's legislation did not permit a prohibition of the death penalty being pronounced, although a prohibition of its execution could be accepted. This objection was accepted by the Committee and, ultimately, by the plenary Conference. As drafted, however, the provision is open to abuse as no time scale for the commutation of the death penalty, if pronounced, is specified. It would seem that the sentencing of individuals to death and their indefinite detention on death row is not a breach of Article 77(5) providing the person is not actually executed. In most cases, however, such behaviour is otherwise prohibited. Article 37(a) of the CRC prohibits capital punishment being imposed for offences committed by children and Article 9 of the ICCPR provides that the death penalty shall not be imposed for crimes committed by persons below 18 years of age.[17] In addition, in many cases such treatment would be inhuman and degrading and, as such, contrary to the detaining power's international obligations under any of a number of human rights treaties.

[17] See also W.A. Schabas, *The Abolition of the Death Penalty in International Law*, Cambridge: Cambridge University Press, 3rd edn, 2002, pp. 136–8.

With regard to what other sanctions can be imposed on child offenders, the 1949 GCs and AP I have little to say. Article 119 of GC IV provides that a detaining power shall take account of a civilian internee's age when imposing any disciplinary penalty on him or her, but this only applies to protected persons under the Convention (and then only with regard to disciplinary punishments imposed on internees). It does not protect children who are POWs or who are not protected persons, the categories into which child soldiers are most likely to fall. The CRC does, however, provide some guidance. Article 37 of the CRC provides that the imprisonment of a child shall only be used as a last resort and for the shortest appropriate period of time, and Article 40, dealing with children's treatment in penal matters, states that children are to be treated in a manner which takes account of the desirability of promoting their reintegration into society; rehabilitation, not retribution, should be the purpose of any sanction imposed on a child offender. However, AP I says nothing about a minimum age of criminal responsibility for offences related to international armed conflicts, although a suggestion was made that it should do so.[18] Nor does the CRC fix a minimum age of criminal responsibility, although it does offer some guidelines.[19] This issue will be discussed at greater length in Chapter 8.

Child soldier POWs and detainees in recent international armed conflicts

In practice, few instances of child soldiers being captured by an adverse party have arisen in recent international armed conflicts. Most contemporary armed conflicts in which child soldiers have been used in any numbers have been internal rather than international in nature. Large numbers of child soldiers, however, did become prisoners of war during the 1980–88 Iran–Iraq War.

Iran made extensive use of child soldiers during the conflict.[20] In February 1984, Hashemi Rafsanjani, Speaker of the Iranian Parliament, called on all Iranian males between 12 and 72 to volunteer for the 'holy war' against Iraq. Fired by religious enthusiasm, and at the urging of their teachers, more than 100,000 children below 16 years of age volunteered. Untrained and barely armed children were put into the front line and called upon to advance across minefields and charge Iraqi machine-gun positions. Many died. Others, some as young as 9 years old, were taken prisoner by the Iraqis; their presence in Iraqi POW camps being verified by both the ICRC and a UN Security Council-mandated fact-finding mission.[21] Child POWs were singled out for indoctrination on the ground that their young minds were more impressionable than those of their adult comrades. However, although concern was expressed by the ICRC both at Iran's recruitment of children into

[18] See Chapter 8, pp. 143–4.
[19] See Chapter 8, pp. 144–6.
[20] See Alain Louyot, *Gosses de Guerre*, Paris: ed. Robert Laffont, 1989.
[21] See ICRC, *1983 Activity Report*; and UN Doc. S/16962 (22 February 1985).

its armed forces[22] and both parties' breach of their international obligations with regard to the treatment of POWs,[23] nothing was said specifically about the situation of child POWs. This may have been because AP I was not applicable to the conflict.[24] It may also have been because the particular situation of child soldiers was only beginning to be recognised or that the issue was overlooked given the prevalence of what were seen as more serious violations of international humanitarian law.

More recently, the USA has held child combatants captured in Afghanistan at its military base at Guantánamo Bay in Cuba. The US Administration has denied that any of the Guantánamo detainees benefit from the protections provided by the 1949 GCs, but has stated that its treatment of them is in conformity with the standards set out in GC III.[25] A number of the detainees were reported to be children aged between 13 and 15 years old.[26] It appears that juvenile detainees are accommodated separately from the adults in 'Camp Iguana'; that their guards are selected for their experience in working with young people; and that they receive some schooling, including English lessons, and regular group-therapy sessions.[27] Human Rights Watch has alleged that the US authorities are in breach of their obligations under Article 7 of the OP to cooperate in the rehabilitation and social reintegration of persons who are victims of acts contrary to the Protocol.[28] This seems to be on the basis that their continued detention does not promote these aims. The ICRC has stated that it does 'not consider Guantánamo Bay an appropriate place to detain juveniles'.[29] However, the real issue seems to be whether the USA is entitled to detain the Guantánamo detainees without permitting them access to a tribunal to determine their legal status, an issue which arises with regard to all of the detainees, adults and children alike.[30] The USA appears to have

[22] See P. Tavernier, 'La Guerre du Golfe – Quelques Aspects de l'Application du Droit des Conflits Armés et du Droit Humanitaire' (1984) 30 AFDI 43, p. 57.

[23] The ICRC made three public appeals during the conflict. See Y. Sandoz, 'Appel du CICR dans le Cadre du Conflit entre l'Irak et l'Iran' (1983) 29 AFDI 161; E. David, 'La Guerre du Golfe et le Droit International' (1987) 20 RBDI 153; and S.H. Lamar, 'The Treatment of Prisoners of War: The Role of the International Committee of the Red Cross in the War between Iran and Iraq' (1991) 5 Emory International Law Journal 243.

[24] Iran had only signed, but not ratified AP I, while Iraq had neither signed nor ratified, so the treaty was not in force between them.

[25] See White House Fact Sheet, 'Status of Detainees at Guantanamo: United States Policy', 7 February 2002.

[26] See Human Rights Watch, 'Letter to Secretary Rumsfeld on Child Detainees at Guantanamo', 24 April 2003.

[27] T. Conover, 'In the Land of Guantanamo', *New York Times Magazine*, 29 June 2003.

[28] *Op. cit.* note 26.

[29] ICRC, 'US Detention Related to the Events of 11 September 2001 and its Aftermath – the Role of the ICRC', operational update, 14 May 2004.

[30] For discussion of the issue, see R.K. Goldman and B.D. Tittemore, 'Unprivileged Combatants and the Hostilities in Afghanistan: Their Status and Rights Under International Humanitarian Law', American Society of International Law Task Force on Terrorism,

acted in a manner consonant with the requirements of Article 77 of AP I, even though not a party to that treaty. One might consider the US authorities' actions inconsistent with Article 37 of the CRC, requiring that the detention of a child shall be only as a last resort and for the shortest appropriate period of time, but the USA is not a party to the CRC either. In early 2004, the US authorities released three youths from Guantánamo.[31] However, as of mid-May 2004 it appeared that two children continued to be detained there.

Child soldiers in the power of an adverse party in internal armed conflicts

Similar, if more rudimentary, provisions apply to children captured in internal armed conflicts. Article 4(3)(d) of AP II provides that: 'The special protection provided by this Article to children who have not attained the age of fifteen years shall remain applicable to them if they take a direct part in hostilities despite the provisions of sub-paragraph (c) and are captured'. Children captured in internal armed conflicts shall be provided with the care and aid they require, which specifically includes schooling.[32] Although there is no requirement in AP II to provide separate quarters for child and adult detainees, such an obligation does exist in Article 37(c) of the CRC. As with AP I, child detainees cannot be recruited into the forces of the party into whose hands they have fallen.

However, in internal armed conflicts those taking part in hostilities do not benefit from any immunities by virtue of their status as combatants. Insurgents can be punished for having violated national law.[33] They can be prosecuted for treason for taking up arms against their government or for murder for the killing of government soldiers. With regard to child soldiers, however, this conclusion is subject to two caveats. First, no child can be punished for any acts committed when aged below the minimum age of criminal responsibility. Second, international law imposes a number of limits on the penalties that can be imposed in children for offences committed by them relating to armed conflicts, and the provisions regarding the imprisonment of children and their treatment in penal affairs apply in internal as they do in international armed conflicts. Article 37 of the CRC provides that:

December 2002; and M. Happold, 'The Detention of Al-Qaeda Suspects at Guantánamo: United Kingdom Perspectives' (2004) 4 Human Rights Law Review 57.

[31] N. Khan, 'Freed Afghan youth tells of Guantanamo', *Boston Globe*, 12 February 2004.

[32] Article 4(3)(c) AP II.

[33] See Y. Sandoz, C. Swinarski and B. Zimmermann (eds), *Commentary on the Additional Protocols of 8 June 1977 to the Geneva Conventions of 12 August 1949*, Geneva: ICRC, 1987, p. 1325.

> States Parties shall ensure that:
> […]
> (b) No child shall be deprived of his or her liberty unlawfully or arbitrarily. The arrest, detention or imprisonment of a child shall be in conformity with the law and shall be used only as a measure of last resort and for the shortest appropriate period of time;
> (c) Every child deprived of liberty shall be treated with humanity and respect for the inherent dignity of the human person, and in a manner which takes into account the needs of persons of his or her age. In particular, every child deprived of liberty shall be separated from adults unless it is considered in the child's best interest not to do so and shall have the right to maintain contact with his or her family through correspondence and visits, save in exceptional circumstances;
> (d) Every child deprived of his or her liberty shall have the right to prompt access to legal and other appropriate assistance, as well as the right to challenge the legality of the deprivation of his or her liberty before a court or other competent, independent and impartial authority, and to a prompt decision on any such action.

Article 40 of the CRC imposes a number of fair-trial guarantees, as well as requiring that:

> every child alleged as, accused of, or recognized as having infringed the penal law … be treated in a manner consistent with the promotion of the child's sense of dignity and worth, which reinforces the child's respect for the human rights and fundamental freedoms of others and which takes into account the child's age and the desirability of promoting the child's reintegration and the child's assuming a constructive role in society.[34]

In other words, if child insurgents are treated as criminals, they are all entitled to the rights which any child accused of a criminal offence has under the Convention. In any event, they may not be imprisoned unlawfully or arbitrarily. Article 37(c) of the CRC refers back to a state party's other international obligations under international humanitarian law or international human rights law, whichever is applicable in the circumstances. Accordingly, in situations where an armed conflict does not exist (or where the government does not admit of its existence) child insurgents cannot be interned without trial unless the government has lawfully derogated from its international obligations.

The disarmament, demobilisation and reintegration of child soldiers

The Machel report argued that the official acknowledgement of children's participation in war was vital, as without it there could be no effective recognition of their special needs in demobilisation programmes. Reintegration programmes should re-establish contact between child soldiers and their families and communities.

[34] Article 40(1) CRC.

Education, especially the completion of primary schooling, should be a priority, with vocational training and preparation for employment being provided for older children.[35] General Assembly resolution 51/77, in addition to welcoming the publication of the Machel report, urged:

> States and all other parties to armed conflict to adopt all necessary measures to end the use of children as soldiers and to ensure their demobilization and reintegration into society, including through adequate education and training, in a manner that fosters their self-respect and dignity, and ... [invited] the international community to assist in this endeavour.[36]

The resolution also recommended that: 'humanitarian concerns relating to children in armed conflict and their protection be fully reflected in United Nations field operations'.[37] This message was reiterated in subsequent General Assembly resolutions, and the issue has continued to be highlighted by the Secretary-General's Representative on Children in Armed Conflict and increasingly been integrated into UN diplomacy and peacekeeping efforts.

Article 39 of the CRC provides that:

> States Parties shall take all appropriate measures to promote physical and psychological recovery and social reintegration of a child victim of: any form of neglect, exploitation or abuse; torture or any other form of cruel, inhuman or degrading treatment or punishment; or armed conflicts. Such recovery and reintegration shall take place in an environment which fosters the health, self-respect and dignity of the child.

Child soldiers, particularly those who have been illegally recruited, would seem to fall into the category of victims of neglect, exploitation, abuse, cruel, inhuman or degrading treatment and/or armed conflict. Accordingly, Article 39 places on states parties to the Convention an obligation to take 'all appropriate measures' to promote their social reintegration.

Article 7 of the OP imposes additional obligations on states parties. It states:

> 1. States Parties shall cooperate in the implementation of the present Protocol, including in the prevention of any activity contrary thereto and in the rehabilitation and social reintegration of persons who are victims of acts contrary thereto, including through technical cooperation and financial assistance. Such assistance and cooperation will be undertaken in consultation with the States Parties concerned and the relevant international organizations.
> 2. States Parties in a position to do so shall provide such assistance through existing multilateral, bilateral or other programmes or, inter alia, through a voluntary fund established in accordance with the rules of the General Assembly.

[35] *Impact of Armed Conflict on Children*: Report of the Expert of the Secretary-General, Ms Graça Machel, submitted pursuant to General Assembly Resolution 48/157, UN Doc. A/51/206 (26 August 1996), paras 50–7.

[36] Para. 24, GA Res. 51/77 On the Rights of the Child (12 December 1996).

[37] *Ibid.*, para. 21.

States Parties are obliged not only to promote the social reintegration of former child soldiers but also to cooperate with other states parties attempting to do so. A similar provision appears in ILO Convention 182. Article 1 of the Convention provides that states parties 'shall take immediate and effective measures to secure the prohibition and elimination of the worst forms of child labour as a matter of urgency'. Article 8 then requires that they 'take appropriate steps to assist one another in giving effect to the provisions of this Convention through enhanced international cooperation and/or assistance including support for social and economic development, poverty eradication programmes and universal education'. However, the provision seems to be little more than hortatory. During the International Labour Conference, the ILO Legal Adviser was asked to what extent Article 8 would create a binding obligation for states parties to assist one another. In reply, he explained that: 'no obligation would arise ... for ratifying member States in relation to a particular level or form of cooperation or assistance. There was only an obligation to take appropriate steps towards enhanced international partnership, and it was up to individual States to decide on those appropriate steps'.[38] On this reading, the obligation is a very weak one. One might consider the obligation contained in Article 7 of the OP to be similar, in particular given the stress in the second paragraph of the article on states parties' discretion as to the manner of their assistance. Developed states have on occasion proved willing to assist programmes for the demobilisation and rehabilitation of child soldiers. In his commentary on ILO Convention 182, Michael Dennis pointed out that the USA was the world's largest donor to the ILO International Programme on the Elimination of Child Labour,[39] while the World Bank and donor governments undertook to provide $500 million to support the demobilisation and reintegration of combatants in the Great Lakes region following a Security Council request for such assistance.[40] However, states have been anxious to minimise their legal obligations to provide financial or other assistance.

The Machel report pointed out that as of the date of its compilation no peace agreement had formally recognised the existence of child combatants.[41] This was the case even in situations where the use of child soldiers had been notorious. Examination of a number of contemporaneous peace processes in which the UN was involved shows this clearly.

[38] International Labour Conference, 87th Session, Geneva, June 1999, Report of the Committee on Child Labour, para. 242. See also M.J. Dennis, 'The ILO Convention on the Worst Forms of Child Labor' (1999) 93 AJIL 943, p. 947.

[39] Dennis, *ibid.*, p. 947.

[40] See Report of the Secretary-General: Children and Armed Conflict, 26 November 2002 (S/2002/1299), para. 55.

[41] *Op. cit.* note 32, para. 49.

Liberia (1996–67)

In Liberia the peace process was intended primarily to end hostilities and provide for elections.[42] There was a ceasefire and a demobilisation, but no efforts were made by the parties to ensure former child soldiers were rehabilitated and reintegrated back into Liberian society.[43] Of 4,326 child soldiers who were demobilised between November 1996 and February 1997 (itself a number well below the original estimate of 9,000 child combatants), only around 800 identified themselves as in need of family tracing (a prerequisite to qualify for support under the UN Humanitarian Assistance Office in Liberia (UNHACO) disarmament and demobilisation plan). Of them, some 600 children ended up in transit homes. All unprotected children received was a package of vegetable oil and bulgar wheat and, with no vehicles to transport them from the demobilisation points to their places of origin, many simply returned to their commanders in the bush.[44] As a result, interviews with NGO staff in Monrovia in November 1997 reported an increased number of street children and heightened delinquent behaviour among urban youth.[45] Many child soldiers are believed to have continued fighting across the border in Sierra Leone.[46]

In other peace agreements, where the reintegration of ex-combatants did form part of the process, the needs of former child soldiers were ignored.

El Salvador

In El Salvador, 1,500–1,600 children were among the 8,552 Farabundo Martí National Liberation Front (FMLN) combatants demobilised between February and December 1992, 105 of them between the ages of 11 and 15. However, children under 16 were excluded from the most popular reincorporation programme, which provided ex-combatants with a small plot of land on credit and some agricultural training, and the 105 former child soldiers under 16 ultimately received no benefits at all. Indeed, it was only after arduous renegotiations that the government permitted those between 16 and 18 to take advantage of the land option.[47]

Guatemala

Similarly, in Guatemala, although the peace agreement provided for the reintegration of Unidad Revolucionaria Nacional Guatemalteca (URNG) combatants and

[42] See I. Cohn, 'The Protection of Children in Peacemaking and Peacekeeping Processes' (1999) 12 Harvard Human Rights Journal 129, p. 159.

[43] *Ibid.*, p. 162. See also I. Cohn, 'The Protection of Child Soldiers During the Liberian Peace Process' (1998) 6 IJCR 179.

[44] *Ibid.*, pp. 195–8.

[45] *Op. cit.* note 35, p. 172.

[46] Report of the Secretary-General: Children and Armed Conflict, 19 July 2000 (A/55/163-S/2000/712), para. 45.

[47] *Ibid.*, pp. 166–7.

affiliates into national life and some 836–883 (about 30 per cent) of the demobilised URNG combatants were between 10 to 20 years old, there were no special programmes targeting children during the demobilisation.[48]

Since the Machel report, however, the issue has become more prominent. The Secretary-General's Special Representative on Children and Armed Conflict has been active in encouraging parties to conflicts to incorporate provisions on the rights and protection of children in their peace agreements, and the Security Council has, on several occasions, called for the demobilisation of child soldiers.[49] A number of peace agreements have included provisions of the demobilisation and rehabilitation of child combatants, although they remain the exception.

Sierra Leone

The 1999 Lomé peace agreement between the Government of Sierra Lone and the Revolutionary United Front,[50] provided that:

> The Government shall accord particular attention to the issue of child soldiers. It shall, accordingly, mobilize resources, both within the country and from the International Community, and especially through the Office of the UN Special Representative for Children in Armed Conflict, UNICEF and other agencies, to address the special needs of these children in the existing disarmament, demobilization and reintegration processes.[51]

Sudan/Uganda

In the 1999 agreement between Sudan and Uganda,[52] in which Sudan agreed to end its sponsorship of the LRA in return for Uganda's ceasing to support the southern Sudanese insurgents, the two parties made a commitment to:

> Make a special effort to locate any abductees, especially children, who have been abducted in the past and return them to their families. All information about such cases will be shared with the Carter Center, UNICEF, and other international organizations and we will cooperate fully in the search and rescue of these victims, beginning immediately with those who can be identified.[53]

The two states also agreed to 'offer amnesty and reintegration assistance to all former combatants who renounce the use of force'.[54]

[48] *Ibid.*, pp. 172–3.
[49] See Chapter 3, pp. 43–4 and 49–51.
[50] Peace Agreement Between the Government of Sierra Leone and the Revolutionary United Front of Sierra Leone, Lomé, Togo, 7 July 1999.
[51] *Ibid.*, Article XXX.
[52] Agreement Between the Governments of Sudan and Uganda, 8 December 1999.
[53] *Ibid.*, Article 8.
[54] *Ibid.*, Article 10.

Democratic Republic of Congo

The 1999 Lusaka ceasefire agreement[55] between parties to the conflict in the Democratic Republic of Congo, provided that the agreed ceasefire would entail the cessation of 'all acts of violence against the civilian population by respecting and protecting human rights', including by ending of the recruitment and use of child soldiers.[56] The agreement also provided that there would be a mechanism for the disarmament of militias and armed groups,[57] but did not go into any greater detail and or make any mention of the specific needs of child combatants.

Burundi

In the 2000 Arusha peace and reconciliation agreement for Burundi,[58] the parties agreed to demobilise members of both the Burundian armed forces and the combatants of the political parties and movements who did not meet (unspecified) age criteria.[59] The agreement also included a provision on vulnerable groups, which stated that:

> The Government shall ensure that, through special assistance, the protection, rehabilitation and advancement of vulnerable groups, namely child heads of families, orphans, street children, unaccompanied minors, traumatised children, widows, women heads of families, juvenile delinquents, the physically and mentally disabled, etc.[60]

Child soldiers, however, although they might fall within any of a number of categories mentioned, do not appear on the list.

Liberia

The 2003 Liberian peace agreement[61] also includes provisions on vulnerable groups. It does, however, specifically mention child soldiers. Article XXXI of the agreement provides that:

> 1a The NTGL [National Transitional Government of Liberia] shall accord particular attention to the issue of the rehabilitation of vulnerable groups or war victims (Children, women, the elderly and the disabled) within Liberia, who have been severely affected by the conflict in Liberia.
>
> b With the support of the International Community, the NTGL shall design and implement a program for the rehabilitation of such war victims.

[55] Ceasefire Agreement, Lusaka, 10 July 1999.
[56] *Ibid.*, Article 3(c).
[57] *Ibid.*, Article 22. See also Annex A, Articles 7.4 and 8.2.
[58] Arusha Peace and Reconciliation Agreement for Burundi, 28 August 2000.
[59] *Ibid.*, Protocol II, Article 21(7).
[60] *Ibid.*, Protocol IV, Article 10.
[61] Comprehensive Peace Agreement Between the Government of Liberia and the Liberians United for Reconciliation and Democracy (LURD) and the Movement for Democracy in Liberia (MODEL) and Political Parties, Accra, Ghana, 18 August 2003.

2a The NTGL shall, in addition, accord special attention to the issue of child combatants.

b It shall, accordingly, mobilize resources with the assistance of the International Community, especially in cooperation with the Office of the U.N. Special Representative for Children in Armed Conflict, UNICEF, the African Committee of Experts on the Rights and Welfare of the Child and other relevant agencies, to address their special demobilization and re-integration needs.

3 The NTGL, in formulating and implementing programs for national rehabilitation, reconstruction and development, for the moral, social and physical reconstruction of Liberia in the post-conflict period, shall ensure that the needs and potentials of the war victims are taken into account and that gender balance is maintained in apportioning responsibilities for program implementation.

These agreements are only some of the peace agreements concluded in the period since the Machel report. Other conflicts which have seen the recruitment and use of child soldiers have been concluded without the inclusion of similar provisions in the peace agreements ending them. Indeed, with the exception of the Sudan–Uganda agreement, none of these peace agreements are binding in international law, which does not govern agreements made between governments and insurgents, even when sponsored by other states and international organisations.[62] The provisions on the demobilisation and rehabilitation of child soldiers are, however, important because they show what the parties to the agreements consider their international obligations to be. Although explicable by the Special Representative's involvement in the drafting of several of them, the similarity in language – the fact that each agreement builds upon its predecessors – adds force to this argument. The lack of such provisions in other agreements, on the other hand, can be explained as being the result of political rather than legal considerations. As Margaret McCallin said in relation to the peace process in Mozambique: 'public recognition that children had been actively involved in the conflict was considered a political liability, and their demobilisation was inconvenient'.[63]

It might be said that the presence of such provisions in peace agreements is in itself meaningless. What is important is whether they are implemented or, to put it another way, what is important is how children's rights and needs are dealt with following any peace agreement, not whether they are explicitly recognised in the agreement itself. However, the presence of such provisions makes it more likely that there will at least be attempts to comply with the legal requirements. As Ilene Cohn has written: 'in the post-conflict setting most donor funding and support as well as the attention of the international monitoring agencies is directed to the

[62] See *Prosecutor* v. *Morris Kallon*, Case No. SCSL-2004-15-AR72(E), decision on challenge to jurisdiction: Lomé Accord amnesty, 13 March 2004, Appeals Chamber, Special Court for Sierra Leone, paras 36–49.

[63] See Margaret McCallin, 'The Reintegration of Ex-combatants into Civilian Life', ILO: 1995, p. 120.

issues agreed upon in the peace negotiations'.[64] It is the peace agreement that sets the agenda for subsequent action. If the peace agreement provides for the demobilisation and reintegration of child combatants, it is more likely that real efforts, directed specifically to children's needs, will be undertaken to such an end.

What constitutes appropriate measures towards the demobilisation and reintegration of former child soldiers will obviously vary from situation to situation. However, a number of common elements have been identified. In his fourth report on children and armed conflict, the Secretary-General listed several 'over-reaching considerations' that should inform any disarmament, demobilisation and reintegration programmes for children. These included that:

(i) In disarmament, demobilization and reintegration processes, separate and child-specific programmes should be organised for demobilized children;
(ii) From the start of the process, there should be a clear definition of who is a child and of the criteria of eligibility of children for the disarmament, demobilization and reintegration programme. Eligibility criteria should be broad enough to ensure that all children associated with armed forces and groups have access to the programme;
(iii) Reintegration programmes should take an integrated community approach and interventions should not single out former child soldiers;
(iv) Monitoring and follow-up of demobilized children should be undertaken to ensure successful reintegration and delivery of benefits;
(v) Local civil society groups, such as elders and religious leaders, should be provided with the support and resources to allow them to play a role in the process;
(vi) Longer-term community reintegration is required to prevent re-recruitment. Progress for demobilized children must represent a viable alternative to military life; and
(vii) Special attention must be given to the specific needs of girls and their stigmatisation.[65]

In resolution 1539, the Security Council reiterated its request to all parties concerned to continue to ensure that all children associated with armed forces and groups are systematically included in every disarmament, demobilisation and reintegration process, bearing in mind the Secretary-General's assessment of best practices.[66]

Article 39 of the CRC does not refer to child soldiers or child combatants, or even to children who have been recruited into armed forces or groups or used to participate actively in hostilities. It speaks of child victims of armed conflict. Its scope is wide. As the Secretary-General's guidelines state, when designing and implementing disarmament, demobilisation and reintegration programmes, care

[64] *Op. cit.* note 42, p. 181.

[65] Report of the Secretary-General: Children and Armed Conflict, 10 November 2003 (A/58/546-S/2003/1053*), para. 65.

[66] SC Res. 1539 of 22 April 2004 On Children and Armed Conflict, para. 9.

must be taken to ensure that they include all war-affected children that might benefit from them. In the view of Save the Children:

> 'Children associated with armed forces' is the term preferred … in referring to any child under 18 years of age who is a part of, or is attached to, any kind of armed force, whether or not there is an armed conflict. This definition is not limited to children who are carrying or have carried arms, but includes those involved in any other capacity, such as cooks, domestic workers, porters, messengers, spies, decoys, couriers, guards and those accompanying such groups other than purely as family members. It includes girls as well as boys, and children recruited for sexual purposes and forced 'marriage'. It apples to all children in armed forces, regardless of whether they have been forced to join, or appear to have done so voluntarily, and applies equally to government and non-government forces. This definition is consistent with the Cape Town Principles as set down in the Cape Town Plan of Action (1997).[67]

In situations of demobilisation, use of the definition of child soldiers in the Cape Town principles would seem appropriate to determine who should be included in the process. Only one caveat should be added. Not all recruitment of children is illegal. Accordingly, it is difficult to see that states are under any legal obligation to demobilise child soldiers who have been lawfully recruited, unless for some other reason they fail to fall within the scope of Article 39 of the CRC.

Both the Secretary-General's assessment of best practices and the Cape Town principles also highlight that any demobilisation programme must ensure the inclusion of girl children associated with armed forces. In Liberia, hardly any girls were demobilised, and a subsequent study found that girl children faced greater barriers to going through the official demobilisation process and greater difficulties reintegrating with their families and communities.[68] As the Secretary-General's first report on children and armed conflict stated: 'The social stigma attached to girls' experiences makes them reluctant to seek medical assistance or emotional support. They are often not adequately catered for in post-conflict educational and vocational training opportunities. Their special needs are rarely provided for in demobilization and reintegration programmes'.[69] Although girls do serve as combatants, they are often found in auxiliary roles or as the 'wives' of adult soldiers. Programmes that focus on combatants, by requiring, for example, the handing in of a serviceable weapon as a condition of demobilisation, may well exclude them. Armed groups may be more loath to release girls, seeing their relationships with adult soldiers as private matter in which they should not meddle. Girl children associated with armed forces have particular needs that need to be addressed in any demobilisation and reintegration process, such as the psychological, physical and social consequences of sexual abuse, forced marriage and pregnancy.

[67] Save the Children UK, *When Children Affected by War Go Home: Lessons Learned from Liberia* London: Save the Children UK, 2003, p. 7.

[68] *Ibid.*, at pp. 142–52.

[69] *Op. cit.* note 41, para. 35.

In addition, although the discussion so far has concentrated on the demobilisation and reintegration of children associated with armed groups in the context of peace agreements and peace processes, there is nothing in Article 39 of the CRC that restricts its temporal scope. This point was specifically made in the Secretary-General's assessment of best practice, which states that: 'The demobilization of child soldiers should be sought at all times during conflict'.[70] The obligations states have not to recruit and use child soldiers and to take all appropriate measures to promote the physical and psychological recovery and social reintegration of child victims of armed conflict run in tandem. If a state had recruited child soldiers illegally, it is under an obligation to demobilise them immediately in a manner that, to the best of its abilities, ensures the children's physical and psychological recovery and social reintegration. Indeed, one can go further and argue that the obligation applies to any child soldiers who fall into the hands of a state party to the CRC. In non-international armed conflicts, child soldiers belonging to armed opposition groups who have been illegally recruited and who fall into the hands of government forces should be disarmed, demobilised and reintegrated into the community in preference to being detained as rebels. Indeed, the Secretary-General argues that; 'Children who escape, are released or captured from any armed forces or groups should not be considered or treated as enemy combatants'.[71] In practice, child soldiers have been demobilised during a number of conflicts, both by governments and insurgent groups.

Added strength is given to this argument when one considers that Article 39 of the CRC addresses itself solely to states parties to the Convention, as do Article 7 of the OP and Article 8 of ILO Convention 182 to their respective parties. The provisions regarding the rehabilitation and reintegration of war-affected children only bind states, not armed opposition groups. Armed opposition groups are under a negative obligation: not to recruit children under 15 (or, in some cases, 18) or use them to participate actively in hostilities. The only positive obligation they have arises if they breach this primary obligation: they are obliged to demobilise illegally recruited children. In addition, Article 2(1) of the CRC requires that states parties shall ensure the rights set out in the Convention without discrimination of any kind. If states were not obliged to act to aid their recovery and reintegration, most demobilised child soldiers would find themselves without legal protection. Thus far most governments have been unable or unwilling to comply with their legal obligations. As we have seen, however, they are at least becoming more willing to acknowledge them.

[70] *Op. cit.* note 59, para. 65(a).
[71] *Ibid.*, para. 65(b).

8

The recruitment of child soldiers as a war crime

Introduction

Article 8 of the Rome Statute of the International Criminal Court (ICC)[1] includes in its list of war crimes within the jurisdiction of the Court:

> (b) … serious violations of the laws and customs applicable in international armed conflict, within the established framework of international law, namely the following acts:
> […]
> (xxvi) Conscripting or enlisting children under the age of fifteen years into the national armed forces or using them to participate actively in hostilities.
>
> (c) … serious violations of the laws and customs applicable in armed conflicts not of an international character, within the established framework of international law, namely any of the following acts:
> […]
> (vii) Conscripting or enlisting children under the age of fifteen into armed forces or groups or using them to participate actively in hostilities.

On 8 September 2003, in his report to the Second Assembly of States Parties to the Rome Statute of the International Criminal Court, the ICC Prosecutor, Mr Luis Moreno-Ocampo, reported that he had selected the situation in Ituri in the Democratic Republic of Congo (DRC) as the first situation meriting analysis with a view to commencing a formal investigation.[2] In a description of the atrocities being committed in Ituri, the Prosecutor made specific reference to the recruitment and use of child soldiers, stating that: 'Between 8,000 and 10,000 children are serving as soldiers in the strife-torn Ituri region. In total, it is estimated that more than 30,000 child soldiers serve among the ranks of the various belligerents in the entire DRC, representing between 40 and 60 per cent of the soldiers fighting

[1] UN Doc. A/CONF.183/9* (1998).

[2] International Criminal Court, Second Assembly of States Parties to the Rome Statute of the International Criminal Court, Report of the Prosecutor of the ICC, Mr Luis Moreno-Ocampo, 8 September 2003.

this war'.[3] On 19 April 2004, the Prosecutor announced that the Government of the DRC has referred the situation in the country to the Court,[4] and on 23 June his Office opened its first investigation into that situation.[5]

On 29 January 2004, the Prosecutor announced that Uganda had referred the situation concerning the Lord's Resistance Army (LRA), and that he had determined there was a sufficient basis to start planning for an investigation. The LRA is particularly notorious for its abduction and forcible recruitment of children, some as young as 8 years old. A conservative estimate places the number of children kidnapped by the LRA during the course of the conflict between it and the Ugandan Government at more then 20,000, and it appears that the number of abductions has risen massively in recent years.[6]

On 5 July 2004, the Presidency of the ICC assigned the situations in DRC and Uganda to Pre-Trial Chambers I and II.[7] Given the nature of these two situations, it seems likely that the first prosecutions before the ICC will include charges of recruiting children. Indeed, individuals are already being prosecuted on charges of child recruitment before another tribunal: the Special Court for Sierra Leone.

Mirroring the provisions, of the Rome Statute, the Statute of the Special Court for Sierra Leone, in its Article 4 on other violations of international humanitarian law, includes 'conscripting or enlisting children under the age of 15 years into armed forces or groups or using them to participate actively in hostilities', as a crime within the jurisdiction of the Court. All of the defendants before the Special Court have been indicted for conduct within Article 4(c).

However, in the Secretary-General's draft statute Article 4(c) appeared in a different form. In his report on the establishment of a Special Court for Sierra Leone,[8] the Secretary-General stated that:

> While the prohibition on child recruitment has by now acquired a customary international law status, it is far less clear whether it is customarily recognized as a war crime entailing the individual criminal responsibility of the accused.
>
> Owing to the doubtful customary nature of the ICC Statutory crime which criminalizes the conscription or enlistment of children under the age of 15, whether forced or

[3] *Ibid.*, p. 3. Human Rights Watch, in its report *Ituri: 'Covered in Blood': Ethnically Targeted Violence in Northeastern DR Congo*, New York: HRW, 2003, pp. 46–7, stated that all the armed groups fighting in Ituri had large numbers of children fighting in their ranks.

[4] Press release, Office of the Prosecutor, ICC, 'Prosecutor Receives Referral of the Situation in the Democratic Republic of Congo', 19 April 2004.

[5] Press release, Office of the Prosecutor, ICC, 'The Office of the Prosecutor of the International Criminal Court Opens its First Investigation', 23 June 2004.

[6] See Human Rights Watch, *Stolen Children: Abduction and Recruitment in Northern Uganda*, New York: HRW, 2003. The report, published in March 2003, estimated that about 5,000 children had been abducted since June 2002, more than in any previous period.

[7] See Decision Assigning the Situation in the Democratic Republic of Congo to Pre-trial Chamber I, ICC-01/04, 5 July 2004; and Decision Assigning the Situation in Uganda to Pre-trial Chamber II, ICC-02/04, 5 July 2004.

[8] UN Doc. S/2000/915 (4 October 2000).

> 'voluntary', the crime which is included in article 4 (c) of the Statute of the Special Court is not the equivalent of the ICC provision. While the definition of the crime as 'conscripting' or 'enlisting' connotes an administrative act of putting one's name on a list and formal entry into the armed forces, the elements of the crime under the proposed Statute of the Special Court are: (a) abduction, which in the case of the children of Sierra Leone was the original crime and is itself a crime under common article 3 of the Genera Conventions; (b) forced recruitment in the most general sense – administrative formalities, obviously, notwithstanding; and (c) transformation of the child into, and its [*sic*] use as, among other degrading uses, a 'child-combatant'.[9]

Accordingly, article 4(c) of the draft statute only criminalised: 'Abduction and forced recruitment of children under the age of 15 years into armed forces or groups for the purpose of using them to participate actively in hostilities'.

The Security Council, however, did not agree with the Secretary-General. In the only amendment proposed to the list of crimes within the jurisdiction of the Court, the Council suggested that draft article 4(c) be amended to cover 'Conscripting or enlisting children under the age of 15 years into armed forces or groups or using them to participate actively in hostilities'.[10] The Council asked that the provision be so modified 'so as to conform it to the statement of the law existing in 1996 and as currently accepted by the international community'.[11] The amendment was accepted by the Government of Sierra Leone[12] and was included in the Statute of the Special Court annexed to the Agreement between the UN and Sierra Leone establishing the Court.

The Security Council's action took place following a campaign by NGOs to have the draft statute so modified as to reflect the provisions of the Rome Statute.[13] This does not necessarily mean that the Council was wrong in its view of what the law was in 1996 but it does raise the question of whether their decision to overrule the Secretary-General's conclusions was based more on political expediency than legal considerations.

All of the defendants before the Special Court have been indicted on charges of child recruitment. Unsurprisingly, however, an accused, Samuel Hinga Norman, challenged the Court's jurisdiction on the ground that it had no right to try him for crimes under Article 4(c) of its Statute since the crime of child recruitment was not part of customary international law at the times relevant to the indictment. The

[9] *Ibid.*, at paras 17–18 (paragraph numbers omitted).

[10] Letter dated 22 December 2000 from the President of the Security Council addressed to the Secretary-General, UN Doc. S/2000/1234, Annex.

[11] *Ibid.*, at p. 2.

[12] Ninth report of the Secretary-General on the United Nations Mission in Sierra Leone, UN Doc. S/2001/228 (14 March 2001), at para. 54.

[13] See, e.g., Amnesty International news release, 'The Special Court for Sierra Leone', 20 October 2000, AFR 51/081/2000: Human Rights Watch, 'Justice and the Special Court: Letter to the United Nations Security Council', 1 November 2000; and Coalition to Stop the Use of Child Soldiers, 'Appeal on Sierra Leone: Special Court Should Prosecute Recruiters, not Child Soldiers', 7 November 2000.

Appeals Chamber of the Court held to the contrary, finding that customary law has crystallised so as to criminalise child recruitment prior to November 1996 (the beginning of the Court's temporal jurisdiction), although it did so in the face of a strong dissenting opinion from Justice Robertson.[14] However, it will be seen that there are a number of problems with the Special Court's conclusions. The question of whether the Rome Statute codified existing customary international law criminalising the recruitment of under-15s or whether it saw an exercise in progressive development of the law cannot be seen as having been conclusively determined. This might be thought as being of academic interest only. However, given the general view that war crimes are not subject to any period of limitations[15] and the increasing use of Article 1F(a) of the Geneva Convention Relating to the Status of Refugees to exclude persons from refugee status,[16] the answer to the question could have important consequences to other individuals who participated in the recruitment of children prior to 1998.

The recruitment of children under 15 as a war crime

War crimes are violations of the laws and customs of war incurring individual criminal responsibility.[17] The four GCs and AP I provide for a regime of 'grave breaches' of their provisions. Violations of Article 77(2) of AP I do not figure in the list of grave breaches set out in Article 85 of the Protocol. However, it is generally agreed that not only grave breaches are criminal. It is well established that the failure of a rule of international humanitarian law to address the prohibition to individuals or specifically provide for criminal sanctions for its breach is not determinative of the issue whether such breach is criminalised.[18] As the Trial Chamber of the International Criminal Tribunal for the former Yugoslavia stated in the *Tadić* case: 'The individual criminal responsibility of the violator need not be explicitly stated in a convention for its provisions to entail individual

[14] *Prosecutor* v. *Samuel Hinga Norman*, Case No. SCSL-2004-14-AR729E, Special Court for Sierra Leone (Appeals Chamber), decision on preliminary motion based on lack of jurisdiction (child recruitment), 31 May 2004.

[15] See Antonio Cassese, *International Criminal Law*, Oxford: Oxford University Press, 2003, pp. 317–19 for discussion of the issue.

[16] 189 UNTS 150 (1951). See also the Protocol Relating to the Status of Refugees 606 UNTS 267 (1967). Article 1F provides, *inter alia*, that the Refugee Convention 'shall not apply to any person with respect to whom there are serious reasons for considering that: (a) he has committed a crime against peace, a war crime, or a crime against humanity, as defined in the international instruments drawn up to make provision in respect of such crimes'.

[17] See *Prosecutor* v. *Tadić (Jurisdiction)*, Case IT-94-1-A, decision of the Appeals Chamber, 2 October 1995, 105 ILR 453, p. 503.

[18] See *Trial of German Major War Criminals*: Proceedings of the International Military Tribunal Sitting at Nuremberg, Germany, Part 22, pp. 445 and 467: *US* v. *Ohlendorf et al.* (the '*Einsatzgruppen* case') 4 CCL No. 10 Trials 411, pp. 460–1; and *Tadić*, *ibid.*, p. 524.

criminal responsibility'.[19] The distinction between grave and 'non-grave' breaches of international humanitarian law is concerned with jurisdiction rather than criminality. All states are obliged to prosecute or extradite persons suspected of having committed grave breaches. However, although states are obliged to 'respect and ensure respect'[20] of the other provisions of the GCs and APs, they have some discretion as to how this is to be achieved.

How to distinguish a violation of international humanitarian law that incurs individual criminal responsibility from one that does not is, however, less clear. There seems to be three main approaches to the issue. The first asks whether the breach is of a certain type: for example, whether it causes 'appreciable injury'.[21] Such conduct is to be contrasted with 'technical' violations of international humanitarian law such as the failure by a commander of a POW camp to keep a complete record of disciplinary punishments[22] or the failure of the commander of a civilian internment camp to ensure that its canteen sells tobacco or soap 'at prices not higher than local market prices'.[23] The second approach is a more positivist one. One has to show that violation of a rule of international humanitarian law has been specifically criminalised in international law.[24] 'For a violation of a rule of *jus in bello* to produce the special legal effect of entailing the criminal responsibility of the individual who commits it, one should prove not only the existence of the violated rule in international law, but also the parallel existence of a secondary rule, usually a customary one, ascribing to the former rule this special legal effect in case of violation'.[25] No difficulties arise using this approach when violation of the rule has consistently been considered a war crime by national or international courts, or is described as a war crime in the statute of an international tribunal. Problems arise, however, when the case law and statutes of international tribunals are silent. In such cases, according to Antonio Cassese, in seeking to answer the question one may have resort to military manuals and national legislation or, if answers are lacking there, to the general principles of criminal justice, and the

[19] *Prosecutor* v. *Tadić (Jurisdiction)*, Case IT-91-1-T, decision of the Trial Chamber, 10 August 1995, 105 ILR 427, p. 449.

[20] Common Article 1, 1949 GCs and Article 1(1), AP I.

[21] See H. Lauterpacht, 'The Law of Nations and the Punishment of War Criminals' (1944) BYIL 58, at pp. 78–9; and B.V.A. Röling, 'The Law of War and the National Jurisdiction since 1945' (1960) 1000 *Hague Recueil* 323, at p. 340.

[22] In breach of Article 96 of GC III. The example is given in S.R. Ratner, 'War Crimes, Categories of', in R. Gutman and D. Rieff (eds), *Crimes of War: What the Public Should Know*, New York: W.W. Norton & Co., 1999.

[23] In breach of Article 87 of GC IV. The example is taken from Y. Sandoz, 'Penal Aspects of International Humanitarian Law', in M.C. Bassiouni (ed.), *International Criminal Law*, Ardsley: Transnational, 2nd edn 1999), p. 408.

[24] Cassese, *op. cit.*, note 15, p. 51.

[25] G. Abi-Saab, 'The Concept of "War Crimes"', in Sienho Yee and Wang Tieya (eds), *International Law in the Post-Cold War World: Essays in Memory of Li Haopei*, London: Routledge, 2001, p. 112.

legislation and judicial practice of the state to which the accused belongs or on whose territory the crime was allegedly committed.[26] Although the first approach may be suitable for clear cases, it is too vague for borderline ones, which are precisely those with regard to which a workable test is needed. As Georges Abi-Sabb states: 'It is not enough … simply to use adjectives, by describing the violation as "serious" or "grave" or the violated norm as "fundamental". Such a question-begging approach is neither valid nor operational as a distinguishing criterion'.[27] In addition, it seems to leave the issue of what is a war crime entirely up to the judge in any particular case. This is inappropriate given, in particular, the principle of *nullum crimem sine lege.*

A third approach, however, takes the view that all violations of the laws and customs of law are criminal.[28] There is substantial authority for this proposition,[29] although it would seem to contradict the views of the Appeals Chamber in *Tadić*. The Chamber held that in order for Article 3 of the Tribunal's Statute (on violations of the laws and customs of war other than grave breaches) to apply the violation must constitute a breach of a rule of international humanitarian law and the violation of the rule must entail the individual criminal responsibility of the person breaching it.[30] It is implicit that the Chamber did not consider that all breaches of rules of international humanitarian law are war crimes; otherwise the second condition would be otiose. Earlier cases took the same view,[31] as did all of the judges of the Appeals Chamber of the Special Court in *Hinga Norman.* Nevertheless, this third approach does have the virtue of simplicity. Its basis is the view that 'violations of the international laws of war have traditionally been regarded as criminal under international law'.[32] There is considerable weight to this argument, but it is presently the minority view. Nonetheless, most violations of international humanitarian law are war crimes.

Whichever view one accepts, one cannot consider the situation to be wholly satisfactory. The difficulty would seem to lie in the use of the customary law process to create criminal offences. The same issue, it might be said, arises from the development of the common law through judicial interpretation from case to case.[33]

[26] Cassese, *op. cit.* note 15.

[27] *Ibid.*

[28] See Christopher Greenwood, 'International Humanitarian Law and the *Tadić* Case' (1996) 7 EJIL 265.

[29] See the provisions in the UK, US and Canadian military manuals cited by Greenwood, *ibid.*, p. 280, fn 49 and accompanying text.

[30] *Op. cit.* note 14, at pp. 503–4.

[31] See *Trial of Heinz Hagendorf*, 13 Law Reports of Trials of War Criminals 146.

[32] *Op. cit.* note 28, p. 280.

[33] See *R* v. *R* [1991] 1 WLR 767, where the House of Lords abolished the marital exception to rape. On a subsequent application by the defendant to the European Court of Human Rights, the Court found no violation of Article 7 of the European Convention (no punishment without law): see *C.R.* v. *UK*, judgment of 22 November 1995, ECHR Series A No. 335-C.

However, the development of customary international law cannot be assimilated to the accretion of judicial decisions that make up the common law. There is no one body of published decisions, whose respective weight can be assessed by application of the doctrine of *stare decisis*. Instead, the sources are far more heterogeneous, often difficult to access, and frequently the subject of differing interpretations. The creation of common law offences is now generally frowned on. One might consider that there should be a similar moratorium on the use of the customary process to create offences under international law.

International humanitarian law and international human rights law

Although the prohibition of the recruitment of children under 15 was first promulgated as a rule of international humanitarian law, it might be said that it has since migrated to become a part of international human rights law. With a few exceptions, breach of human rights provisions does not incur individual criminal responsibility[34] unless specifically criminalised by the adoption of a treaty norm.[35]

In form, the prohibition seems a part of international humanitarian law. Article 77(2) of AP I is addressed to states, to the 'Parties to the conflict', rather than formally conferring rights on individuals, that is, the children subject to recruitment and use in hostilities. Indeed, this form of drafting was followed in Article 38 of the CRC, in distinction from most of the other substantive provisions of the Convention, which refer to states recognising 'the right to the child' to some good. For René Provost, this distinction is significant in that the humanitarian standards enunciated 'although grounded in the principle of humanity, are not directly attached to the human person, but instead stem from international public order requirements'.[36] However, as Theodor Meron has shown, as early as the 1949 GCs rights have been conferred upon individuals in international humanitarian law.[37] All that can probably be said is that the wording of Article 38 shows its origins as an international humanitarian law provision.

[34] A state may be in default of its obligations if it fails to investigate and – if the evidence warrants – prosecute and punish certain serious human rights violations. However, in such cases it is the state that will be responsible under international law. Proceedings against the alleged violator take place under domestic law; it is simply that the adequacy of the proceedings is tested by reference to the state's human rights commitments and if they are held inadequate the state is itself responsible. Crimes against humanity, which are crimes under international law, must be part of a widespread or systematic attack on the civilian population.

[35] See, e.g. Articles 5 and 7, Convention Against Torture and Other Cruel, Inhuman or Degrading Treatment or Punishment, (1985) 24 ILM 535.

[36] René Provost, *International Human Rights and Humanitarian Law*, Cambridge: Cambridge University Press, 2002, p. 34.

[37] Theodor Meron, 'The Humanization of Humanitarian Law' (2000) 94 AJIL 239.

However, there also exist arguments of substance rather than form. The nature of the prohibition means that it is primarily directed to restricting the ways in which states can act towards their own nationals. International humanitarian law has traditionally concerned itself with how states treat other states' nationals.[38] It has been international human rights law that has covered how governments treat their own citizens. In addition, the prohibition applies in times of peace as well as in times of war. War crimes can only be committed during periods of armed conflict.[39] It seems odd that breach of a rule incurs individual criminal responsibility only if committed at a particular time.

In response to the first of these arguments, although international humanitarian law traditionally has been restricted to regulating how states treat other states' nationals, this is less and less the case. We have already seen how Part II of GC IV applies to the whole of the populations of countries in conflict, not just to 'protected persons'.[40] This development was taken further in AP I, in particular in Part IV on the civilian population.[41] Article 77 is situated in Section III of Part IV, which is specifically said to be 'additional to the rules concerning humanitarian protection of civilians and civilian objects in the power of a Party to the conflict contained in the Fourth Convention'.[42] AP II, expanding the basic provisions in Common Article 3 of the GCs, further extended the ambit of international humanitarian law into non-international armed conflicts, thus interfering with states' relations with their nationals in a very obvious way. Both the Yugoslavia and Rwanda tribunal have held violations of international humanitarian law applicable in internal armed conflicts to be criminal.[43] And, in addition, the Appeals Chamber of the International Criminal Tribunal for Yugoslavia (ICTY) has held that whether a victim of a war crime is a protected person 'should not be determined on the basis of formal national characterisations, but rather on an analysis of the substantial relations', such as ethnicity and allegiance.[44] In other words, a war crime in an international armed conflict can be perpetrated by a person of the same formal nationality as the person against whom the crime is committed.

The second argument is more attractive, at least initially. It is odd that international law decides whether particular conduct is criminal by determining whether

[38] The majority of the provisions of the four GCs apply only to 'protected persons' *Prosecutor* v. *Tadić (Jurisdiction)*, *op. cit.* note 17, at p. 513.

[39] *Tadić*, *op. cit.* note 17 at p. 488.

[40] See Chapter 4, pp. 55–6.

[41] Article 50(2) AP I defines the civilian population as 'all persons who are civilians'. Similarly, Article 52(1) defines civilian objects as 'all objects which are not military objectives'. There is no nationality requirement.

[42] Article 72 AP I. Indeed, the section is said to be additional to, in particular, Parts I and III of GC IV, that is, the parts which only provide protection for protected persons.

[43] *Prosecutor* v. *Tadić*, *op. cit.* note 17, p. 523; and *Prosecutor* v. *Akayesu*, judgment of 2 September 1998, Trial Chamber, ICTR, paras 608–9 and 616.

[44] *Prosecutor* v. *Delalić et al.*, Case No. IT-96-21/A, judgment of the Appeals Chamber, 20 February 2001, para. 84.

it is linked to an armed conflict. Nevertheless, this oddity is inherent in the concept of war crimes, as they are violations of the laws and customs of war or, to put it in a more contemporary idiom, of international humanitarian law. Ultimately it is a product of the concept's history. To use it as an argument that the recruitment or use to participate directly in hostilities of children under 15 years of age is not a war crime seems wrong. The argument is over-inclusive. Several sorts of conduct are prohibited in times of peace as well as times of war but only give rise to criminal sanctions when linked to an armed conflict. If the argument were effective it would repeal quite a number of war crimes. More specifically, the prohibition on the recruitment and use of child soldiers was originally linked to situations of armed conflict. Its application in times of peace as well as war was only confirmed in the CRC.

It might be argued that there are two separate customary law rules on the subject: one a rule of international humanitarian, breach of which incurs individual criminal responsibility (but only in times of armed conflict); the other a rule of international human rights law, breach of which can only engage state responsibility. Such a situation does not seem impossible but it does appear unlikely. It is far more difficult to see how the two rules developed separately than it is to see how a single rule crystallised. Indeed, as we have already seen, it is on the basis of the evidence of states' positions during both the drafting of the two APs and the CRC that a rule of customary law can be founded.[45]

The prohibition of the recruitment of children can be seen as straddling both international human rights and international humanitarian law. However, in one respect in particular, it sits firmly on the international humanitarian law side of the fence. International human rights law binds only states. A state cannot be held responsible for the actions of non-state actors, such as armed opposition groups, unless it is in breach of its obligation to effectively investigate allegations of human rights violations, as such groups and their members are not organs or agents of the state. This is very different from international humanitarian law, which imposes numerous obligations on armed opposition groups.[46] We have already seen in Chapters 4, 5 and 6 that the recruitment and use of child soldiers by armed opposition groups is subject to extensive regulation, both as a matter of treaty and customary international law.[47] Indeed, we have also seen that such groups' activities are increasingly subject to scrutiny by international institutions, not least by the Security Council.

States did not explicitly criminalise the recruitment of children below 15 years of age in any treaty dealing with the issue prior to the Rome Statute. There is

[45] See pp. 89–90.

[46] See generally, L. Zegveld, *The Accountability of Armed Opposition Groups in International Law*, Cambridge: Cambridge University Press, 2002.

[47] See, e.g., Inter-American Commission on Human Rights, Third Report on the Human Rights Situation in Colombia, OEA/Ser.L/V/II.102, Doc. 9 rev. 1, 26 February 1999, at ch. XIII, paras 63–4.

evidence that at least some states thought they were innovating when they adopted Articles 8(2)(b)(xxvi) and 8(2)(e)(vii). A few states had reservations about the provisions. Indeed, the USA specifically argued the prohibition of the recruitment of children under 15 was more a human rights than a criminal law provision.[48] On the other hand, when some states suggested raising the minimum age for recruitment from 15 to 18, this was rejected as not reflecting customary law.[49] This seems to indicate that most states thought that there was a customary rule prohibiting the recruitment of children below 15 years of age. It might also be said to show that the majority states considered that there was also a customary rule criminalising violations of the prohibition. This seems to have been the view of the situation taken by the Security Council in 2002,[50] although the extent to which one should credit retrospective views on *opinio juris* is another matter.

The decision of the Special Court in *Prosecutor* v. *Samuel Hinga Norman*

However, there now exists a ruling of an international tribunal on the point, an interlocutory decision of the Appeals Chamber of the Special Court for Sierra Leone in *Prosecutor* v. *Samuel Hinga Norman*. The Applicant, Chief Samuel Hinga Norman, was charged together with Moinina Fofana and Allieu Kondewa on an indictment containing eight counts, the last of which alleged his command responsibility for a serious violation of international humanitarian law, namely: 'At all times relevant to this indictment ... Enlisting children under the age of fifteen years into armed forces or groups or using them to participate actively in hostilities'. He applied by preliminary motion to the Appeals Chamber of the Special Court, arguing that the Court had no jurisdiction to try him for crimes under Article 4(c) of the Court's Statute. To do so, he argued, would violate the principle of *nullum crimen sine lege* as no such crime existed at any times relevant to the indictment. The majority of the Appeals Chamber of the Special Court for Sierra Leone (Justices Ayoola, Gelaga King and Winter) disagreed. They held that; 'Child recruitment was criminalized before it was explicitly set out as a criminal prohibition in treaty law and certainly by November 1996, the starting point of the time frame relevant to the indictments'.[51]

The Court considered that prior to November 1996, the prohibition on child recruitment had crystallised as customary international law, on the grounds of the wide ratification of the GCs, AP II and the CRC and the lack of reservations made by States to Article 38 of the CRC.[52] The Court adopted the ICTY's conclusion in

[48] See H. von Hebel and D. Robinson, 'Crimes within the Jurisdiction of the Court', in R.S. Lee (ed.), *The International Criminal Court: The Making of the Rome Statute: Issues, Negotiations, Results*, Ardsley: Transnational, 1999, p. 117.

[49] *Ibid.*, pp. 117–18.

[50] See text to note 8.

[51] *Op. cit.* note 11 para. 53.

[52] *Ibid.*, paras 17–20.

the *Tadić* case that it was necessary to show that the violation must constitute an infringement of a rule of international humanitarian law; it must be 'serious'; and it must entail the individual criminal responsibility of the person breaching the rule.[53] However, the Court emphasised that the prohibition of the recruitment and use of children to participate in hostilities was one of the 'fundamental guarantees' in AP II, which was itself an expansion of Common Article 3 of the GCs. Reference was also made to a 1996 Security Council resolution on the situation in Liberia,[54] which condemned the 'inhuman and abhorrent' practice of recruiting, training, and deploying children for combat.[55] Indeed, to an extent the Court seems to have elided the second and third criteria, purporting to adopt the conclusions of the International Criminal Tribunal for Rwanda (ICTR) in *Akayesu* that a breach of a rule protecting important values was a 'serious violation' entailing individual responsibility.

The Court emphasised that war crimes within the jurisdiction of the ICC were stated to be 'within the established framework of international law'. On the basis that at the second session of the Preparatory Committee it had been proposed that the ICC should have power to prosecute serious violations of Common Article 3 and AP II, even though the inclusion of child recruitment as a crime was not specifically suggested until December 1997, it concluded that: 'The discussion during the preparation of the Rome Statute focused on the codification and effective implementation of the existing customary norm rather than the formation of a new one'.

Moving on to consider Article 4(2) of the OP, which requires states parties to take all feasible measures to prevent the recruitment and use in hostilities of children by armed groups, 'including the adoption of legal measures necessary to prohibit and criminalize such practices', the Court argued that the provision demonstrated that 'the aim at this stage was to raise the standard of the prohibition of child recruitment form age 15 to age 18, proceeding from the assumption that the conduct was already criminalized at the time in question'. The Court concluded this stage of its decision by stating that:

> The prohibition of child recruitment constitutes a fundamental guarantee and although it is not enumerated in the ICTR and ICTY Statutes, it shares the same character and the same gravity of the violations that are explicitly listed in those Statutes. The fact that the ICTY and the ICTR have prosecuted violations of Additional Protocol II provides further evidence of the criminality of child recruitment before 1996.[56]

The Court also considered that the wording of Articles 38 ('all feasible measures') and 4 ('all appropriate legislative ... measures') of the CRC included criminal

[53] It might be thought that the second criterion was jurisdictional rather than substantive.
[54] SC Res. 1071 of 30 August 1996 On the Situation in Liberia.
[55] *Ibid.*, at para. 29.
[56] *Ibid.*, para. 39.

sanctions as means of enforcement.[57] The Court found that a few states had criminalised child recruitment prior to 1996.[58] However, the Court also considered it significant that other states had prohibited child recruitment in military law, had done so indirectly by criminalising any breaches of law by civil servants generally, or had made it impossible for individuals to recruit children.[59] The Court concluded by holding that 'the period during which the majority of states criminalized the prohibited behaviour ... was the period between 1994 and 1996'.[60] The Applicant's motion was dismissed.

Justice Robertson, in his dissenting opinion, took a very different line. He considered that the more narrowly drawn offence in the Secretary-General's draft Statute was a war crime by November 1996, as it amounted to a most serious breach of Common Article 3'.[61] However, Article 4(c), as adopted, was in a different form, and could be committed in three different ways:

(i) by conscripting children (which implies compulsion, albeit in some cases through force of law)
(ii) by enlisting them (which merely means accepting and enrolling them when they volunteer), or
(iii) by using them to participate actively in hostilities (i.e. taking the more serious step, having conscripted or enlisted them, of putting their lives directly at risk in combat).

Offence number (ii) extended liability considerably, as the prosecution would need only to show that the defendant know that the person he enlisted was under 15 at the time. Justice Robertson commented that:

> It might strike some as odd that the state of international law in 1996 in respect to criminalization of child enlistment was doubtful to the UN Secretary-General in October 2000 but very clear to the President of the Security Council only two months later. If it was not clear to the Secretary-General and his legal advisers that international law by 1996 criminalized the enlistment of child soldiers, could it really have been any clearer to Chief Hinga Norman or any other defendant at that tome, embattled in Sierra Leone? ... If international criminal law adopts the common law principle that in cases of real doubt as to the existence or definition of a criminal offence, the benefit of that doubt must be given to the defendant, then this would appear to be such a case.[62]

Following the language of Security Council resolution 1071 relied upon by the majority, Justice Robertson agreed that the enlistment of under-15s was 'abhorrent' but stressed that abhorrence alone did not make conduct a crime in international

[57] *Ibid.*, at para. 41.
[58] *Ibid.*, at para. 45.
[59] *Ibid.*, at para. 47.
[60] *Ibid.*, at para. 51.
[61] Dissenting Opinion of Justice Robertson, at para. 4.
[62] *Ibid.*, at para. 6.

law.[63] Justice Robertson emphasised that showing that child enlistment – as distinct from the forcible recruitment of children or their subsequent use in combat – was a war crime required not only showing that child enlistment was prohibited as a matter of international law but also that the rule had 'metamorphosed' into a rule of criminal law for breach of which individuals might be punished.[64] He laid particular stress on the *nullum crimen sine lege* principle, which he considered should be interpreted strictly.

Justice Robertson, as did the majority, referred to the *Tadić* case. However, he relied on a passage from the decision of the Appeals Chamber, rather than from that of the Trial Chamber, which stated that:

> The Nuremberg Tribunal considered a number of factors relevant to its conclusion that the authors of particular prohibitions incur individual responsibility: the clear and unequivocal recognition of the rules of warfare in international law and State practice indicating an intention to criminalise the prohibition, including statements by government officials and international organisations as well as punishment of violations by national courts and military tribunals. Where these conditions are met, individuals must be held criminally responsible.[65]

Justice Robertson did not consider these criteria fulfilled in 1996 in relation to the prohibition on child enlistment. The material supplied by UNICEF in its *amicus* brief upon which the majority had relied did not evidence that the majority of states had explicitly criminalised child enlistment prior to November 1996, and there had been no suggestion of any prosecution for such an offence having taken place under the national law of any state.[66] Justice Robertson concluded that:

> What had emerged, in customary international law, by the end of 1996 was a humanitarian rule that obliged states, and armed factions within states, to avoid enlisting under fifteens or involving them in hostilities, whether arising from international or internal armed conflict. What had not, however, evolved was an offence cognisable by international criminal law which permitted the trial and punishment of individuals accused of enlisting (i.e. accepting for military service) volunteers under the age of fifteen. It may be that in some states this would have constituted an offence against national law, but this cannot be determinative of the existence of an international law crime.[67]

Justice Robertson's dissent clearly exposed the weaknesses in the majority opinion. The evidence relied upon by the majority to support their finding that child recruitment was criminalised in the period 1994–96 is not convincing. The language of Security Council resolution 1071 actually argues against their conclusion. If the Council had considered such behaviour unlawful, it might have been expected

[63] *Ibid.*, at para. 9.
[64] *Ibid.*, at para. 10.
[65] *Prosecutor* v. *Tadić*, Case No. IT-94-1-AR72, at p. 520, para. 128. *Ibid.*, at para. 23.
[66] *Ibid.*, para. 23.
[67] *Ibid.*, para. 33.

to say so expressly, as it has since done with regard to instances of child recruitment in elsewhere. The Court's interpretation of CRC and the OP are not generally accepted and seem to ignore the distinction between obligations upon states to make particular conduct criminal in their national law and the creation of international crimes. The evidence of the negotiations of the Rome Statute, as we have already seen, is mixed, and the instances of state practice relied upon weak. Indeed, although the Court argued that they had to show that the prohibition had been criminalised, at times the standard applied seems close to a simple requirement that the conduct be of a particular level of seriousness. Such judgments are inherently subjective and lack legal certainty.

However, Justice Robertson's conclusions cannot be said to be entirely convincing either. Although, following the Secretary-General, he stated that he considered the conscription of children under 15 years of age and their use to participate actively in hostilities to have been war crimes at all relevant times, he did not explain why. It will be recalled that the Secretary-General's report stated that the abduction of children violated Common Article 3, while their transformation into 'child combatants' amounted to degrading treatment. The problem is, however, is that Common Article 3 does not specifically prohibit such conduct, nor is there any evidence additional to that adduced in the majority opinion to suggest that states had criminalised it prior to 1996. Applying Justice Robertson's own standards, one might consider that no case can be made that any recruitment or use of children to participate in hostilities was a war crime prior to the adoption of the Rome Statute.

The recruitment of children as a war crime in contemporary international law

All of the judges in *Hinga Norman*, however, agreed that the recruitment of use of children under 15 to participate actively in hostilities was a war crime in contemporary international law. There seems no reason to doubt this conclusion. Although not made explicit in the President of the Security Council's letter to the Secretary-General, it seems that the Council considered the recruitment of under-15s or their use to participate actively in hostilities to be a customary crime regardless of the nature of the conflict during which it was committed, as the Sierra Leone conflict was an internal armed conflict. Numerous states are now incorporating the provision into their domestic criminal law in compliance with their obligations as parties to the Rome Statute.

In the Elements of Crimes adopted by consensus by the ICC Assembly of State Parties, the elements of the war crime of using, conscripting or enlisting children under Article 8(2)(b)(xxvi) of the Rome Statute are that:

1. The perpetrator conscripted or enlisted one or more persons into the national armed forces or used one or more persons to participate actively in hostilities.

2. Such person or persons were under the age of 15 years.
3. The perpetrator knew or should have known that such person or persons were under the age of 15 years.
4. The conduct took place in the context of and was associated with an international armed conflict.
5. The perpetrator was aware of the factual circumstances that established the existence of an armed conflict.

The elements of the war crime of using, conscripting or enlisting children under Article 8(2)(e)(vii) are very similar, being that:

1. The perpetrator conscripted or enlisted one or more persons into an armed force or group or used one or more persons to participate actively in hostilities.
2. Such person or persons were under the age of 15 years.
3. The perpetrator knew or should have known that such person or persons were under the age of 15 years.
4. The conduct took place in the context of and was associated with an armed conflict not of an international character.
5. The perpetrator was aware of factual circumstances that established the existence of an armed conflict.

Save for differences arising out of the different characteristics of international and non-international armed conflicts, the two provisions are near identical. This was intentional and reflects the Rome Statute. However, a number of additional comments can be made.

In the first place, whereas Article 77(2) of AP I and Article 38 of the CRC prohibit all recruitment of children under 15, the Rome Statute only criminalises such conduct if the perpetrator knew or should have known that the persons recruited were under 15 years of age. Apparently, at the Preparatory Commission for the ICC, some states argued that there should be no mental element to the crime.[68] If a person recruited children under 15 he would be guilty of the offence regardless of whether he had any reason to know or suspect what their age was. This approach was justified on the basis that it was for recruiters to satisfy themselves that recruits were not underage. On the other hand, it was argued that such an approach was inconsistent with Article 67(1)(i) of the Rome Statute, which provides that an accused before the ICC has the right not to have imposed on him any reversal of the burden of proof or any onus of rebuttal.[69] Strictly speaking, this counter-argument missed the point, as making an offence a crime of strict liability does neither of those things. However, Article 30(1) of the Statue provides that: 'Unless otherwise provided, a person shall be criminally responsible and liable for punishment for a crime within the jurisdiction of the Court only if the material elements are committed with knowledge and intent'.

[68] K. Dörmann, *Elements of War Crimes under the Rome Statute of the International Criminal Court: Sources and Commentary*, Cambridge: Cambridge University Press, 2003, p. 375.

[69] *Ibid.*

Articles 8(2)(b)(xxvi) and 8(2)(e)(vii) do not provide otherwise. Article 30(3) states that for the purpose of the article '"knowledge" means awareness that a circumstance exists', so the prosecutor must prove that the accused was aware of that the relevant circumstances existed. However, there was general agreement at the PrepCom that such a stringent test should not apply.[70] This seems not unreasonable given that Article 77(2) of AP I and Article 38 of the CRC require the taking of 'all feasible measures' to prevent children under 15 taking a direct part in hostilities. However, adolescents develop physically at different rates and the systems for the recording of births are rudimentary and ineffective in many countries, not least those embroiled in conflict. The drafting adopted avoids penalising persons who recruited children whom they genuinely considered to be over 15 years of age and who took reasonable measures to confirm their belief, while requiring good faith efforts from recruiters to ensure that those recruited are not underage.

However, whereas Article 77(2) of AP I and Article 38 of the CRC prohibit children under 15 from taking 'a direct part in hostilities', Articles 8(2)(b)(xxvi) and 8(2)(e)(vii) and the Elements of Crimes criminalise using children under 15 to 'participate actively in hostilities'. As we have already seen,[71] there are two views on this: the first, which looks at the term's history and the view of the ICTR, is that 'direct' and 'active' are synonyms; the second, which looks to the negotiating history of the Rome Statute, sees 'active' participation in hostilities as meaning all participation.

It seems likely that this issue will remain open until a decision of the ICC on the point. However, if the interpretation of 'active participation' referred to by the PrepCom is followed, conduct would be criminalised which did not breach the international law rules applicable to states. An individual could be convicted under the Rome Statute in circumstances in which state responsibility could not be incurred. In general, the intention of the drafters of the Rome Statute was to codify rather than develop international criminal law. In this instance, the Statute may have developed international law. If this is correct, however, it does appear that individuals' duties under international law may be wider that states' obligations. Individual criminal responsibility is not derivative of state responsibility, but even so it seems odd that a person acting as a state agent might be criminally responsible for something that the state itself is entitled to do. Alternatively, it may be that states' obligations under customary international law have also widened in a corresponding manner to extend beyond those set out in AP I and the CRC.

Another issue arises with regard to the use of the term 'national armed forces' in Article 8(2)(b)(xxvi). It would appear that it is only recruitment into national armed forces that is criminalised in international armed conflicts. Excluded from the ambit of the offence are those persons who conscript or enlist children under 15 years of age into other military groups participating in such conflicts: guerrillas,

[70] *Ibid.*
[71] See pp. 97–9.

resistance groups, and all other forms of 'private armies'. Enlistment and conscription lead to the same result: the induction of a person into military service. It is simply that enlistment is voluntary, whereas conscription is compulsory. There is no requirement that any further use be made of the person recruited. The enrolment of a child below 15 years of age into the national armed forces in and of itself incurs individual criminal responsibility

It appears that the term was introduced into Article 8(2)(b)(xxvi) to assuage concerns among Arab states that otherwise the participation of Palestinian youth in the *intifada* would be criminalised.[72] This is a misguided concern insofar as the provision does not criminalise children's participation in hostilities. It has nothing to say if children below 15 spontaneously take up arms without adult help or encouragement. However, even if the recruitment of children under 15 into military groups which are not national armed forces is not prohibited under Article 8(2)(b)(xxvi), their use to participate actively in hostilities is criminal. This is, of course, precisely what the Israeli Government alleges the Palestinian leadership does.[73] Whether and, if so, to what extent, such allegations are correct is another matter. They do, however, encourage questions as to what is encompassed by the term 'using' in Article 8(2)(b)(xxvi) and 8(2)(e)(vii). It might be thought, however, that given the purpose of the provisions, the term should be construed broadly. It seems that an unprincipled distinction has been drawn between recruitment into national armed forces and other armed groups involved in international armed conflicts. It could be said that the Rome Statute follow Article 77(2) of AP I, in that that provision only prohibits the recruitment of children under 15 years of age into state parties' armed forces.[74] This is correct but misses the point. Article 77(2) is framed in such a manner because of to whom it is addressed, the states party to it. Article 8(2)(b)(xxvi), by contrast, is addressed not to states but to individuals.

The recruitment and use of child soldiers as the crime of enslavement

It may well be, however, that even prior to 1998, if not a violation of the laws and customs of war, the recruitment and use of child soldiers was an international crime – at least in some circumstances. The Secretary-General's draft of the Statute of the Sierra Leone Special Court listed the '[a]bduction and forced recruitment of children under the age of 15 years into armed forces or groups for the purpose of using them to participate actively in hostilities' as a serious violation of international humanitarian law. The wording of the provision suggests that

[72] The Israeli–Palestinian conflict, it is alleged, is an international armed conflict because the Palestinians are fighting against alien occupation in exercise of their right of self-determination. See Article 1(4) of AP I (to which Israel is not a party).

[73] For the views of the Legal Adviser to the Israeli Foreign Ministry, see A. Baker and H. Ben-Ari, 'The Use of Children in Armed Conflict', *Justice*, No. 26, winter 2000, p. 7.

[74] See Chapter 4, pp. 62–3.

what was objectionable was not the recruitment of children under 15 *per se* but their recruitment by forcible or coercive means and their use for a particular degrading purpose.

Holding a person in slavery or servitude or subjecting him or her to forced or compulsory labour is contrary to international law. It is prohibited in a number of treaties[75] and under customary international law.[76] GC IV prohibits the employment of interned protected persons as forced labourers,[77] and, while other protected persons can be compelled to work, the circumstances in which this can be done are severely limited, with guarantees in respect of wages, hours of work and working conditions.[78] In the Charter of the International Military Tribunal 'deportation to slave labour' was listed as one of the war crimes as within the Tribunal's jurisdiction, while 'enslavement' was included within the list of crimes against humanity. Enslavement was also listed as a crime against humanity in Control Council Law No. 10, and is a crime within the jurisdiction of the ICTY, the ICTR, the ICC and the Special Court for Sierra Leone.

International law originally emphasised the elimination of 'chattel slavery', that is, the situation where the enslaved person is assimilated to a piece of property owned by another. However, the prohibition has progressively widened to include not only slavery but also servitude and forced and compulsory labour. According to the *travaux* to the International Covenant on Civil and Political Rights, slavery has a limited and technical meaning, implying the destruction of the juridical personality. It is primarily a legal category. Servitude, on the other hand, is a more general idea, encompassing all possible forms of humankind's domination over human beings.[79] Tribunals ruling on charges of enslavement have taken the wider view, looking to the factual situation to determine whether the crime has been committed. Cases after the Second World War included forced or compulsory labour under enslavement as a crime against humanity.[80]

[75] Slavery Convention, 60 LNTS 253 (1926); Convention Concerning Forced or Compulsory Labour, 39 UNTS 55 (1930); Supplementary Convention on the Abolition of Slavery, the Slave Trade and Institutions and Practices Similar to Slavery, 266 UNTS 3 (1956); European Convention on Human Rights, ETS No. 5 (1950); International Covenant on Civil and Political Rights, 999 UNTS 171 (1966), American Convention on Human Rights; African Convention on Human and Peoples' Rights; AP II, *op. cit.* note 10.

[76] See *Barcelona Traction* case (*Belgium* v. *Spain*), ICJ Reports (1970) 3, at p. 32; and American Law Institute, *Restatement of the Law, the Third, the Foreign Relations Law of the United States* (1987), vol. 2, para. 702.

[77] Article 95, GC IV.

[78] Articles 40 (concerning the treatment of aliens in the territory of a party to the conflict) and 51 (concerning the treatment of protected persons in occupied territories), GV IV.

[79] See Marc J. Bossuyt, *Guide to the 'Travaux Préparatoires' of the International Covenant on Civil and Political Rights*, Dordrecht: Martinus Nijhof, 1987 p. 167.

[80] See the cases cited in *Prosecutor* v. *Kunarac and others*, Case No. IT-96-23-T and IT-96-23/1-T, judgment of the Trial Chamber, 22 February 2001, paras 523–7.

A recent case before the ICTY, *Prosecutor* v. *Kunarac, Kovać and Vuković*, sets out the contours of the offence. Kunarac and Kovać were charged with enslavement as a crime against humanity under Article 5(c) of the Tribunal's Statute in respect of acts committed during the period 1992–23. Accordingly, the Trial Chamber had to determine the customary international law content of the offence at the relevant time. It held that: 'at the time relevant to the indictment, enslavement as a crime against humanity in customary international law consisted of the exercise of any or all of the powers attaching to the right of ownership over a person'.[81] The *actus reus* of the offence was the exercise of any or all of the powers attaching to the right of ownership over a person. The *mens rea* was that the exercise of such powers was intentional.[82] This definition can be seen as including instances of slavery, servitude, and forced and compulsory labour. One has to look at the factual indicia in order to determine whether the crime had been committed.

> [I]ndications of enslavement include elements of control and ownership; the restriction or control of an individual's autonomy, freedom of choice or freedom of movement; and, often, the accruing of some gain to the perpetrator. The consent or free will of the victim is absent. It is often rendered impossible or irrelevant by, for example, the threat or use of force or other forms of coercion; the fear of violence, deception or false promises; the abuse of power; the victim's position of vulnerability; detention or captivity, psychological oppression or socio-economic conditions. Further indications of enslavement include exploitation; the exaction of forced or compulsory labour or service, often without remuneration and often, though not necessarily, involving physical hardship; sex; prostitution; and human trafficking. … The 'acquisition' or 'disposal' of someone for monetary or other compensation is not a requirement for enslavement.[83]

The Appeals Chamber agreed that whether a particular phenomenon is a form of enslavement depends on the operation of the factors identified by the Trial Chamber.[84] It too considered that the Trial Chamber's definition of the crime of enslavement reflected customary international law at the time the alleged crimes were committed.[85]

Enslavement is listed as a form of crime against humanity within the ICC's jurisdiction in Article 7(1)(c) of the Rome Statute. The ICTY's definition of the crime of enslavement is largely reproduced in the ICC Elements of Crimes. The elements of the crime against humanity of enslavement are that:

1. The perpetrator exercised any or all of the powers attaching to the right of ownership over one or more persons, such as by purchasing, selling, lending or bartering such persons or persons, or by imposing on them a similar deprivation of liberty.

[81] *Ibid.*, para. 539.
[82] *Ibid.*, para. 540.
[83] *Ibid.*, para. 542.
[84] Judgment of the Appeals Chamber, 12 June 2002, para. 119.
[85] *Ibid.*, para. 124.

2. The conduct was committed as part of a widespread or systematic attack directed against a civilian population.
3. The perpetrator knew that the conduct was part of or intended the conduct to be part of a widespread or systematic attack directed against a civilian population.

Element 1, with its emphasis on the ability to transfer ownership as an example of a power attaching to the right of ownership, seems to hark back to the original concentration on chattel slavery. However, the provision also refers to 'similar' deprivations of liberty. A footnote states that such deprivations of liberty could, in appropriate circumstances, include exacting forced labour or otherwise reducing a person to servile status. This would seem to reflect the fact-sensitive approach of the ICTY.

It is clear that child soldiers have been subject to treatment within the definition of enslavement. However, conscription for military service, at least of adults, is generally viewed as lawful. Although individuals have a right not to be subjected to slavery or servitude, or be required to perform forced or compulsory labour, an exception is usually made for service of a military character.[86] Children under 15, however, are immune from conscription (as they all from all forms of recruitment into armed forces and groups), so it is difficult to see how the exception could apply to their recruitment if it falls within the legal definition of enslavement. Strength is added to this argument by the provisions of ILO Convention 182 Concerning the Prohibition and Immediate Action for the Elimination of the Worst Forms of Child Labour. The Convention defined 'the worst forms of child labour' as including: 'all forms of slavery or practices similar to slavery, such as the sale and trafficking of children, debt bondage and serfdom and forced or compulsory labour, including forced or compulsory recruitment of children for use in armed conflict'.[87] It is apparent from the wording of the provision that the states adopting the Convention in July 1999 considered that the forced or compulsory recruitment of children for use in hostilities already amounted to enslavement. Indeed, given the similarity in the wording of Article 3(a) of ILO Convention 182 and article 4(c) of the draft Statute of the Special Court, one can deduce that the former was one of the sources of the latter. In other words, the Secretary-General's draft might be thought to reflect existing customary law because the forced or compulsory recruitment of children for use in armed conflict is a form of enslavement, which is incontestably a crime in customary international law.[88]

[86] See Article 4(3)(b), European Convention on Human Rights, ETS No. 5; (Article 8(c)(ii), ICCPR, *op. cit.* note 43; and Article 6(3)(b), American Convention on Human Rights (1970) 9 ILM 673.

[87] Article 3(a), ILO Convention 182.

[88] The other obvious influences on draft article 4(c) were Article 77(2) of AP I, Article 4(3)(c) of AP II and Article 38 of the CRC. The provision only encompassed the abduction or forced recruitment of children below the age of 15 because the recruitment of children over the age of 15 is lawful. As has been seen, however, ILO Convention 182 categorises the forced or compulsory recruitment of all children as a slavery-type practice. Indeed, it

However, the draft Statute also included enslavement *per se* as a crime against humanity within the jurisdiction of the Special Court.[89] This can be explained as the result of a concern that a particular form of behaviour characteristic of the conflict in Sierra Leone be specifically criminalised in the Statute. On the other hand, the inclusion of enslavement as a crime against humanity and the forced or compulsory recruitment of children for use in armed conflict as a war crime could also be seen as reflecting some confusion about how to categorise the offence.[90] For behaviour to amount to a war crime, it must have taken place during an armed conflict and there must be a link between the armed conflict and the commission of a crime. Crimes against humanity, by contrast, can be committed in times of peace as well as war, but must be part of a widespread or systematic attack against the civilian population. It is submitted that in characterising the forced or compulsory recruitment of children under the age of 15 for the purpose of using them to participate actively in hostilities as a war crime, rather than a crime against humanity, the Secretary-General erred. The offence is merely a sub-set of the crime against humanity of enslavement. Characterisation of the offence as a crime against humanity rather than a war crime would not restrict its applicability in any real manner, as armed forces and groups which do indulge in such behaviour tend to do so systematically.[91]

Conclusions

To sum up, there are two offences related to the recruitment of children into armed forces and groups and their use to participate in hostilities. In the first place, it is a war crime to conscript or enlist children under the age of 15 into armed forces or groups or use them to participate actively in hostilities. In the second, the abduction and forced recruitment of children under the age of 15 years into armed forces or groups can amount to the crime against humanity of enslavement. Indeed, the abduction and use of children for war-related activities and sexual purposes, amounts to enslavement even if they are not formally enrolled into an armed force or group or used to actively participate in hostilities. Both offences are crimes under customary international law. However, the conscription or enlistment of children under the age of 15 into armed forces or groups or their use to participate actively in hostilities may have only recently become a crime under customary

might be thought that provided the elements of the crime of enslavement are made out the forced or compulsory recruitment of any child (or, indeed, any person) is a crime against humanity.

89 The provision also appears in the adopted Statute, as Article 2(e).

90 Indeed, it will be recalled that the Secretary-General appears to have considered that child abduction was a breach of Common Article 3 of the 1949 GCs. See text to note 4.

91 Indeed, it might expand the applicability of the offence.

law, although it seems to have crystallised as custom, at the latest, with the adoption of the ICC Statute in 1998.

The war crime of conscripting or enlisting children under the age of 15 into armed forces and groups or using them to participate in hostilities can be committed in both international and non-international armed conflicts. However, an armed conflict must be in existence at the time the offence was committed and there must be a link between the conflict and the commission of the crime. This latter requirement, it might be thought, is not a particularly onerous one. However, the offence is committed if only one child under 15 years of age is recruited or used to participate actively in hostilities. There is no need to show the existence of any policy to recruit or use such individuals. By contrast, while to prove the crime against humanity of enslavement there is no requirement to show the existence of an armed conflict, it does have to be shown that the offence was part of a widespread or systematic attack against the civilian population.

A final word: what if the facts as alleged in a particular case fall within the definitions of both offences, in other words, if a single act amounts to both crimes? According to the Appeals Chamber of the ICTY in *Prosecutor* v. *Delalić and others*: 'Multiple criminal convictions entered under different statutory provisions but based on the same conduct are permissible only if each statutory provision involved has a materially distinct element not contained in the other. An element is materially distinct from another if it requires proof of a fact not required by the other'.[92] Applying it to the instant situation, it can be seen that proving each offence does require proof of facts not required to prove the other. To prove a war crime one must show that the commission of the crime was linked to an armed conflict. This element need not to be proved to prove the commission of a crime against humanity, but one must show that the offence was part of a widespread systematic attack on the civilian population, which element is in turn not required to prove a war crime. Accordingly, the two offences may be charged cumulatively and the tribunal may convict the defendant of both. However, although the accused can be sentenced for both offences, the two sentences should be served concurrently.

[92] Case No. IT-96-21-A, Appeals Chamber, judgment of 20 February 2001, at para. 339. This test is known as the *Blockburger* test in common law countries after the decision of the US Supreme Court in *US* v. *Blockburger* 284 US 299 (1932) and the 'principle of reciprocal specialty' in civil law jurisdictions. See Cassese, *op. cit.* note 15.

9

The responsibility of child soldiers for war crimes

Introduction

Having considered in the previous chapter the criminality of those who recruit and use child soldiers, in this chapter we will consider the circumstances in which child soldiers themselves might be held criminally responsible for their actions. Child soldiers often act in an undisciplined manner, and the use of child soldiers to commit atrocities is a real problem. However, it will be seen that it is a problem to which international law has been slow to respond.

Governments often seek to penalise child soldiers for their activities, in particular – but not only – when they are members of insurgent groups. In late 2002 the Ugandan authorities brought treason charges against two former LRA fighters: two boys aged 14 and 16. According to Human Rights Watch, the boys had been kidnapped and forcibly inducted into the LRA and had voluntarily surrendered to the Ugandan People's Defence Force.[1] In an open letter, Human Rights Watch urged the Ugandan Government to drop the charges and release the boys to a rehabilitation centre. In April 2003 the Ugandan Government indicated that it would withdraw the charges were the two boys to apply for amnesty, which, on the advice of the Ugandan Director of Public Prosecutions, they promptly did.[2]

In another example, in 2001 Human Rights Watch intervened with the Government of the DRC to urge that death sentences imposed on four child soldiers should not be carried out.[3] The four had been aged between 14 and 16 years old at the time they were arrested, and tried, convicted and sentenced by the Court of Military

[1] Human Rights Watch, 'Uganda: Letter to Minister of Justice', 19 February 2003. See also Human Rights Watch press release, 'Uganda: Drop Treason Charges Against Child Abductees', 4 March 2003.

[2] See J. Eremu, 'Treason Suspects Apply for Amnesty', *New Vision*, 5 April 2003; and 'Treason Charges Against Child Soldiers Dropped', Human Rights Watch, monthly e-mail update, April 2003.

[3] 'Human Rights Watch Letter to Foreign Minister of Democratic Republic of Congo', 2 May 2001.

Order. In the event, the four were not executed,[4] but it appears that earlier, in January 2000, the Congolese Government did execute a 14-year-old child soldier.[5]

In these cases, the crimes charged were based upon domestic law. In internal armed conflicts, incumbent governments are entitled to punish those taken in arms against them. Rebels can be found guilty of treason and, unlike in international armed conflicts, insurgents who kill their opponents in combat are liable to be charged with murder. But conduct can be criminal under domestic law and international law. In a number of recent armed conflicts, child soldiers have behaved in ways that violate international humanitarian law. In Sierra Leone, for example, child soldiers committed numerous atrocities against the civilian population. The negotiations of the Statute of the Special Court for Sierra Leone were marked by controversy over whether the Court should have jurisdiction to prosecute individuals who were children at the time they allegedly committed crimes.

All persons, whether combatants or not,[6] have a duty to comply with international humanitarian law. Failure to do so can give rise to criminal sanctions. However, one of the reasons why armed forces and groups recruit child soldiers is that they are more suggestible than adults. Children are less socialised, and more docile and malleable than adults, and hence are more obedient and more easily coerced into committing atrocities. Even if not specifically recruited for such purposes, children's lack of mettle and moral development may mean that they are more prone to behave badly than adult troops. In addition, children often do not serve willingly, but because they have been abducted or forcibly recruited; they are subjected to abuse and brutalising treatment; and their continued participation is maintained through threats and coercion. At times child soldiers have been given drugs and/or alcohol by their commanders to lessen their inhibitions. The question is: to what extent should such factors serve to exclude, or at least mitigate, child soldiers' legal culpability for their actions?

Accordingly, we will consider the consequences of children's mental and moral immaturity for their criminal responsibility for their actions, and the availability of a defence of duress in respect of child soldiers' responsibility for atrocities, given that their participation in hostilities is frequently coerced. It will, however, be seen that international law provides only vague guidelines with regard to the minimum age of criminal responsibility and only permits duress as a defence to international crimes in very limited circumstances. We will also look at the scope of the defence of intoxication, although it will be seen quickly that this defence raises fewer issues, as it applies to children in much the same manner as it does to adults.

[4] 'Congo Spares Child Soldiers', Human Rights Watch, monthly e-mail update, June 2001.

[5] 'Congo: Don't Execute Child Soldiers: Four Children to be Put to Death', Human Rights Watch press release, 2 May 2001.

[6] See *Heinrich Gerike and others*, British Military Court sitting at Brunswick, verdict of 3 April 1946, in G. Brand (ed.), *Trial of Heinrich Gerike*, William Hodge & Co.: London, Edinburg and Glasgow, 1950; and *Bruno Tesch and Others*, British Military Court sitting at Hamburg, verdict of 8 March 1946, I Law Reports of Trials of War Criminals 93.

Infancy and individual criminal responsibility

Most systems of criminal law take the view that before a person can be held blameworthy and, hence, punishable, his behaviour must have contained an element of fault. To be guilty of a crime, particularly with regard to serious offences, it is not enough simply to have done a particular prohibited act; there must be the requisite *mens rea* as well as the *actus reus*.[7] Consequently, it is possible to escape criminal liability by showing that one was lacking a guilty mind, for example that the act was committed accidentally rather than intentionally, or while in a state of automatism.

In respect of one class of person, however, a lack of *means rea* is presumed. As Simester and Sullivan write in relation to the defence of infancy: 'Although it is a defence of status (no-one under 10 years of age [the minimum age of criminal responsibility in England and Wales] can commit a crime), the status is predicated on assumptions concerning a person's mental development and consequent moral irresponsibility for her actions'.[8] Children are considered *doli incapax*: incapable of evil. By virtue of this presumption, they escape criminal liability for their acts.[9] However, with regard to the criminal responsibility of child soldiers, a problem immediately arises. It is unclear what the minimum age of criminal responsibility in respect of international crimes actually is. Indeed, it is unclear whether international law fixes a minimum age of criminal responsibility at all. Although it is clear that too low a national minimum age of criminal responsibility will breach international law, where the line is to be drawn has not been specified.

Additional Protocol I

The issue arose in during the negotiations of AP I. There, the representative of Brazil proposed that what is now Article 77(5) of the Protocol[10] be amended to add the sentence: 'Penal proceedings shall not be taken against, and sentence not pronounced on, persons who were under sixteen years at the time the offence was committed'.[11] The proposed amendment was not accepted. However, the Italian representative, without objecting to the article as it was adopted, stated that he would have wished that it included an additional paragraph prohibiting any criminal prosecution and conviction of children for offences which at the time of

[7] See A. Ashworth, *Principles of Criminal Law*, Oxford: Oxford University Press, 3rd edn, 1999, pp. 87–8.

[8] A.P. Simester and G.R. Sullivan, *Criminal Law: Theory and Doctrine*, Oxford: Hart, 1st edn, 2000, p. 541.

[9] *Ibid.*, pp. 644–5.

[10] Article 77(5) prohibits the execution of the death penalty for offences related to an international armed conflict on persons who had not attained the age of 18 years at the time when the crime was committed.

[11] O.R. III, p. 307, CDDH/III/325.

commission they were too young to understand the consequences of their actions.[12] Committee III, to whom the draft article had been assigned, agreed that there was a general principle that a person cannot be convicted of an offence if, at the time he committed it, he was unable to understand the consequences of his act. The Committee decided, however, to leave the issue to national regulation. One might consider such a rule a general principle of law and, as such, a rule of international law.[13] However, the rule would seem to permit states either to fix a minimum age below which children are presumed not to be criminally responsible or to determine culpability on an individual basis, by applying a test of whether an accused understood the consequences of his acts at the time he committed them.

It has occasionally been argued that Article 77(2) itself fixes the minimum age of criminal responsibility for war crimes at 15. Such a reading of the provision is based on the idea that if a child under 15 is too young to fight he should also be considered to be too young to be held criminally responsible for his actions. Such a reading of Article 77(2) is, however, unwarranted. It is unsupported by the text itself, which makes no reference to child soldiers' criminal responsibility. And, as we have already seen, the negotiators specifically decided to include no such provision in the final text of Article 77. This is not to say, however, that the ideas standing behind such a reading of Article 77(2) have not been influential in debates about what should be the minimum age of criminal responsibility for international crimes.

The CRC

The CRC took matters a little further. Article 40(3)(a) provides that state parties to the CRC shall seek to establish a minimum age below which children shall be presumed not to have the capacity to infringe the criminal law. However, no minimum age of criminal responsibility is stipulated. All that the CRC requires of states is that they establish a minimum age of criminal responsibility. It is left to each state to decide what that age should be.

The relevant provisions of the United Nations Standard Minimum Rules on the Administration of Juvenile Justice ('the Beijing Rules') and their commentary[14] are, however, more enlightening. Article 40 of the CRC was drafted so as to reflect the approaches to juvenile justice taken in the Beijing Rules,[15] and although the Rules and their commentary are not in themselves binding, they do provide an indication of the shared thinking of states on the issue. Rule 4, on the age of

[12] O.R. XV, p. 219, CDDH/II/SR.59.

[13] See also G. Van Bueren, *The International Law on the Rights of the Child*, Dordrecht: Martinus Nijhof, 1995, p. 173.

[14] G.A. Res. 40/33, annex, 40 UN GAOR Supp. (No. 53) at 207, UN Doc. A/40/53 (1985).

[15] See S. Detrick, *A Commentary on the United Nations Convention on the Rights of the Child*, Dordrecht: Martinus Nijhof, 1998, p. 700.

criminal responsibility, is not particularly helpful, merely stating that: 'In those legal systems recognising the concept of the age of criminal responsibility for juveniles, the beginning of that age shall not be fixed at too low an age limit, bearing in mind the facts of emotional, mental and intellectual maturity'. This seems to require even less than the CRC, as there is no obligation to establish a minimum age of criminal responsibility. However, the commentary to the rule is more interesting. It sees disparities in national minimum ages of criminal responsibility as the product of historical and cultural differences. It goes on to say that:

> The modern approach would be to consider whether a child can live up to the moral and psychological components of criminal responsibility; that is, whether a child, by virtue of his or her individual discernment and understanding, can be held responsible for antisocial behaviour. If the age of criminal responsibility is fixed too low or if there is no lower age limit at all, the notion of responsibility would become meaningless.

In other words, criminal responsibility should only be imposed when there is some element of fault, that is, sufficient mental and moral awareness on the part of the individual committing the prohibited act of the consequences or potential consequences of his actions. The commentary also links the imposition of criminal responsibility to the granting of civil rights, such as the right to marry and the right to vote. Such rights, of course, are frequently only granted from age 16, 17 or 18. The commentary ends by stating that efforts should be made to agree an international standard minimum age of criminal responsibility. Unfortunately, no such agreement has yet been possible.

Elucidation of the requirements of Article 40(3)(a) of the CRC has been given by the Committee of the Rights of the Child, established under the CRC to monitor states' compliance with its provisions.[16] In its comments on states' periodic reports, on a number of occasions the Committee has expressed concern when it appears that no minimum age of criminal responsibility has been fixed.[17] In a general discussion on the administration of juvenile justice,[18] the Committee considered that criminal responsibility should not be determined by reference to subjective factors, such as 'the attainment of puberty, the age of discernment or the personality of the child',[19] as doing so led to invidious discrimination. The implication is that only objective factors, such as age, are appropriate criteria. The reason for this was given during discussion of Senegal's initial report to the Committee. There, a Committee member stated that:

> She was concerned that children's judges were given the possibility of considering that a child could be criminally responsible on the basis of his personality. However,

[16] See Article 43 CRC.

[17] See the instances listed in R. Hodgkin and P. Newell, *Implementation Handbook for the Convention on the Rights of the Child*, London: UNICEF, 1998, p. 551.

[18] See Committee on the Rights of the Child, Report on the Tenth Session (Geneva, 30 October–17 November 1995), UN Doc. CRC/C/46 (18 December 1995), paras 203–38.

[19] *Ibid.*, para. 218.

> if there was a minimum age below which the law recognized that no child could infringe the criminal law, then there could be no possibility for differences of interpretation.[20]

However, the Committee has been less definite on at what age the minimum age of criminal responsibility should be fixed. The Committee has frequently expressed concern that the minimum age set by states has been too low,[21] but it has not expressed a view on what it should be.

The European Court of Human Rights

An interesting discussion of this issue did take place in the recent judgments of the European Court of Human Rights in *T.* v. *United Kingdom* and *V.* v. *United Kingdom.*[22] Both T and V were 10 years old when they abducted and killed a 2-year-old boy. Aged 11, they were tried in public in an adult court before a judge and jury (although some allowances were made for their age), convicted of murder and abduction, and sentenced to an indefinite period of detention. They applied to the European Court of Human Rights on the ground, among others, that their treatment had violated Article 3 of the European Convention on Human Rights, which prohibits torture and other inhuman or degrading treatment or punishment.

The Court concluded that the attribution to the applicants of criminal responsibility for their acts did not violate Article 3. It found Article 4 of the Beijing Rules and Article 40(3)(a) of the CRC of little help, even though the Committee on the Rights of the Child had recommended that the UK give serious consideration to raising its minimum age of criminal responsibility.[23] Nor did it consider that there was any common standard as to the minimum age of criminal responsibility among the Member States of the Council of Europe.[24] At the time, the age of criminal responsibility was 7 in Cyprus, Ireland, Liechtenstein and Switzerland; 8 in Scotland; 13 in France; 14 in Austria, Germany, Italy and many eastern European States; 15 in the Scandinavian states; 16 in Andorra, Portugal and Poland; and 18 in Belgium, Luxembourg and Spain. Consequently, the Court held that: 'Even if England and Wales is among the few European jurisdictions to retain a low age of criminal responsibility, the age of ten cannot be said to be so young as to differ disproportionately from the age-limit followed by other European States. The Court concludes that the attribution of criminal responsibility does not in itself give rise to a breach of Article 3 of the Convention'.[25]

[20] UN Doc. CRC/C/SR/248, at para. 26.

[21] See Hodgkin and Newell, *op. cit.* note 17, at pp. 551–2.

[22] *T* v. *United Kingdom* and *V* v. *United Kingdom* (2000) 30 EHRLR 121. The two cases were heard together.

[23] Concluding Observations on the United Kingdom's Initial Report, UN Doc. CRC/15/add. 34 (1995), at para. 34. See *ibid.*, pp. 145–6.

[24] *Op. cit.* note 22, p. 146.

[25] *Ibid.*, p. 176.

One might consider that a practice is not unusual is not, of itself, enough to legitimise it. A number of common practices breach the human rights of those subjected to them. In addition, in basing its conclusions on the lack of consensus among the contracting states, the Court granted states a wide margin of appreciation in respect of an issue within the scope of Article 3, which is an absolute, non-derogable right. In a joint partly dissenting opinion, Judges Pastor Ridruejo, Ress, Makarcyzk, Tulkens and Butkevych disagreed with the majority's assessment. Standards could be ascertained from the relevant international instruments and the practice of the Member States of the Council of Europe. In the dissenting judges' view:

> Only four Contracting States out of forty-one are prepared to find criminal responsibility at an age as low as, or lower than, that applicable in England and Wales. We have no doubt that there is a general standard among the member States of the Council of Europe under which there is a system of relative criminal responsibility beginning at the age of thirteen or fourteen – with special court procedures for juveniles – and providing for full criminal responsibility at the age of eighteen or above. … Even if Rule 4 of the Beijing Rules does not specify a minimum age of criminal responsibility, the very warning that the age should not be fixed too low indicates that criminal responsibility and maturity are related concepts. It is clearly the view of the vast majority of Contracting States that this kind of maturity is not present in children below the age of thirteen of fourteen.[26]

Taking the age of criminal responsibility together with the trial procedure and sentencing, there had been a breach of Article 3.[27] The minority stated that: 'Bringing the whole weight of the adult criminal process to bear on children as young as eleven is, in our view, a relic of times where the effect of the trial process and sentencing on a child's physical and psychological conditions and development as a human being was scarcely considered, if at all'.[28] At least with regard to whether there are any emerging standards as to the minimum age of criminal responsibility, it is submitted that the reasoning of the minority of the Court is to be preferred.

The Statute of the Special Court for Sierra Leone

Consideration of the minimum age of criminal responsibility also recently took place during the drafting of the Statute of the Special Court for Sierra Leone. The statutes of international criminal tribunals drafted previously had ignored or avoided the issue. The statutes of the ICTY and the ICTR did not include any provisions governing the age of criminal responsibility[29] and neither tribunal has indicted any

[26] *Ibid.*, p. 203.
[27] *Ibid.*, p. 202.
[28] *Ibid.*
[29] See the Report of the Secretary-General Pursuant to para. 2 of SC Res. No. 808 (1993), UN Doc. S/25704, reprinted in (1993) 32 ILM 1170, at para. 58: 'The international tribunal [for the former Yugoslavia] will have to decide on various personal defences which may relieve a person of individual criminal responsibility, such as minimum age or mental incapacity, drawing upon the general principles of law recognised by all nations'.

person below the age of 18. The issue was addressed in the Rome Statute of the ICC, but not in any enlightening manner. Article 26 of the Statute provides that: 'The Court shall have no jurisdiction over any person who was under the age of 18 at the time of the alleged commission of the offence'. It is clear both from the language of the article and its drafting history that the provision is procedural rather than substantive in nature. It is simply the jurisdiction of the ICC that is excluded, leaving the treatment of child war criminals to national courts.[30] Indeed, it appears that one of the reasons for this exclusion of jurisdiction was to avoid arguments as to what the minimum age of responsibility for international crimes should be.[31] The NGO Caucus on Children's Rights in the ICC had called for the Statute to determine a minimum age at which individuals could be held criminally responsible for crimes within the Court's jurisdiction, which they argued should be 18.[32] However, national approaches differ considerably and during the negotiations suggestions as to where the minimum age of criminal responsibility should be fixed varied between 12 to 18 years of age.[33] A jurisdictional solution was adopted to sidestep these disagreements.

However, with regard to the Statute of the Special Court for Sierra Leone, the issue could not be avoided. In the conflict there, child soldiers tortured, maimed, raped and killed. Those same children, however, had frequently been abducted and forcibly recruited into armed groups, and subjected to sustained abuse by their comrades. In his report on the establishment of a Special Court, the UN Secretary-General acknowledged the difficulty of prosecuting child soldiers for war crimes and crimes against humanity, given their dual status as both victims and perpetrators.[34] His report described considerable disagreement as to how juvenile offenders should be dealt with. According to the Secretary-General:

> The question of child prosecution was discussed at length with the Government of Sierra Leone both in New York and in Freetown. It was raised with all the interlocutors of the United Nations team; the members of the judiciary, members of the legal profession and the Ombudsman, and was vigorously debated with members of civil society, non-governmental organizations and institutions actively engaged in child-care and rehabilitation programmes.
>
> The Government of Sierra Leone and representatives of Sierra Leone civil society clearly wish to see a process of judicial accountability for child combatants presumed

[30] See R.S. Clark and O. Triffterer, 'Article 26: exclusion of jurisdiction over persons under eighteen', in O. Triffterer (ed.), *Commentary on the Rome Statute of the International Criminal Court: Observers' Notes, Article by Article*, Baden-Baden: Nomos Verlag, 1999, p. 499.

[31] *Ibid*., p. 497.

[32] Caucus on Children's Rights in the ICC, 'Recommendations and Commentary for the December 1997 Preparatory Committee Meeting on the Establishment of an International Criminal Court'.

[33] Clark and Triffterer, *op. cit.* note 30, p. 495.

[34] Report of the Secretary-General on the Establishment of a Special Court for Sierra Leone, UN Doc. S/2000/915, 4 October 2000.

> responsible for the crimes falling within the jurisdiction of the Court. It is said that the people of Sierra Leone would not look kindly upon a court which failed to bring to justice children who committed crimes of that nature and spared them the judicial process of accountability. The international non-governmental organizations responsible for child-care and rehabilitation programmes, together with some of their national counterparts, however, were unanimous in their objections to any kind of judicial accountability for children below 18 years of age for fear that such a process would place at risk the entire rehabilitation programme so painstakingly achieved.[35]

Similarly, when in October 2000 eleven members of the Security Council visited Sierra Leone, they reported that:

> The possibility that children should be prosecuted by the Special Court was the subject of animated debate in Sierra Leone and there appeared to be no prevailing view. In the view of the Government of Sierra Leone, the Court should prosecute those child combatants who freely and willingly committed indictable crimes. On the other hand, non-governmental and United Nations agencies, especially those engaged in the protection of children, favoured excluding those under the age of 18 years.[36]

In the end, the mission made no recommendations in relation to the establishment of the Special Court, stating that the issues required further discussion by the Security Council.[37]

Article 7(1) of the Secretary-General's draft Statute provided that; 'The Special Court shall have jurisdiction over persons who were 15 years of age at the time of the alleged commission of the crime'. Why the Secretary-General fixed 15 as the minimum age of criminal responsibility was not made clear, but it seems likely that the decision was made to mirror the provisions of the two APs and the CRC, on the ground that if children under 15 are too young to be recruited, they must be too young to be held responsible for their actions. The Secretary-General's draft also provided that:

> At all stages of the proceedings, including investigation, prosecution and adjudication, an accused below the age of 18 (hereinafter 'a juvenile offender') shall be treated with dignity and a sense of worth, taking into account his or her young age and the desirability of promoting his or her rehabilitation, reintegration into and assumption of a constructive role in society.[38]

There followed a number of guarantees for juvenile offenders: only exceptionally should a juvenile offender be denied bail; a juvenile offender should be tried before a specially constituted 'Juvenile Chamber'; a juvenile offender's trial should be separated from those of any co-accused adults; the parent or legal guardian of a juvenile offender should be permitted to participate in the proceedings; the Special

[35] *Ibid.*, paras 34–5.

[36] Report of the Security Council mission to Sierra Leone, UN Doc. S/2000/992 (16 October 2000), para. 50.

[37] *Ibid.*, para. 54(b).

[38] Article 7(2), draft statute, *ibid.*, enclosure.

Court should provide protective measures, including but not limited to the protection of his identity and *in camera* proceedings, to ensure the juvenile offender's privacy; the Court could not punish a juvenile offender by imprisonment. These provisions closely followed (and went beyond) those concerned with juvenile justice in the ICCPR and the CRC.[39]

The Secretary-General's advocacy of these provisions cannot be seen as unreserved. In his report, he simply stated that he considered 'that it would be most prudent to demonstrate to the Security Council for its consideration how provisions on prosecution of persons below the age of 18 ... before an international jurisdiction could be formulated'.[40] Indeed, he concluded by saying that: 'ultimately, it will be for the Prosecutor to decide if, all things considered, action should be taken against a juvenile offender in any individual case'.[41] However, all the Security Council did to Article 7 was to shorten it so that it read that:

> Should any person who was at the time of the alleged commission of the crime below 18 years of age come before the Court, he or she shall be treated with dignity and a sense of worth, taking into account his or her young age and the desirability of promoting his or her rehabilitation, reintegration into and assumption of a constructive role in society, and in accordance with human rights standards, in particular the rights of the child.[42]

This was, it might be thought, less satisfactory than the Secretary-General's draft, as it failed to set out the human rights standards that should apply to the trial of any juvenile offenders. Even more significantly, the revised Article 7 failed to include any minimum age of criminal responsibility for crimes within the Special Court's jurisdiction. However, the wording of the revised provision implied that any such prosecutions would be exceptional. Such a reading is confirmed in the Security Council's comments on the Secretary-General's draft; 'the simplified and more general formulations suggested' were considered appropriate because the Council considered that the Special Court should concentrate on prosecuting persons who played a leadership role in the conflict in Sierra Leone.[43] Instead, the Council considered that the Truth and Reconciliation Commission established under the Lomé Peace Agreement[44] should play the major role in the case of juvenile offenders.

In his reply to the Council, the Secretary-General suggested amendments to the revised Article 7. He stated that even if jurisdiction of the Court was limited to persons bearing the greatest responsibility for crimes committed during the conflict

[39] See, in particular, Articles 10(2)(b), 10(3), 14(1) and 14(4) of the ICCPR; and Articles 37(b), 37(c), 37(d), 40(1), 40(2)(b)(ii), 40(2)(b)(vii) and 40(4) of the CRC.

[40] *Ibid.*, para. 36.

[41] *Ibid.*, para. 38.

[42] Letter dated 22 December 2000 from the President of the Security Council addressed to the Secretary-General, UN Doc. S/2000/1234, Annex.

[43] *Ibid.*, para. 1.

[44] UN Doc. S/1999/777.

in Sierra Leone, the determination of which individuals bore such responsibility would be made, in the first instance, by the Prosecutor, and would therefore 'have to be reconciled with an eventual prosecution of juveniles ... even if such prosecutions are unlikely'.[45] The Secretary-General expressed his understanding that the Security Council's revised draft was not intended to allow the prosecution of persons for crimes committed below 15 years of age and that the reference to human rights standards encompassed all the guarantees of juvenile justice set out in his draft,[46] and suggested that Article 7 be amended to read that:

> 1. The Special Court shall have no jurisdiction over any person who was under the age of 15 at the time of the alleged commission of the crime. Should any person who was at the time of the alleged commission of the crime between 15 and 18 years of age come before the Court, he or she shall be treated with dignity and a sense of worth, taking into account his or her young age and the desirability of promoting his or her rehabilitation, reintegration into and assumption of a constructive role in society, and in accordance with international human rights standards, in particular the rights of the child.
> 2. In the disposition of a case against a juvenile offender, the Special Court shall order any of the following: care guidance and supervision orders, community service orders, counselling, foster care, correctional, educational and vocational training programmes, approved schools and, as appropriate, any programmes of disarmament, demobilization and reintegration or programmes of child protection agencies.

Paragraph 2 reproduced *verbatim* the provisions of Article 7(3)(f) of the Secretary-General's original draft. The Secretary-General's suggested amendments were accepted by the Security Council and the Government of Sierra Leone and were incorporated into the Statute of the Special Court.

None of the persons indicted by the Prosecutor of the Special Court is accused of crimes committed while a child, and it does not appear that the Special Court will see any prosecutions of juvenile offenders. The Special Court's Statute provides that its function is 'to prosecute persons who bear the greatest responsibility' for the atrocities committed during the conflict in Sierra Leone'.[47] Security Council Resolution 1315,[48] which requested the Secretary-General to negotiate an agreement with the Government of Sierra Leone establishing the Special Court, stated that Court:

> Should have personal jurisdiction over persons who bear the greatest responsibility for the commission of the crimes referred to in paragraph 2 [crimes against humanity, war crimes and other serious violations of international humanitarian law, as well as crimes under relevant Sierra Leonean law committed within the territory of

[45] Letter dated 12 January 2001 from the Secretary-General Addressed to the President of the Security Council, UN Doc. S/2001/40, para. 2.

[46] *Ibid*., paras 7–8.

[47] Statute of the Special Court for Sierra Leone, Article 1(1).

[48] SC Res. 1315 of 14 August 2000.

> Sierra Leone], including those leaders who, in committing such crimes, have threatened the establishment of and implementation of the peace process in Sierra Leone.[49]

The Secretary-General's draft omitted the leadership criterion, arguing that the term 'persons most responsible' should be viewed as including not only the political and military leadership but also others responsible for particular grave or serious crimes.[50] On this reading, according to the Secretary-General, children could fall within the Court's personal jurisdiction.[51] However, the Security Council restored the reference to those persons who played a leadership role,[52] and the Special Court's Statute again categorises 'those leaders who, in committing such crimes, have threatened the establishment and implementation of the peace process' as among those persons most responsible. Given this focus, it was always unlikely that any juvenile offenders would be tried before the Special Court.[53] The general view, expressed by both the Security Council[54] and the Secretary-General,[55] was that juvenile offenders were best dealt with by the Truth and Reconciliation Commission. Indeed, the Prosecutor took an early opportunity to state that, as a matter of policy, he did not intend to indict persons for crimes committed when children.[56]

Conclusions

A number of tentative conclusions can be drawn from this rather disparate material. States are obliged to establish a minimum age of criminal responsibility, which should be fixed and not determined on an individual basis by reference to an accused's personal characteristics. However, although international law dictates that states have a minimum age of criminal responsibility, it does not purport to tell them what that age should be. It does, however, offer a number of guidelines. First, the age should not be so low as to result in the punishment of children for offences in respect of which, at the time of their commission, they were too young to understand the consequences of their actions. This would seem to be a general principle of law. Second, there may a trend to standardise the minimum age of criminal responsibility somewhere in the mid-teens (13, 14, 15). This was the approach taken by the minority in the *T* and *V* Cases and by the UN

[49] *Ibid.*, para. 3.
[50] *Op. cit.* note 34, para. 30.
[51] *Ibid.*, para. 31.
[52] *Op. cit.* note 44, para. 1.
[53] See the comments of Hans Corell, UN Under-Secretary-General for Legal Affairs, in C. McGreal, 'Unique Court to Try Killers of Sierra Leone', *Guardian*, 17 January 2002, and David Crane, Special Court Prosecutor, in R. Dowden, 'Justice Goes on Trial in Sierra Leone, *Guardian*, 3 October 2002.
[54] See text to note 42.
[55] *Op. cit.* note 45, para. 9.
[56] 'Special Court Prosecutor Says He Will Not Prosecute Children', Special Court for Sierra Leone, Public Affairs Office, Press Release, 2 November 2002.

Secretary-General (with whom the Security Council agreed) when drafting the Special Court's Statute.[57] Third, even children above the age of criminal responsibility should be treated differently from adults. Here the drafting history of the Statute of the Special Court is particularly relevant. The Statute closely follows Article 40 of the CRC and emphasises that the purpose of juvenile justice is rehabilitation. The Secretary-General's draft also set out a list of guarantees of juvenile justice. Indeed, in some respects it went further than the relevant human rights instrument: providing that all trials of children be held *in camera* and prohibiting the Court from imprisoning juvenile offenders. In the final version of the Statute much of this language disappeared but a requirement that the Court adhere to international human right standards was retained. Moreover, both the Security Council and the Secretary-General were *ad idem* that prosecution before the Special Court should be a last resort. Their attitude that juvenile offenders be dealt with by the Truth and Reconciliation Commission mirrors Article 40(3)(b) of the CRC, which provides that states shall seek to promote, 'whenever appropriate and desirable, measures for dealing with such children without resorting to judicial proceedings'.

However, even if the Statute and practice of the Special Court can be seen as an example of 'best practice', states are still left with a considerable amount of discretion. Indeed, the to-and-fro between the Secretary-General and the Security Council, and the variety of opinions expressed by the Government of Sierra Leone, local civil society and international NGOs serve to show serious differences about and uncertainties as to how children alleged to have committed serious crimes should be dealt with.

Difficulties arising

That states retain considerable discretion as to when to fix their minimum age of criminal responsibility can be seen as giving rise to difficulties. It is generally admitted that the perpetrators of genocide, war crimes and crimes against humanity are subject to universal jurisdiction.[58] Any state into whose hands they fall may prosecute and punish them. Indeed, state parties to the Geneva Conventions and Additional Protocols are obliged to do so in the case of persons who have committed 'grave breaches' of the Conventions and Protocols.[59] In cases involving child soldiers, it would appear perfectly proper for states to apply their own domestic law as to the minimum age of criminal responsibility providing such law falls within the broad limits set out above. This might be seen as likely to lead to arbitrariness and unfairness. To a large extent, whether a child soldier can be prosecuted for international crimes would seem to depend on the minimum age of

[57] Which was, of course, adopted by the Security Council and the Government of Sierra Leone.

[58] See Ian Brownlie, *Principles of Public International Law*, Oxford: Oxford University Press, 5th edn, 2003, pp. 303–5.

[59] Articles 49/50/129/146, 1949 GCs and Article 85, AP I.

criminal responsibility of the state prosecuting him. A suspect found in a country with a low minimum age of criminal responsibility might be prosecuted, when his comrades, who had escaped to a state with a higher one, could not be. Alternatively, a child soldier might be under the age of criminal responsibility of the state in which he committed atrocities, but having fled elsewhere, to somewhere with a lower minimum age, might open himself to criminal prosecution.

It might be thought that this problem is a somewhat theoretical one. Certainly, states have not shown themselves eager to prosecute child soldiers who fall into their hands. When child soldiers have been prosecuted, as has been seen, it has been for domestic crimes. Indeed, this writer knows of no examples of prosecutions of child soldiers by states other than those in which the alleged crimes have taken place. In recent years, however, at least some states have displayed a greater willingness to prosecute international crimes, even in cases where their own nationals have not been involved either as perpetrators or victims. In addition, there is already one context in which the issue is a live one. Under Article 1F(a) of the Convention relating to the Status of Refugees, states are obliged to refuse refugee status to any persons 'with respect to whom there are serious reasons for considering that ... he has committed ... war crime or a crime against humanity'. Former child soldiers can be, and have been, excluded from refugee status by the application of Article 1F.[60]

Duress as a defence

But what if the child soldier is above the minimum age of criminal responsibility? As with any other accused, child soldiers might be able to avail themselves of any of a number of grounds for excluding criminal responsibility. One defence seems immediately relevant. Given that children's' recruitment into armed forces and groups is often coerced, it might be thought that if faced with prosecution they should be able to avail themselves of the defence of duress by threats.

Duress differs as a defence from infancy. Although formally a status defence, infancy as a defence derives its rationale from a belief that children lack the necessary mental and moral development to comprehend fully the consequences of their actions. Accordingly, a lack of *mens rea* is presumed. A defendant who claims duress, however, is not saying that he did not intend to do what he did,[61] but rather that, faced with an imminent and unavoidable threat aimed at persuading him to

[60] See UNHCR, 'The Exclusion Clauses: Guidelines on Their Application' (December 1995), reproduced in P.J. van Krieken (ed.), *Refugee Law in Context: The Exclusion Clause*, The Hague: T.M.C. Asser Instituut, 1999, p. 22; and S. Kaepferer, 'Exclusion Clauses in Europe – a Comparative Overview of State Practice in France, Belgium and the United Kingdom' (2000) 12 IJRL 194, p. 214.

[61] See J.C. Smith, *Smith and Hogan: Criminal Law*, London: Butterworths, 10th edn, 2002, pp. 252–3.

commit the offence, he had no viable alternative but to do as he was told.[62] Duress is a defence because: 'Threats of immediate death or serious personal violence so great as to overbear the ordinary power of human resistance should be accepted as a justification for acts which would otherwise be criminal'.[63] In such circumstances, society cannot seriously expect individuals to refuse to comply with the demands made upon them and, given this, they should not be held criminally liable for their actions. Morally, such a refusal might be laudable, but it is praiseworthy because it goes beyond what might reasonably be expected of a person and, in such circumstances, the criminal law will not demand that we all be heroes.[64] Although the law does not approve of the conduct of a person acting under duress, it is not considered blameworthy and, hence, punishable.

However, an issue arises in relation to the ambit of the defence. The defence of duress is not the same in all legal systems. Whereas, in general, duress can constitute a complete defence to all criminal charges in civil law systems,[65] in almost all common law legal systems it is not a defence to charges of murder.[66] This might be thought to be unsatisfactory. Take one hypothetical example. Two child soldiers face prosecution in a state with a common law legal system which does not permit duress as a defence to murder. Both are over the minimum age of criminal responsibility. It transpires that they were each required by their commanders, under threat of immediate execution, to cut of a person's hands. In both cases, the intention was not to kill the person, but merely to inflict grievous bodily harm so that the victims would serve as living examples of the armed group's ruthlessness towards its opponents. However, the person mutilated by Child A dies of his wounds, while the person mutilated by Child B does not. In that case, Child A could be convicted of murder (as an intention to inflict grievous bodily harm is sufficient to provide

[62] In English law, the threats must have been such that 'a sober person of reasonable firmness' would not have resisted them: see *R* v. *Graham* (1982) 74 Cr App R 255 (CA). However, in *R* v. *Bowen* [1985] Crim LR 220, the Court of Appeal refined the issue: the relevant question is what a sober person of reasonable firmness sharing the characteristics of the defendant (including his age) would have done.

[63] *Attorney-General* v. *Whelan* [1934] IR 518, *per* Murnaghen J at p. 526 (Irish Court of Criminal Appeal). Strictly speaking, of course, in most circumstances the defence provides an excuse for, rather than a justification of, the defendant's conduct: see Paul H. Robinson, 'Criminal Law Defences: a Systematic Analysis (1982) 82 Columbia LR 245.

[64] See J.C. Smith, *Justification and Excuse in Criminal Law*, London: Stevens, 1988, p. 94.

[65] See the provisions in the penal codes of France, Belgium, the Netherlands, Spain, Germany, Italy, Norway, Sweden, Finland, Nicaragua, Chile, Panama, Mexico and Yugoslavia reproduced in *Prosecutor* v. *Drazen Erdemović*, Case No. IT-96-22-T, Judgment of the Appeals Chamber of the ICTY, 7 October 1997, Joint Separate Opinion of Judges McDonald and Vohrah, para. 59.

[66] For the situation in English law, see *Abbott* v. *The Queen* [1977] AC 755 (PC); *R* v. *Howe* [1987] AC 417 (HL), and *R* v. *Gotts* [1992] 2 AC 412 (HL). For an examination of recent English and American approaches to the issue, see Alan Reed, 'Duress and Provocation as Excuses to Murder: Salutary Lessons from recent Anglo-American Jurisprudence' (1997) 6 Journal of Transnational Law & Policy 51.

the *mens rea* for the crime of murder) and could not rely on the defence of duress, but Child B, charged with inflicting grievous bodily harm, could.[67] Indeed, the present situation in English law has been the subject of extensive and cogent academic criticism.[68] However, the policy reasons given by the House of Lords for maintaining the distinction between murder and attempted murder and other crimes would seem to apply with equal force to murder-type crimes, such as war crimes and crimes against humanity involving killing. In such situations, given the sanctity afforded to human life, it may be that the law does require that we all be heroes and refuse to save our own lives at the expense of those of others.[69]

This was the view taken by the majority of the Appeals Chamber of the ICTY in the *Erdemović* case.[70] Erdemović had been charged with a crime against humanity and a war crime in respect of his participation in a Bosnian Serb firing squad following the fall of Srebrenica in 1995. Before a Trial Chamber of the Tribunal, he pleaded guilty to the charge of a crime against humanity, but added that he would have been killed had he refused to join the firing squad.[71] The Trial Chamber accepted Erdemović's guilty plea and sentenced him to ten years' imprisonment.[72] Erdemović appealed against his sentence. In determining his appeal, the Appeals Chamber examined whether a plea of duress, rather than serving as a mitigating factor, could serve as a defence to war crimes and crimes against humanity involving killing.

The majority of the Appeals Chamber (Judges McDonald, Vohrah and Li) considered that it could not. Judges McDonald and Vohrah did so largely on the grounds put forward by the British House of Lords.[73] Judge Li accepted the submissions of the prosecutor that tribunals since the Second World War had laid down a rule of customary international law that duress could only be pleaded in mitigation.[74] However, in his separate and dissenting opinion, President Cassese gave a lengthy and convincing rebuttal to this argument.[75] Like Judges McDonald and Vohrah, President Cassese was unable to discover any international rules determining whether duress was a valid defence to international crimes involving killing. Unlike them, however, he held that as it was a general principle of law that duress did amount to a defence to criminal behaviour,[76] if no exception to the rule could

[67] A similar example is given in J.C. Smith, *op. cit.* note 64, p. 94.

[68] See, for example, J.C. Smith, *ibid.*, pp. 73–98 and [1987] Crim LR 48; and P. Alldridge, 'Duress, Murder and the House of Lords' (1988) 52 Journal of Criminal Law 186.

[69] See the comments of Lords Griffiths and Mackay of Clashfern in *R* v. *Howe*, *op. cit.* note 66, pp. 439 and 456.

[70] *Prosecutor* v. *Drazen Erdemović*, *op. cit.* note 65.

[71] *Ibid.*, para. 4.

[72] *Ibid.*, para. 10.

[73] *Ibid.*, Joint Separate Opinion of Judges McDonald and Vohrah, paras 73–8.

[74] *Ibid.*, Separate and Dissenting Opinion of Judge Li, paras 4–12.

[75] *Ibid.*, Separate and Dissenting Opinion of Judge Cassese, paras 20–9.

[76] Judges McDonald and Vohrah had merely found that it was a general principle of law that an accused person is less blameworthy and less deserving of full punishment when he performs a prohibited act under duress; *op. cit.* note 75, para. 65.

be found, then it should apply. Finally, Judge Stephen also dissented, but on narrower grounds. He found that the reasons given by national courts for not permitting duress as a defence to charges of murder did not refer to situations where an individual, acting under duress, killed persons who would have been killed regardless of that individual's participation in their deaths.[77]

What is even less clear is whether the rule laid down by the majority of the Appeals Chamber in *Erdemović* as to the unavailability of a defence of duress to international crimes involving killing was meant to be binding on national courts. It is suggested that it was not. In the Appeals Chamber, only Judge Li considered that international law governed the issue[78] and his reasons for so concluding were comprehensively exploded by President Cassese. Judges McDonald, Vohrah, Cassese and Stephen were all agreed that there were no rules of international law regarding the availability or otherwise of duress as a defence to the killing of innocent persons. However, as judges of a court of criminal appeal, it was not open to them to declare a *non liquet*. All four judges were agreed that they were obliged to determine Erdemović's appeal. It was in respect of the process by which they were entitled to come to their decision that they disagreed.

Since *Erdemović*, however, the issue has been addressed in the Rome Statute of the International Criminal Law. Article 31 of the Statute provides that:

> 1. In addition to other grounds for excluding criminal responsibility provided in this Statute, a person shall not be criminally responsible if, at the time of that person's conduct:
>
> [...]
>
> (d) The conduct which is alleged to constitute a crime within the jurisdiction of the Court has been caused by duress resulting from a threat of imminent death or of continuing or imminent serious bodily harm against that person or another person, and the person acts necessarily and reasonably to avoid this threat, provided that the person does not intend to cause a greater harm than the one sought to be avoided.

The Rome Statute is now in force. It might be asked, however, whether the rule in Article 31(1)(d) applies other than in proceedings of the ICC. In other words, does the provision reflect a rule of customary international law? If it does, it is, at least according to the majority of the ICTY in *Erdemović*, a rule that has crystallised remarkably quickly. What is of particular interest, however, is that the rule as enunciated in the Rome Statute applies in relation to all crimes within the jurisdiction of the ICC; that is, it applies in relation to war crimes and crimes against humanity involving killing. To this extent, *Erdemović* has been overruled. Consequently, it is difficult to argue that international law prohibits the permitting of

[77] Such as in Erdemović's case, where he was one member of an execution squad; *op. cit.* note 67, Separate and Dissenting Opinion of Judge Stephen, para. 64.

[78] Specifically, the decisions of military tribunals, both national and international, applying international law; *op. cit.* note 76, para. 4. The reference seems to be to Article 38(1)(d) of the Statute of the International Court of Justice.

a defence of duress to charges of war crimes and crimes against humanity involving killing.

It might be argued that no rule of international law governs the issue. Article 31(1)(d) has been criticised as being the result of a compromise and as wrongly encompassing both the defences of duress and necessity.[79] If so, states have freedom of action: they apply their own rules at to the scope of the defence. Alternatively, and perhaps more convincingly, one might see the Rome Statue as, if not crystallising, at least providing the *fons et origo* of a new rule. As with previous 'law-making' conventions, such as the two Additional Protocols and the 1982 United Nations Convention on the Law of the Sea, the Rome Statute might serve as a focus for concordant state practice. National courts, in particular, might be thought likely to refer to the Statute to determine what international criminal law requires, while national legislatures are already incorporating its provisions into their domestic law. Already, the ICTY has held that to a large extent the rules set out in the Rome Statute represent the expression of the *opinio juris* of the vast majority of states.[80]

With regard to the particular situation of child soldiers, however, three points deserve to be emphasised. First, the fact that a child soldier was recruited by coercive means is insufficient to found duress. It must be shown that there was a direct threat aimed at inducing the child soldier to commit the particular crime for which he is being prosecuted and which led him to commit that crime. Second, it is probably the case that voluntary membership of an organisation notorious for committing atrocities prevents use of the defence of duress in cases where a member of the group is threatened to induce him to commit such crimes. Such a rule, known as the doctrine of prior fault, has been applied in domestic proceedings with regard to membership of violent criminal gangs and paramilitary organisations.[81] However, while the rationale for the rule would seem to apply with equal, if not greater, force with regard to war crimes and crimes against humanity, whether it should apply with regard to child soldiers is more doubtful. The recruitment of all children under 15 is unlawful. This can be seen as indicating that under-15-year-olds are not viewed as having the maturity to make a real choice whether or not to join an armed group. If so, it would seem unfair to penalise them for joining a criminal one. Application of the rule to children of 15 years or over remains, however, an open question, as only the conscription of such children is prohibited. Finally, the obverse of the second point is that a child soldier should not be

[79] See Albin Eser, 'Article 31: Grounds for excluding criminal responsibility', in Triffterer (ed.), *op. cit.* note 30.

[80] See *Prosecutor* v. *Furundzija*, Case No. IT-95-17/1-T, Trial Chamber, ICTY, judgment of 10 December 1998, para. 227; and *Prosecutor* v. *Tadić*, Case No. IT-94-1-A, Appeals Chamber, ICTY, judgment of 15 July 1999 para. 223.

[81] See *R* v. *Sharp* [1987] QB 853 (CA); *R* v. *Fitzpatrick* [1977] NI 20 (Northern Ireland CCA); and *State* v. *Bradbury* 1967 (1) SA 387 (Appellate Division of the SA Supreme Court).

penalised simply because he is a member of an armed group whose members committed atrocities. He must have, in some way, whether as principal or accessory, participated in such offences. This last point might be thought too obvious to mention. However, it is a point that has often been ignored when deciding to exclude individuals from refugee status under Article 1F(a) of the Refugee Convention, an issue which we will examine in the next chapter.

Intoxication as a defence

As we saw earlier,[82] there are numerous reports of child soldiers being given drugs and/or alcohol, particularly before battle, so as to lessen their fear and reduce their inhibitions. If such treatment left them unable to appreciate what they were doing or to control themselves, it might be argued that they should not be held liable for any crimes committed.

A defence of intoxication exists in international law.[83] Article 31 of the Rome Statute provides that:

> a person shall not be criminally responsible if, at the time of that person's conduct:
> […]
> (b) The person is in a state of intoxication that destroys that person's capacity to appreciate the unlawfulness of nature of his or her conduct, or capacity to control his or her conduct to conform to the requirements of law, unless the person has become voluntarily intoxicated under such circumstances that the person knew, or disregarded the risk, that, as a result of the intoxication, he or she was likely to engage in conduct constituting a crime within the jurisdiction of the Court …

Accordingly, a child who was coerced into drinking or taking drugs before going into battle could rely on the defence, but a child who drunk or drugged himself so as to make easier or blot out what he was going to do could not. The intoxication must be so great as to negate *mens rea*, but this would seem easier to show in the case of children than of adults. Other than that, however, the defence does not seem to raise any issues as regards its applicability to the criminal conduct of child soldiers.

[82] See pp. 16–17.
[83] Cassese, *International Criminal Law*, Oxford University Press: Oxford, 2003, pp. 228–9.

10

Child soldiers as asylum seekers and refugees

Recruitment as a child soldier as a basis for refugee status

Children often wish to avoid recruitment into armed forces and groups, and child soldiers often face harsh treatment from their commanders and comrades. They may seek to flee such recruitment or treatment; leaving their country and travelling abroad. The question is: in such circumstances, can they found a successful claim for refugee status on the basis that the harm they sought to avoid amounted to persecution for one of the reasons specified in the 1951 Convention Relating to the Status of Refugees?[1]

The Refugee Convention provides that contracting states shall grant refugee status to persons who are outside their country of origin and cannot return due to a well-founded fear of persecution because of their race, religion, nationality, membership of a particular social group or political opinion.[2] It seems easy to say that the treatment many child soldiers suffer amounts to persecution. Although the concept of persecution is a flexible one, with no universally accepted definition,[3] there appears to be general agreement that violating an individual's fundamental (or core) human rights amounts to persecution.[4] Recruiting children under the age of 15 years is viewed as a sufficiently serious breach of international law so as to give rise to individual criminal responsibility. Indeed, in many cases when recruitment is forced or compulsory, it amounts to slavery or, at least, a practice similar to slavery. There is no doubt that the enslavement of a person is in breach of his fundamental human rights. In consequence, one might consider that the

[1] 189 UNTS 150. See also the 1961 Protocol Relating to the Status of Refugees, 606 UNTS 267.

[2] Article 1A(2), Refugee Convention, *ibid.*

[3] See UNHCR, *Handbook on Procedure and Criteria for Determining Refugee Status Under the 1951 Convention and the 1967 Protocol Relating to the Status of Refugees* (1992), at para. 92.

[4] See J.C. Hathaway, *The Law of Refugee Status*, Toronto: Butterworths, 1991, pp. 106–7; and G.S. Goodwin-Gill, *The Refugee in International Law*, Oxford: Oxford University Press, 2nd edn, 1996, pp. 66–9.

forcible or compulsory recruitment of any child or the recruitment *per se* of any child under 15 amounts to persecution within the meaning of the Refugee Convention. In addition, even if a child soldier does not suffer persecution solely because of the fact of his recruitment, his subsequent treatment may amount to such. Physical maltreatment and sexual assault have frequently been recognised as types of persecution, as has (less frequently) interference with a person's private and family life.

In general, deserters and draft evaders are not seen as eligible for refugee status because the treatment they fear from the authorities on account of their actions is considered punishment for their refusal to obey the law of the land rather than persecution. Asylum seekers are required to show that the conscription they sought to avoid was conducted in a discriminatory manner so as to amount to persecution; or that their desertion or evasion was to avoid participating in an illegitimate conflict or (possibly) as the result of a conscientious objection to military service. In Germany, for example, the Federal Office for the Recognition of Foreign Refugees (Bundesamt für die Anerkennung von ausländischen Flüchtlingen) labels former child soldiers deserters and considers that any persecution suffered was not inflicted because of the former child soldier's opinions or membership of a relevant group. As a result, former child soldiers' applications for asylum in Germany have been uniformly unsuccessful.[5] However, applying this general rule to child draft evaders or deserters seems wrong. While international law permits the conscription of adults, it prohibits all recruitment of under-15-year-olds and the forced or compulsory recruitment of all children. Treatment that is legally acceptable when inflicted upon an adult becomes persecution when inflicted on a child.

In the US case of *Lukwago* v. *Ashcroft*,[6] the petitioner argued that as a 15-year-old boy he had been kidnapped by the Ugandan LRA and forced to fight for them. Before the US Court of Appeals for the Third Circuit, the US Immigration and Naturalisation Service argued that forced military conscription did not amount to persecution. The Court disagreed, although it distinguished between conscription by a government acting lawfully from forcible abduction by a rebel guerrilla organisation. In appropriate circumstances such treatment could constitute persecution. The Court described Lukwago's treatment by the LRA as 'enslavement'.[7] It concluded that:

> Lukwago's persecution by the LRA was not limited to forced military service. He also endured physical and psychological abuse. He was forced to kill his friend, to watch the murder of his parents, and to view the mutilation of innocent civilians. Thus, to the extent that the BIA [Board of Immigration Appeals] rejected Lukwago's claim of past persecution because it equated forced captivity with conscription into a government's armed services, it erred as a matter of law. Lukwago's confinement

[5] See M. Ludwig, 'Former Child Soldiers as Refugees in Germany', Terre des homes/ Bundesfachverband Unbegleitete Minderjährige Flüchtlinge, 2004.

[6] 329 F.3d 157 (2003).

[7] *Ibid.*, p. 169.

> and treatment by the LRA may constitute persecution under the INA [Immigration and Nationality Act].[8]

The distinction between recruitment by government and rebel forces is problematic. However, it should be recalled that Lukwago was 15 years old at the time he was kidnapped by the LRA, so his recruitment by the Ugandan Government would not have been unlawful under international law.[9] In addition, the requirement that governmental conscription be lawful referred to conscription under a domestic law of general application, leaving room for arguments that recruitment not authorised by a state's own law, imposed in a discriminatory manner, or in breach of international law, would constitute persecution for the purposes of the Refugee Convention.

It is more difficult, however, to argue that any such persecution is on account of one of the specified grounds (race, religion, nationality, membership of a particular social group or political opinion). One might argue that children who are liable to be recruited into armed forces or groups have a well-founded fear of persecution because of their membership of a particular social group, that of children from a particular country or region who, by reason of their age and (in most cases) gender, are potential recruits (generally, though not always, adolescent boys). Although it has been argued that the existence of a particular social group requires a degree of cohesiveness, cooperation or interdependence between its members,[10] which would exclude children from the category, the majority view has denied such a requirement.[11] Persecution on account of membership of a particular social group means:

> Persecution that is directed towards an individual who is a member of a group of persons all of who share a common, immutable characteristic. The shared characteristic might be an innate one such as sex, color, or kinship ties, or in some circumstances it might be a shared past experience such as former military leadership or land ownership. The particular kind of group characteristic that will qualify under this construction remains to be determined on a case-by-case basis. However, whatever the common characteristic that defines the group, it must be one that members

[8] *Ibid.*, p. 170.

[9] Uganda is a party to both ILO Convention 182 and the OP but was not at the time of Lukwago's abduction.

[10] See *Sanchez-Trujillo* v. *Immigration and Naturalization Service*, 801 F.2d 1571 (1986), at 1577 (US Court of Appeals for the Ninth Circuit)); and *R* v. *Secretary of State for the Home Department, ex parte Shah* [1998] 1 WLR 74 (Court of Appeal), *per* Staughton LJ at 93. See also *Gomez* v. *Immigration and Naturalization Service*, 947 F.2d 660, at 664, where the US Court of Appeals for the Third Circuit stated that: 'Possession of broadly-based characteristics such as youth and gender will not by itself endow individuals with membership of a particular social group'.

[11] *Matter of Acosta*, 19 I. & N. Dec. 211 (B.I.A. Lexis 1985). See also *Applicant A* v. *Minister for Immigration and Ethnic Affairs* (1997) 142 ALR 331; *Canada (Attorney General)* v. *Ward* [1993] SCR 689; *In re GJ* [1998] INLR 387; and *R* v. *Secretary of State for the Home Department, ex parte Shah* [1999] 2 AC 629 (HL).

> of the group cannot change, or should not be required to change because it is fundamental to their individual identities or consciences.[12]

Although children's common characteristic is not immutable, it is not something they can change voluntarily. Only time can transform children into adults. However, to say that the treatment child soldiers receive amounts to persecution because they are children is not to say that they are persecuted because they are children.

In *Lukwago*, the petitioner argued that he had been persecuted because of his membership of a particular social group of 'children from Northern Uganda who are abducted and enslaved by the LRA and oppose their involuntary servitude'.[13] The Board of Immigration Appeals (BIA) held that he had failed to show that the LRA's persecution was based on any of the enumerated grounds. In turn, the US Court of Appeals for the Third Circuit held that: 'Based on the evidence in the record, the BIA's findings that the LRA did not target Lukwago for persecution based on his age is supported by substantial evidence. The BIA found that the LRA abducted Lukwago due to its need for labor, not on account of his membership in any "particular social group" ... The evidence does not compel a conclusion contrary to the BIA's finding'.[14] Although the Court did not hold that children facing recruitment could never constitute a particular social group, it did express some scepticism, stating that:

> It is undeniable that youth is an important component of a child's identity. Children share many general characteristics, such as innocence, immaturity and impressionability. However, unlike innate characteristics, such as sex or color, age changes over time, possibly lessening its role in personal identity. Moreover, children as a particular social group represent an extremely wide and diverse group and children, even within a single neighbourhood, have a wide degree of varying experiences, interests and traits.[15]

The Court also pointed out that the existence of a particular social group must exist independently of the persecution suffered by its members. However, the Court of Appeals based its determination that Lukwago's persecution was not because of his membership of a particular social group on the facts as found by the Board, which findings the Court was legally required to treat as 'conclusive unless any reasonable adjudicator would be compelled to conclude to the contrary'.[16] Evidence had been put before the BIA that the LRA targeted children between 13- to 16 years old for abduction; and that it was a systematic choice based on certain desirable characteristics that the LRA perceived children of such ages as having: 13- to 16-year-olds being strong enough to use weapons and carry heavy loads but young enough to be easily dominated by their captors, physically and

[12] *Matter of Acosta*, *Ibid.*, pp. 53–4.
[13] *Op. cit.* note 6, p. 167.
[14] *Ibid.*, p. 173.
[15] *Ibid.*, pp. 171–2.
[16] *Ibid.*, p. 167.

psychologically. One might consider that in another case a tribunal would consider similar evidence sufficient to establish that the persecution suffered by a former child soldier was on account of his membership of a particular social group.

In many cases, however, child soldiers are not recruited because they are children but for other reasons. When numbers are low, their age may be a matter of indifference to the recruiters. Children are recruited alongside with adults on the basis of who the recruiters can catch. In some cases, it might be argued that children are targeted because they are seen as least likely to resist recruitment, or that they are singled out because of their membership of some other relevant category (an ethnic minority, or a social group such as street children). In others, however, it is difficult to see that the individual's race, religion, nationality, membership of a particular social group or political opinion is the basis for his persecution. This is the major obstacle to the recognition of child soldiers, or children seeking to avoid military service, as refugees.

A person can also, however, be at risk of persecution because of their status as a former child soldier. Demobilised child soldiers are often the object of hatred and suspicion, in particular because of their use to commit atrocities.[17] Former child soldiers are a group of persons sharing a common immutable characteristic; in this case, a shared personal experience.[18] In such circumstances, if reprisals amounting to persecutory acts ensue, they are aimed a former child soldiers because of their membership of a particular social group.[19] In *Lukwago*, although it found no reason to overturn the Board's determinations on the facts, the Court of Appeals did consider Lukwago's claims that he had a well-founded fear of future persecution from both the LRA and the Ugandan Government on the basis of his membership of a particular social group of former child soldiers who have escaped from LRA captivity.

Criminal responsibility and exclusion from refugee status[20]

In recent years, there has been a tendency to subject asylum seekers to closer scrutiny to determine whether, by reason of their previous conduct, they are undeserving

[17] See C.P. Dodge and M. Raundalen, *Reaching Children in War: Sudan, Uganda and Mozambique*, Bergen: Sigma Forlag, 1991.

[18] See in the *Matter of Acosta*, *op. cit.* note 11, where one of the examples given is the shared personal experience of 'former military leadership'.

[19] It might be argued that such treatment was not persecution but punishment for the criminal acts committed by the former child soldiers. Punishment, however, must be individualised, not aimed at members of a group simply because of their membership, and carried out only after a process for determining guilt.

[20] For a more comprehensive discussion of this topic, see M. Happold, 'Excluding Children from Refugee Status: Child Soldiers and Article 1F of the Refugee Convention' (2002) 17 American University International Law Review 1131.

of refugee status.[21] To be eligible for refugee status a person must be able to show both a well-founded fear of persecution and that the persecution feared is on account of the individual's race, religion, nationality, membership of a particular social group or political opinion. However, the Refugee Convention also provides that certain classes of persons are ineligible for refugee status, either because they are not in need of international protection or are receiving it elsewhere, or because they are undeserving of it. Article 1F provides that the Convention: 'shall not apply to any person with respect of whom there are serious reasons for considering that: (a) he has committed a crime against peace, a war crime, or a crime against humanity, as defined in the international instruments drawn up to make provision in respect of such crimes'. Article 1F is framed in mandatory language. It would appear that contracting states have no discretion as to whether or not to grant refugee status to persons suspected of international crimes. Rather, they are prohibited from doing so. It further appears that in applying to 'any person', Article 1F does not distinguish between children and adults, so that the obligation not to grant refugee status to persons who may have committed international crimes applies with respect to both adult and child perpetrators.[22] This has been seen as unsatisfactory. It has been argued that children should never be subject to exclusion from refugee status under Article 1F.[23] Such a view, however, is contrary to both the wording and the drafting history of the provision. In practice, children have been excluded from refugee status as a result of the application of Article 1F.[24]

The exclusion of child soldiers from refugee status

We have already seen that child soldiers have committed atrocities in a number of recent conflicts. Given its terms, one might consider that such individuals, even if otherwise eligible, would be excluded from refugee status by virtue of the operation of Article 1F. Most people, however, would agree that children and adults

[21] See D. McNamara, 'Exclusion Clauses: Closer Attention Paid to the Exclusion Clauses', in International Association of Refugee Judges (ed.), *Refugee and Asylum Law: Assessing the Scope for Judicial Protection*, Nijmegen: Nederlands Centrum Buitenlanders, 1997.

[22] See UNHCR, 'The Exclusion Clauses', *op. cit.* note 3; and 'United Nations High Commissioner for Refugees on Child-Soldiers', reprinted in P.J. van Krieken (ed.), *Refugee Law in Context: the Exclusion Clause*, The Hague: T.M.C. Asser Instituut, 1999.

[23] See the 'Non-Governmental Organisations' Submission to the Standing Committee of the United Nations High Commissioner's Programme', presented at the 10th meeting of the Executive Committee of the UN High Commissioner for Refugees' Programme, referred to in M.K. Niynah, 'Exclusion Under Article 1F: some Reflections on Context, Principles and Practice' (2000) 12 IJRL 295 at 308, note 20.

[24] See UNHCR, 'The Exclusion Clauses', *op. cit.* note 60. See also S. Kaepferer, 'Exclusion Clauses in Europe – a Comparative Overview of State Practice in France, Belgium and the United Kingdom' (2000) 12 IJRL 194, p. 214, which refers to Belgian and French cases where children were excluded.

should not be treated identically in respect of exclusion from refugee status. This perception would seem to comport with Article 1 of the CRC, which provides that; 'In all actions concerning children ... the best interests of the child shall be a primary consideration'. The Article further states that parties to the CRC 'undertake to ensure the child such protection and care as is necessary for his or her well-being'. Even before the adoption of the CRC, the UNHCR Executive Committee, in its Conclusion No. 47 on refugee children, 'stressed that all action on behalf of refugee children must be guided by the principle of the best interests of the child'. The UNHCR applies the CRC to its own work by using the rights laid down in the CRC as guiding principles. Given this, one might conclude that the provisions of the Refugee Convention should be interpreted as far as possible in conformity with the principles set down in the CRC.

We have already seen that child soldiers charged with international crimes might be able to rely on two defences in particular: infancy and duress. However, it might be argued that to exclude a person from refugee status under Article 1F all one needs to show is that there are 'serious reasons' for thinking that the person had committed atrocious acts. If this were the case, then whether a person had a defence would be irrelevant. All that would be needed would be to demonstrate that the person had behaved in a manner amounting to the *actus reus* of a war crime, a crime against humanity, or a crime against peace.

In particular, the argument has been made that, although a defence to criminal proceedings, duress cannot be pleaded in exclusion proceedings. Such a view derives from the US Supreme Court's judgment in *Fedorenko* v. *United States*.[25] In that case, the US Government successfully brought denaturalisation proceedings against Fedorenko on the basis that he had been ineligible for a visa because, as a concentration camp guard during the Second World War, he had participated in the persecution of camp inmates. Fedorenko argued that he had done so under duress, but the Supreme Court ruled that duress was not an available defence. *Fedorenko* was applied to asylum claims by the Board of Immigration Appeals in *Rodriguez-Majano*.[26] There, it was argued that the applicant was ineligible for asylum on the grounds that he had engaged in the persecution of others. The applicant admitted that he had been a member of the guerrillas in El Salvador but argued that he had been forced to join them and had deserted after two months. The Board, however, held that: 'The participation or assistance of an alien in persecution need not be of his volition to bar him from relief [from deportation]', although on the facts of the applicant's case the court found that the guerrillas had not engaged in persecution.

However, the Supreme Court reached its decision in *Fedorenko* solely on its reading of the relevant domestic legislation. The Court saw the issue of one of statutory construction and did not purport to lay down any general rules as to the

[25] 449 US 490 (1981).

[26] *Matter of Rodriguez-Majano*, 19 I. & N. Dec. 811 (B.I.A. 1988).

status of the defence of duress as a matter of international law.[27] Delivering the opinion of the Court, Justice Marshall stated that:

> [W]e conclude that the District Court's construction of the Act was incorrect. The plain language of the Act mandates precisely the literal interpretation that the District Court rejected: an individual's service as a concentration camp armed guard – whether voluntary or involuntary – made him ineligible for a visa. That Congress was perfectly capable of adopting a 'voluntariness' limitation where it felt that one was necessary is plain from comparing s 2(a) with s 2(b), which excludes only those individuals who 'voluntarily assisted the enemy forces ... in their operations ...' Under traditional principles of statutory construction, the deliberate omission of the word 'voluntary' from s 2(a) compels the conclusion that the statute made *all* who assisted in the persecution of civilians ineligible for visas.[28]

In fact, the wording of s 2(a) and (b) of the 1948 Displaced Persons Act[29] was taken verbatim from the 1946 Constitution of the International Refugee Organisation (IRO),[30] the predecessor to the UNHCR. Persons not of concern to the IRO included: 'other persons who can be shown: (a) to have assisted the enemy in persecuting civil populations of countries, Members of the United Nations; or (b) to have voluntarily assisted the enemy forces since the outbreak of the Second World War in their operations against the United Nations'.[31]

The definitions in the Displaced Persons Act were adopted in conformity with the IRO Constitution. Given this, arguments from presumed congressional intent do not appear particularly compelling. Indeed, there is evidence to show that the Supreme Court's interpretation does not conform to that of the drafters of the IRO Constitution. A footnote to Article 2(b) indicates that the word 'voluntarily' was used to exclude from the scope of the provision officials who continued to carry out their normal duties under enemy occupation or persons who cared for sick and wounded enemies.[32] The term was not intended to distinguish between actions performed freely or while under duress.

The Office of the UNHCR succeeded the IRO as the principal UN agency concerned with refugees, while who is a refugee is now defined by the Refugee

[27] See, generally, A.L. Dienstag, '*Fedorenko* v. *United States*: War Crimes, the Defense of Duress and American Nationality Law' (1982) 82 Columbia Law Review 120.

[28] *Op. cit.* note 25, p. 512.

[29] Displaced Persons Act of 1948, Pub. L. No. 775, Stat. 1009 (1948).

[30] Constitution of the International Refugee Organisation and Agreement on Interim Measures to be Taken in Respect of Refugees and Displaced Persons, 18 UNTS 283 (1946).

[31] *Ibid.*

[32] See *Ibid.*, at note 1. The note states that: 'Mere continuance of normal and peaceful duties, not performed with the specific purpose of aiding the enemy against the Allies or against the civil population of territory in enemy occupation, shall not be considered to constitute "voluntary assistance". Nor shall acts of general humanity, such as the care of wounded or dying, be so considered except in cases where help of this nature given to enemy nationals could equally well have been given to Allied nationals and was purposely withheld from them'.

Convention. The Refugee Convention's definition of those persons excluded from refugee status by virtue of their previous conduct is somewhat different from that of the IRO. Not only are the US decisions wrong in principle but they are in no way relevant to the interpretation of Article 1F. Article 1F speaks specifically of 'crimes' rather than of persecution, which would seem to be a clear implication that the general part of criminal law should apply and that, accordingly, duress (and infancy) should be an available defence to attempts to exclude from refugee status. A crime consists of three elements: the *actus reus* (the conduct element), the *mens rea* (the mental element) and the absence of any available defence. Article 1F does not refer to atrocities or persecution; it refers to international crimes. What distinguishes exclusion proceedings from criminal proceedings is simply the standard of proof that is applied (reasonable suspicion rather than beyond reasonable doubt). The burden of proof remains the same and all the elements of the crime must be proved.

Conclusion

It is important to remember that even if a former child soldier is excluded from refugee status under Article 1F(a) it by no means follows that he can necessarily be deported. Article 1F(a) permits the exclusion from refugee status of those in respect of whom, although they have a well-founded fear of persecution for reasons of race, religion, nationality, membership of a particular social group or political opinion, there are serious reasons for considering that they have committed crimes against peace, war crimes or crimes against humanity. Such persons, however, may be protected against *refoulement* for other reasons.

In particular, the European Convention on Human Rights and the Convention Against Torture[33] prohibit the deportation of any person when there are substantial grounds for believing that the individual will be subjected to torture or inhuman or degrading treatment or punishment in the receiving state.[34] This obligation is absolute. It is not affected by an individual's conduct. This was made clear in relation to Article 3 of the European Convention on Human Rights in *Chahal* v. *United Kingdom*.[35] The UK Government had sought to depart Chahal, a Sikh militant, to India on the ground that his presence in the UK was contrary to the public good for reasons of national security and the international fight against terrorism. Chahal claimed that it he were to be deported to India, he would be at serious risk of torture by the Indian security forces. Before the Court, the UK Government argued that the guarantee in Article 3 against deportation was not

[33] Convention Against Torture and Other Cruel, Inhuman and Degrading Treatment or Punishment, GA Res. 46/39 (1985).

[34] See, in particular, *Soering* v. *United Kingdom*, ECHR Series A No. 161 (1989); and *Cruz Varas* v. *Sweden*, ECHR Series A No. 201 (1991).

[35] (1997) 23 EHRR 413.

absolute in cases where an individual posed a threat to the national security of the deporting state. The Court rejected this argument and reaffirmed the blanket nature of Article 3, stating that 'the activities of the individual in question, however undesirable or dangerous, cannot be a material consideration'.[36] There is no indication that this rule does not apply equally to suspected war criminals as it does to suspected terrorists, nor does there seem any justification for it not doing so. The right to be free from torture and inhuman and degrading punishment is an absolute right which cannot be derogated from.

Given the approach of the minority of the European Court of Human Rights in *T.* and *V.*, it may be that the manner in which a child soldier would be prosecuted for war crimes or crimes against humanity in the receiving state might of itself amount to inhuman and degrading treatment. Further, if the result of such a trial might be the execution of the child soldier, this too would be contrary to Article 3.[37] The execution of persons for crimes committed while under the age of 18 is fairly generally agreed to be contrary to international law.

In such circumstances, an exercise of executive discretion granting the former child soldier permission to stay in the state of refuge would seem appropriate. However, there can be problems with such solutions. In the first place, the child may simply be put into a state of legal limbo, unable, in particular, to access the benefits that flow from refugee status. Former child soldiers in Germany, for example, because they are not granted refugee status are unable to obtain permanent residents permits and are subject to a number of restrictions, such as being unable to move from their place of residence or to undertake employment or further education.[38] Over a long period this cannot be seen as satisfactory. In addition, the finding under Article 1F can be the trigger for the person's investigation by the prosecuting authorities of the state of refuge, although the likelihood and nature of such proceedings varies considerably from state to state. What can be concluded, however, is that the law as framed fails to take account of the specific situation and needs of child soldiers.

[36] *Ibid.*, p. 457.

[37] See *Öcalan* v. *Turkey* (2003) 37 EHHR 238. See also Protocol No. 6 to the Convention for the Protection of Human Rights and Fundamental Freedoms Concerning the Abolition of the Death Penalty, 114 ETS 32 (1983). In a number of cases Protocol No. 6 has been held to prohibit state parties from extraditing persons to countries where they might face the death penalty. See *Fidan* (1987) II Recueil Dalloz-Sirey 305 (Conseil d'Etat); *Gacem* (1988) I Semaine Juridique IV-86 (Conseil d'Etat); and *Short* v. *Netherlands* (1990) 76 Rechtspraak van der Week 358, translation in (1991) 29 ILM 221 (Hoge Raad).

[38] See Ludwig, *op. cit.* note 5.

11

Child soldiers in international law: conclusions

In her report on the impact of armed conflict on children,[1] Graça Machel stated that:

> The research conducted for this study uncovered many practical steps to prevent future recruitment. First, governments should work for the finalization and rapid adoption of the draft optional protocol to the Convention on the Rights of the Child on involvement of children in armed conflict. Next, governments must pay much closer attention to their methods of recruitment and, in particular, they must renounce the practice of forced recruitment. They should ensure that all children are registered at birth and receive documentation of age. To be certain that these measures succeed, governments must establish effective monitoring systems and back them up with legal remedies and institutions that are sufficiently strong to tackle abuses.[2]

Much of this has been done. An Optional Protocol has been adopted and most states have renounced the forced recruitment of children. Indeed, the prohibition of the compulsory and forcible recruitment of children may be becoming a rule of customary international law. There is a substantial body of rules governing the recruitment and treatment of child soldiers, and they have been the subject of considerable augementation and development in recent years. It must, however, be asked whether they have been effective, that is, to what extent do the persons – states, non-state armed groups, individuals – to whom the rules are addressed comply with them?

To a large extent, states do comply with the rules governing the recruitment of children into their armed forces. Few states enlist under-15-year-old volunteers into their armed forces or conscript under-18-year-olds. Even fewer states permit such forms of recruitment under their national law, which suggests that they consider such behaviour to be unlawful even if they practise it. However, it might be

[1] Impact of Armed Conflict on Children: 'Report of the Expert of the Secretary-General, Ms Graça Machel, submitted pursuant to General Assembly resolution 48/175', UN Docs A/51/306 and A/51/306/Add.1.

[2] *Ibid.*, at para. 58.

asked whether there is a causal relationship between the existence of the legal norms regulating the recruitment of children and states' general compliance with them. This is not to argue that states do not consider the rules to be legally obligatory but rather to ask whether states would behave in the same manner if they considered that they were not legally obliged to do so. Prior to 1977, few states recruited under-15-years-olds into their armed forces, and minimum ages of recruitment have not changed significantly since the adoption of the two Additional Protocols and the CRC.

There have been some changes. Some states have raised their minimum age for voluntary recruitment and taken measures to ensure that under-18-year-old volunteers are kept out of situations of hostilities. Other states have raised their age for conscription to 18, although only a few states' laws provided for conscription at a lower age. However, the OP to the CRC, the most onerous convention on the subject, which does have the potential to affect states' behaviour quite significantly, has received far fewer ratifications – 72 as opposed to 150 –[3] than ILO Convention 182 on the Worst Forms of Child Labour. Legal developments can be seen as having tracked state practice, not *vice versa*, although the explanation for this may be that NGO campaigning has been more successful at the national rather than at the international level.

Nevertheless, the history of the negotiation of the various treaties governing the recruitment of children shows that states have consistently sought consensus on their provisions. A premium has been put on ensuring universality over raising standards. The negotiations of the two Additional Protocols saw a considerable watering-down of the original ICRC proposals, with the discrepancies between the two provisions being largely due to last-minute amendments made to salvage AP II from total rejection. During the negotiations of Article 38 of the CRC, the objections of a minority to majority attempts to improve on AP I gave rise to considerable acrimony and a very dubious (if politically astute) finding of consensus by the chair. Negotiations on the OP were prolonged and subject to similar minority resistance to attempts to strengthen the law. Although it cannot be disputed that the Protocol does mark a considerable advance on Article 38 of the CRC, claims that its adoption saw the victory of civil society over military interests cannot be accepted. Indeed, the USA became a party to the OP, while remaining unwilling to accede to the CRC. Negotiations in the ILO, seen by some as a way of getting around the impasse in the OP Working Group, were not concluded until the USA (as usual acting as the front representative for a rather larger number of States than would wish to identify themselves publicly) received assurances that ILO Convention 182 solely covered compulsory and forced

[3] See Office of the United Nations High Commissioner for Human Rights, 'Status of Ratifications of the Principal International Human Rights Treaties as of 09 June 2004', available at www.unhchr.ch/html/menu2/6/protocolchild.htm; and ILOLEX: Database of International Labour Standards, available at: www.ilo.org/ilolex/english/index.htm (visited on 14 July 2004).

conscription and had no implications for other forms of military service. With the exception of the African Charter on the Rights and Welfare of the Child, which as a regional rather than a global treaty merely proves the rule, all of the conventions governing the recruitment of children are composed of 'lowest common denominator' provisions. The emphasis has been on rendering the treaties acceptable to all states present at their negotiation. This has meant that states have adopted treaties that largely reflect what they already do.

It might be argued that this method of developing the law has at least the virtue of ensuring that new norms are generally complied with. This is true to a point only. Those states that breach their obligations tend to do so out of weakness rather than bad faith; that is, more as a result of their inabilities to establish functioning systems of conscription, verify the birth dates of their citizens, or impose civilian control over their armed forces. Moreover, the consensual nature of the international legal system and its lack of centralised enforcement mechanisms has meant that several states have been able to continue to recruit and use child soldiers by opting out of new legal developments and flouting those binding them.[4] In addition, much recruitment of children today is not by governments but by armed opposition groups. Recent years have undoubtedly seen developments in how international law governs the activities of such groups, culminating in the prohibition of all recruitment of children by them set out in the OP. However, the growth in legal regulation has not been accompanied by any increase in compliance.

The child-soldier phenomenon cannot be addressed simply by the promulgation of new standards. Indeed, it could be argued that continued stress on a 'straight-18' standard serves to obfuscate the issue. As both the Secretary-General's Representative on Children and Armed Conflict and the Secretary-General himself have stressed, what is needed now is an 'era of application'.[5] Some advances have already been made in this respect. The explicit criminalisation of the recruitment and use in hostilities of children under 15 years of age has shifted the focus onto the individuals who recruit such children. We are already seeing prosecutions before the Special Court for Sierra Leone, and the first two situations being considered by the Prosecutor of the ICC involve the widespread use of child soldiers. Another development has been the 'naming and shaming' of parties to armed conflicts involved in the illegal recruitment and use of child soldiers. More recently, the Secretary-General has proposed, and the Security Council has begun to consider, measures to sanction such parties – whether governments or armed opposition groups – as a means of inducing compliance with their legal obligations. It may be utopian to expect that any sanctions imposed by the Security

[4] Take the example of Burma, which is a party to the 1949 GCs and the CRC, but is not a party to either of the 1977 APs, the OP or ILO Convention 182. It has been estimated that there are around 70,000 children in the Burmese armed forces: see Human Rights Watch, *'My Gun Was as Tall as Me': Child Soldiers in Burma* (2002), at pp. 103–6.

[5] Children and Armed Conflict: Report of the Secretary-General, UN Doc. S/2002/1299, ch. II.

Council will be more than symbolic, but even symbolic sanctions would have a stigmatising effect and might encourage states or groups of states to take their own more substantial measures.

Indeed, examining the issue without looking at how it has been dealt with by the UN is to see less than half the picture. Not only does international law regulate when and under what conditions children can be recruited and used in hostilities, but it has also begun to address the consequences of failures to comply with these rules. There is being developed a body of rules concerning child soldiers themselves, conferring on them both rights and obligations, although such rules have often been extrapolated from more general rules in international humanitarian law or the international law of children's rights and have, as a result, a somewhat rudimentary character. Moreover, the UN and other international institutions now concern themselves with child soldiers far more than they did even a decade ago. Indeed, it is in the debates and practices of various actors within the UN system that many of these rules have been worked out. One cannot consider what is required when demobilising and reintegrating child soldiers without looking at the body of best practices advocated by the UN. Discussion of the minimum age of responsibility for international crimes cannot take place without looking at the debates over the establishment of the Special Court for Sierra Leone. This seems likely to continue and one might consider that it is the development of such practices that are most likely to affect how child soldiers are treated across the world today.

To inject a final note of scepticism, however, one might ask whether the proposed measures to induce compliance will have anything but marginal effects. It has been seen that child soldiers exist for reasons that are deeply embedded in the economic and social structures of the countries where they are being used. Children are a valuable resource in places where up to half the population are under 18 years of age. Lack of educational and employment opportunities, and a desire for security drive children to volunteer to join armed forces and groups. For persons fighting brutal small wars, the UN in New York and the ICC in The Hague may seem far away. Ultimately, one might conclude, it is only by reducing conflict that we are likely to see a durable reduction of child soldiering.

Select bibliography

Abi-Saab, G. 'The Concept of "War Crimes" ', in Yee and Tieya (eds), *International Law in the post-Cold War World: Essays in Memory of Li Haopei*, London: Routledge, 2001.
Akehurst, M. 'Custom as a Source of International Law' (1974–75) 47 *British Year Book of International Law* 1.
Aldrich, G.H. 'Comments on Tavernier's "Combatants and Non-Combatants" ', in Dekker and Post (eds), *The Gulf War of 1980–88: the Iran–Iraq War in International Legal Perspective*, Dordrecht: Martinus Nijhof, 1992.
Amnesty International: *Sierra Leone: Childhood – a Casualty of Conflict*, London: Amnesty International, 2000.
Amnesty International: *United Kingdom: U-18s: Child Soldiers at Risk*, London: Amnesty International, 2000.
Archard, D. *Children: Rights and Childhood*, London: Routledge, 1993.
Ariès, P. *Centuries of Childhood*, New York: Vintage, 1962.
Arzourmanian, N. and Pizzutelli, F. 'Victimes et Bourreaux: Questions de Responsibilité Liées à la Problématique des Enfants-Soldats en Afrique' (2003) *International Review of the Red Cross* No. 852, p. 827.
Ashworth, A. *Principles of Criminal Law*, Oxford: Oxford University Press, 3rd edn, 1999.
Baxter, R.R. 'Multilateral Treaties as Evidence of Customary International Law' (1965–66) 41 *British Year Book of International Law* 275.
Best, G. *War and Law Since 1945*, Oxford: Clarendon Press, 1994.
Bossuyt, M.J. *Guide to the 'Travaux Préparatoires' of the International Covenant on Civil and Political Rights*, Dordrecht: Martinus Nijhof, 1987.
Boudreault, L.S. 'Les réserves apportées au Protocole de Genève sur le Droit Humanitaire' (1989–90) 6 *Revue Québécois de Droit International* 105.
Brett, R. and McCallin, M. *Children: The Invisible Soldiers*, Stockholm: Radda Barnen, rev. edn, 1998.
Van Bueren, G. 'The International Legal Protection of Children in Armed Conflicts' (1994) 43 *International and Comparative Law Quarterly* 809.
Van Bueren, G. *The International Law on the Rights of the Child*, Dordrecht: Martinus Nijhof, 1995.
Caminos, H. and Molitor, M.R. 'Progressive Development of International Law and the Package Deal' (1985) 79 *American Journal of International Law* 871.
Coalition to Stop the Use of Child Soldiers, *Child Soldiers Global Report 2001*.

Coalition to Stop the Use of Child Soldiers, *Child Soldier Use 2003: a Briefing for the 4th Security Council Open Debate on Children and Armed Conflict*, 2003.

Cassese, A. *International Criminal Law*, Oxford: Oxford University Press, 2003.

Clark, R.S. and Triffterer, O. 'Article 26: Exclusion of Jurisdiction over Persons under Eighteen', in Triffterer, O. (ed.), *Commentary on the Rome Statute of the International Criminal Court: Observers' Notes, Article by Article*, Baden-Baden: Nomos Verlag, 1999.

Cohn, I. 'The Protection of Child Soldiers During the Liberian Peace Process' (1998) 6 *International Journal of Children's Rights* 179.

Cohn, I. 'The Protection of Children in Peacemaking and Peacekeeping Processes' (1999) 12 *Harvard Human Rights Journal* 129.

Cohn, I. 'The Protection of Children and the Quest for Truth and Justice in Sierra Leone' (2001) *Columbia University Journal of International Affairs* 1.

deMause, L. 'The Evolution of Childhood', in deMause, L. (ed.), *The History of Childhood*, New York: Harper, 1976.

Dennis, M.J. 'The ILO Convention on the Worst Forms of Child Labor' (1999) 93 *American Journal of International Law* 943.

Dennis, M.J. 'Newly Adopted Protocols to the Convention on the Rights of the Child' (2000) 94 *American Journal of International Law* 798.

Detrick, S. (ed.), *The United Nations Convention on the Rights of the Child: a Guide to the 'Travaux Préparatoires'*, Dordrecht: Martinus Nijhof, 1992.

Detrick, S. *A Commentary on the United Nations Convention on the Rights of the Child*, Dordrecht: Martinus Nijhof, 1998.

Dienstag, A.L. '*Fedorenko* v. *United States*: War Crimes, the Defense of Duress and American Nationality Law' (1982) 82 *Columbia Law Review* 120.

Dodge, C.P., and Raundalen, M. *Reaching Children in War: Sudan, Uganda and Mozambique*, Bergen: Sigma Forlag, 1991.

Dörmann, K. *Elements of War Crimes under the Rome Statute of the International Criminal Court: Sources and Commentary*, Cambridge: Cambridge University Press, 2003.

Dutli, M.T. 'Captured Child Combatants' (1990) *International Review of the Red Cross* No. 278, p. 421.

Eekelaar, J. 'The Emergence of Children's Rights' (1986) 6 *Oxford Journal of Legal Studies* 161.

Ellis, S. *The Mask of Anarchy: The Destruction of Liberia and the Religious Dimension of an African Civil War*, London: Hurst & Co., 1999.

Eser, A. 'Article 31: Grounds for Excluding Criminal Responsibility', in Triffterer, O. (ed.), *Commentary on the Rome Statute of the International Criminal Court: Observers' Notes, Article by Article*, Baden-Baden: Nomos Verlag, 1999.

Farson, R. *Birthrights*, New York: Macmillan, 1974.

Fox, V.C. 'Historical Perspectives on Children's Rights', in Verhellen, E. and Spiesschaert, F. (eds), *Ombudswork for Children: A Way of Improving the Position of Children in Society*, Leuven/Amersfoort: F. Acco, 1989.

Goodwin-Gill, G.S., and Cohn, I. *Child Soldiers: The Role of Children in Armed Conflict*, Oxford: Oxford University Press, 1994.

Goodwin-Gill, G.S. *The Refugee in International Law*, Oxford: Clarendon Press, 2nd edn, 1996.

Greenwood, C. 'Customary Law Status of the 1977 Geneva Protocols', in Delissen, A.J.M. and Tanja, G.J. (eds), *Humanitarian Law of Armed Conflict*, Dordrecht: Martinus Nijhof, 1991.

Greenwood, C. 'International Humanitarian Law and the Tadić Case' (1996) 7 *European Journal of International Law* 265.

Gutman, R. and Rieff, D. (eds), *Crimes of War: What the Public Should Know*, New York: W.W. Norton & Co., 1999.

Happold, M. 'The Optional Protocol to the Convention on the Rights of the Child on the Involvement of Children in Armed Conflict' (2000) 3 *Yearbook of International Humanitarian Law* 226.

Happold, M. 'Child Soldiers in International Law: the Legal Regulation of Children's Participation in Hostilities' (2000) 48 *Netherlands International Law Review* 27.

Happold, M. 'Excluding Children from Refugee Status: Child Soldiers and Article 1F of the Refugee Convention' (2002) 17 *American University International Law Review* 1131.

Hathaway, J.C. *The Law of Refugee Status*, Toronto: Butterworths, 1991.

von Hebel, H. and Robinson, D. 'Crimes within the Jurisdiction of the Court', in Lee, R.S. (ed.) *The International Criminal Court: the Making of the Rome Statute: Issues, Negotiations, Results*, Ardsley: Transnational, 1999.

Helle, D. 'Optional Protocol on the Involvement of Children in Armed Conflict to the Convention on the Rights of the Child' (2000) *International Review of the Red Cross* No. 839, p. 797.

Heywood, C. *A History of Childhood: Children and Childhood in the West from Medieval to Modern Times*, Cambridge: Polity, 2001.

Hodgkin, R. and Newell, P. *Implementation Handbook for the Convention on the Rights of the Child*, London: UNICEF, 1998.

Holt, J. *Escape from Childhood: the Needs and Rights of Children*, New York: E.P. Dutton, 1975.

Human Rights Watch: *Children of the Sudan: Slaves, Street Children and Child Soldiers*, New York, Human Rights Watch, 1995.

Human Rights Watch: *Easy Prey: Child Soldiers in Liberia*, New York: Human Rights Watch, 1994.

Human Rights Watch: *Forgotten Fighters: Child Soldiers in Angola*, New York: Human Rights Watch, 2003.

Human Rights Watch: *Ituri: 'Covered in Blood': Ethnically Targeted Violence in North-eastern DR Congo*, New York: Human Rights Watch, 2003.

Human Rights Watch: *Stolen Children: Abduction and Recruitment in Northern Uganda* New York: Human Rights Watch, 2003.

James, T.E. 'The Age of Majority' (1960) 4 *American Journal of Legal History* 24.

Kaepferer, S. 'Exclusion Clauses in Europe – a Comparative Overview of State Practice in France, Belgium and the United Kingdom' (2000) 12 *International Journal of Refugee Law* 194.

Kalshoven, F. *Constraints on the Waging of War*, Geneva: International Committee of the Red Cross, 1987.

Keairns, Y.E. *The Voices of Girl Child Soldiers: Summary*, Geneva/London: Quaker United Nations Office/Coalition to Stop the Use of Child Soldiers, 2002.

van Krieken, P. (ed.), *Refugee Law in Context: the Exclusion Clause*, The Hague: T.M.C. Asser Press, 1999.

Krill, F. 'The Protection of Children in Armed Conflict', in Freeman, M., and Veerman, P. (eds), *The Ideologies of Children's Rights*, Dordrecht: Martinus Nijhof, 1992.

Kuper, J. *International Law Concerning Child Civilians in Armed Conflict*, Oxford: Oxford University Press, 1997.

Kuper, J. 'Reservations, Declarations and Objections to the 1989 Convention on the Rights of the Child', in Gardner, J.P. (ed.), *Human Rights as General Norms and a State's Right to Opt Out*, London: British Institute of International and Comparative Law, 1997.

Lauterpacht, H. 'The Law of Nations and the Punishment of War Criminals' (1944) *British Year Book of International Law* 58.

Louyot, A. *Gosses de Guerre* Paris: ed. Robert Lafont, 1989.

Ludwig, M. 'Former Child Soldiers as Refugees in Germany', Geneva: Quaker United Nations Office/Terre des Hommes, 2004.

McNamara, D. 'Exclusion Clauses: Closer Attention Paid to the Exclusion Clauses', in International Association of Refugee Judges (ed.), *Refugee and Asylum Law: Assessing the Scope for Judicial Protection*, 1997.

Mann, H. 'International Law and the Child Soldier' (1987) 36 *International and Comparative Law Quarterly* 32.

Meron, T. 'The Geneva Conventions as Customary Law' (1987) 81 *American Journal of International Law* 348.

Meron, T. 'The Humanization of Humanitarian Law' (2000) 94 *American Journal of International Law* 239.

'Out of order', *Guardian*, 25 May 2004.

Niynah, M.K. 'Exclusion Under Article 1F: Some Reflections on Context, Principles and Practice' (2000) 12 *International Journal of Refugee Law* 295

Pictet, J. (ed.) *Commentary on the Geneva Conventions of 12 August 1949*, Geneva: International Committee of the Red Cross, 1955.

Pollock, L. *Forgotten Children: Parent–Child Relations from 1500 to 1900*, Cambridge: Cambridge University Press, 1983.

Provost, R. *International Human Rights and Humanitarian Law*, Cambridge: Cambridge University Press, 2002.

Pupavac, V. 'The Infantilization of the South and the UN Convention on the Rights of the Child' (1998) *University of Nottingham Human Rights Law Review* 3.

Reed, A. 'Duress and Provocation as Excuses to Murder: Salutary Lessons from Recent Anglo-American Jurisprudence' (1997) 6 *Journal of Transnational Law & Policy* 51.

Richards, P. *Fighting for the Rainforest: War, Youth and Resources in Sierra Leone*, Oxford: James Currey, 1996.

Robinson, Paul H. 'Criminal Law Defences: A Systematic Analysis (1982) 82 *Columbia Law Review* 245.

Röling, B.V.A. 'The Law of War and the National Jurisdiction since 1945' (1960) 100 *Hague Recueil* 323.

Roth, K. 'Sidelined on Human Rights', *Foreign Affairs* (March–April 1998), p. 2.

Ryle, J. 'Why Must a Child be Forced to Kill?', *Guardian*, 25 January 1999.

Sandoz, Y., Swinarski, C., and Zimmermann, B. (eds), *Commentary on the Additional Protocols of 8 June 1977 to the Geneva Conventions of 12 August 1949*, Geneva: International Committee of the Red Cross, 1987.

Sandoz, Y. 'Penal Aspects of International Humanitarian Law', in Bassiouni, M.C. (ed.), *International Criminal Law*, Ardsley: Transnational, 2nd edn, 1999.

Save the Children UK: *When Children Affected by War Go Home: Lessons Learned from Liberia*, London: Save the Children UK, 2003.

Schabas, W.A. 'Reservations to the Convention on the Rights of the Child' (1996) *Human Rights Quarterly* 472.

Schabas, W.A. *The Abolition of the Death Penalty in International Law*, Cambridge: Cambridge University Press, 2nd edn, 1997.

Simester, A.P. and G.R. Sullivan, G.R. *Criminal Law: Theory and Doctrine*, Oxford: Hart, 2000.

'Sixth Annual American Red Cross–Washington College of Law Conference on International Humanitarian Law: A Workshop on Customary International Law and the 1977 Protocols additional to the 1949 Geneva Conventions' (1987) 2 *American University Journal of International Law and Policy* 415.

Smith, J.C. *Justification and Excuse in Criminal Law*, London: Stevens, 1988.

Smith, J.C. *Smith and Hogan: Criminal Law*, London: Butterworths, 10th edn, 2002.

Smith, M. 'Britain Bans Boy Soldiers Going to War', *Daily Telegraph*, 29 March 2002.

Smith, M. 'End of an Era for Little Drummer Boys and the Powder Monkeys', *Daily Telegraph*, 29 March 2002.

Surrey Police: *The Deepcut Investigation: Final Report*, London: Stationery Office, 2004.

Tavernier, P. 'Combatants and Non-Combatants', in Dekker, I.F., and Post, H.H.G. (eds), *The Gulf War of 1980–88: The Iran–Iraq War in International Legal Perspective*, Dordrecht: Martinus Nijhof, 1992.

United Nations High Commissioner for Refugees, *Handbook on Procedures and Criteria for Determining Refugee Status*, 1979.

Zegveld, L. *The Accountability of Armed Opposition Groups in International Law*, Cambridge: Cambridge University Press, 2003.

Zelizer, V.A. *Pricing the Priceless Child: The Changing Social Value of Children*, Princeton University Press, 1986.

Index

Milton Keynes UK
Ingram Content Group UK Ltd.
UKHW021330291223
435175UK00009B/97

9 780719 065866